Great Football Moments of the Century

hamlyn

Executive Editor: Julian Brown
Senior Editor: Trevor Davies
Creative Director: Keith Martin
Production Controller: Sarah Scanlon

Produced for Hamlyn by Sport and Leisure Books Ltd

First published in Great Britain in 1999
by Hamlyn, an imprint of
Octopus Publishing Group Limited
2-4 Heron Quays, Docklands, London E14 4JP

Produced by Grafos SA
Printed in Spain

Thanks to Adam Ward, Zoran Jevtic of Audiografix Ltd, Anne Beech and Daniel Kay
for their help in compiling this book.

All pictures from Colorsport,
except for Herald and Evening Times 122;
Hulton Getty 70, 71, 123, 165, 171;
Mirror Syndication 9, 129, 131;
Popperfoto 55, 56, 73, 77, 84, 90, 92, 125, 127, 130, 144, 145, 147, 152.

Contents

Introduction

From the 1928 Wembley Wizards to the 1999 Manchester United 'treble' winners and from Stanley Matthews to the French World Cup winner Zinedine Zidane, there is much to recount about football in the 20th century.

How to do it? To the fan, football is all about the players, the skills, the teams, the magic moments, the excitements and the glory. To convey this best, three of our sections describe the century's great players, great teams and great matches.

With the players, we have tried to identify what made or makes them great, as well as to describe how they played, their greatest moments and the honours they gained. For the teams, there are accounts of their rise and decline, and their star players and triumphs. And for the games, we offer reports which vividly recreate the cut-and-thrust

excitement of these epic struggles.

When it comes to the greatest players, there are probably about five – Maradona, Pele, Cruyff, Di Stefano and Beckenbauer – who would be on everybody's list. Thereafter no two people will agree. The same applies to great teams and matches and, in truth, it would be boring if everybody held the same views. We hope you will enjoy reading our selections, even if you disagree with them.

Of course, great players tend to play for great teams, and to take part in great matches, which could lead to repetition. To minimise overlap, we have emphasised some facts in one section, where they could just as well have been in another. We have not cross-referenced, for to cross-reference, for example, the entries of Sir Alf Ramsey, his England

team, the 1966 World Cup final and Bobby Charlton to each other would quickly become irritating to the reader. We feel the Contents List and the Index will be sufficient to guide readers round the various entries.

We also provide career histories of ten of the greatest British managers, and a section – Dreams and Disasters – which considers some of the humorous, tragic and unforgettable landmarks in the history of the game. We conclude with a narrative section – Milestones – which looks at the history of football and the ways in which the game has changed over the last hundred years or so.

So the book is a mixture of reference, nostalgia and in many cases unashamed hero worship, and we hope the reader will enjoy and find useful this homage to the all-time greats of 20th century football.

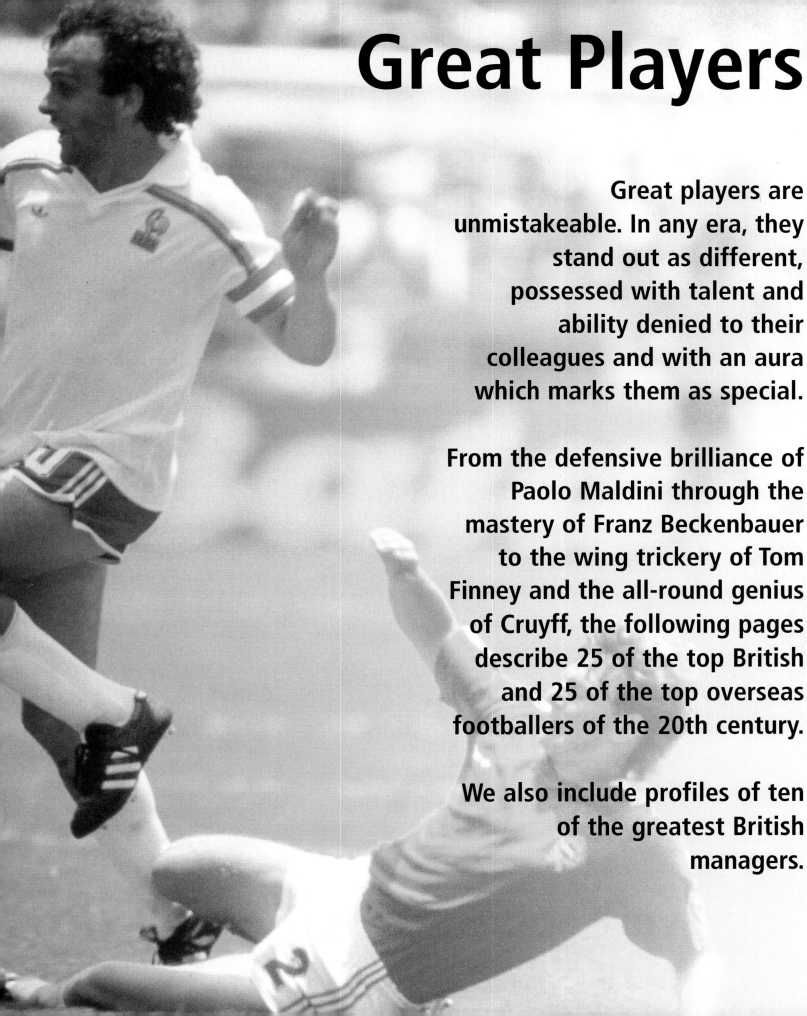

Great Players

Great players are unmistakeable. In any era, they stand out as different, possessed with talent and ability denied to their colleagues and with an aura which marks them as special.

From the defensive brilliance of Paolo Maldini through the mastery of Franz Beckenbauer to the wing trickery of Tom Finney and the all-round genius of Cruyff, the following pages describe 25 of the top British and 25 of the top overseas footballers of the 20th century.

We also include profiles of ten of the greatest British managers.

Gordon Banks

A safe pair of hands for Leicester, Stoke and England

Born:
Sheffield, 30.12.37
Clubs:
Chesterfield 58-59, Leicester City 59-67,
Stoke City 67-75, Fort Lauderdale Strikers
77-78
Club honours:
League Cup 64, 72
International honours:
73 England caps, World Cup 66
Individual honours:
Footballer of the Year 72; OBE 70

Ten years separated Gordon Banks from his first appearance in the public eye, playing for Chesterfield against Manchester United in the FA Youth Cup final, to his triumph in the 1966 World Cup final. In that period he had become one of the greatest goalkeepers in the game.

A tall, strong man, he had excellent positional awareness, safe hands and lightning reflexes, and was a reliable and dependable keeper for club and country. He played his first senior game for Chesterfield in 1958 and, after only 23 games for the club, he went to Leicester City for £7,000 in 1959. He played in two Cup finals for Leicester, against Spurs and Manchester United, losing both, before helping Leicester to win the League Cup in 1964.

His international career was also taking off. He replaced Ron Springett in the England goal for the 1963 game against Scotland, and conceded two goals, one a penalty, scored by the irrepressible Jim Baxter. England lost the match, and they also lost their next game to Brazil.

However, Banks was establishing himself as the regular first-choice keeper, and he kept a clean sheet in the 1966 World Cup finals, until letting in a Eusebio penalty in the semi-final. He was, of course, in goal for the final against West Germany.

A few months after England's victory, Banks was, to many people's surprise, put on the transfer list by Leicester (a young Peter

Shilton was lurking in the Leicester wings, and Banks was now expendable) and moved to Stoke City for £50,000. He had played 293 League games for the Foxes.

In the 1970 World Cup finals, he is best remembered for his miraculous save from Pele and for his inability, thanks to a dodgy bottle of beer the previous evening, to play in the quarter-final against West Germany, making way for Peter Bonetti and a German win.

Back home, in 1972, Stoke won the first major title – the League Cup – in their history, their route to the final being kept open by a Banks save from a Geoff Hurst penalty in extra time in the semi-final. That same year Banks was voted Footballer of the Year.

One year later, Banks had retired from the game at the age of 35. A car accident had sent windscreen glass into his right eye, and he was partially blinded. He tried to continue playing but, aside from a short spell in America, he couldn't go on.

Ironically, Shilton, his replacement as England goalkeeper, remarked before the crash: 'He's the best in the world and could go on playing for England for years.'

Not for nothing was he known as 'Banks of England'. He gained 73 caps for England, losing only nine games and keeping 35 clean sheets, a remarkable record given the strength and quality of the opposition he faced in his career.

Jim **Baxter**

The dazzling Slim Jim of Ibrox

Mention Jim Baxter's name to Scottish fans of a certain vintage, and their minds drift inexorably and gleefully back to Wembley 1967, the year that Scotland beat England 3-2 and became 'unofficial World Champions', inspired by Baxter's outrageous skill and trickery, his 'keepie-uppie' on the pitch, and his teasing and tormenting of the bewildered English team.

Baxter was class and audacity, a seemingly languid playmaker with supreme confidence bordering on arrogance. Arguably the finest left-sided player ever to have come out of Scotland, he had the wit and quick intelligence to dictate the pattern of the game and the ability to thread himself through defences with a shrug and a feint. And he could pass the ball sublimely. Although he sometimes considered tackling a rather pedestrian waste of his talents, and he didn't waste much time in the air, he was nonetheless the lynchpin of the great Rangers team of the early 1960s.

Starting his career at Raith Rovers in 1957, he was spotted by Rangers and signed for the club in 1960 for £17,500. Playing alongside Ibrox legends Willie Henderson, Davie Wilson, Jimmy Millar and Ian McMillan, Baxter was in his element, controlling the game and sweeping the ball up to the predatory forwards in his inimitable regal style. In his period at the club Baxter helped Rangers to three League titles, three Cups and four League Cups, including the 'treble' in 1964. His stage was Ibrox Stadium and he was the darling of the fans, particularly as he loved to turn it on against Celtic.

He was first capped for Scotland in 1960 in the 5-2 drubbing of Northern Ireland at Hampden, and he went on to acquire 34 caps for his country. He managed to avoid the 9-3 thrashing by England the following year, but achieved some revenge for the national humiliation in 1963 when he scored both goals in Scotland's 2-1 victory over 'the auld enemy' at Wembley.

His stature was confirmed when he was selected for The Rest of the World against England the following year. He was unlucky never to play in the World Cup finals, Scotland missing out in 1962 and narrowly failing to qualify for England 1966. But his high spot was 1967...

He left Rangers for Sunderland in 1965 for a fee of £72,500 but did not do himself any real justice there, and in 1967 moved to Nottingham Forest to even less effect ('I let Nottingham down. I didn't play at all', he apologised). A free transfer took him back to Rangers in 1969 where he played for one more season, and he retired from the game in 1970, at the early age of 30, to move into the pub trade.

Baxter possessed many of the faults of genius. He tended to irresponsibility, had a self-destructive streak and was very much his own man, often to a fault. His self-confessed fondness for alcohol and his playboy lifestyle detracted from his talent and led to illness in later life. However, in his pomp Slim Jim was a magical footballer, and no-one can take that away from him.

Born:
Hill o'Beath, Fife, 29.9.39
Clubs:
Raith Rovers 57-60, Glasgow Rangers 60-65, Sunderland 65-67, Nottingham Forest 67-69, Glasgow Rangers 69-70
Club honours:
Scottish League Championship 60/1, 62/3, 63/4; Scottish Cup 62, 63, 64; Scottish League Cup 61, 62, 64, 65
International honours:
34 (3) Scotland caps

George Best

The first pop star footballer

George Best was the first player to cross the line from football stardom to media celebrity. The Belfast-born attacker was the most gifted British forward of his generation. At his peak with Manchester United, he was probably the best in the world. But, unlike previous generations – who played in the days of the maximum wage – Best made headlines off the pitch as well as on it.

He boasted the ideal image for the swinging 60s – young, handsome, and talented. When he scored twice as United took Benfica apart 5-1 in the 1966 European Cup quarter-final, it was typical that the Lisbon press dubbed him 'El Beatle'. Best was news. His house was news. His girl friends were news. But he found it difficult to handle the trappings of fame.

Matt Busby wasn't used to dealing with celebrity footballers, and perhaps that's why he was reluctant to build a team around Best, after the waning of great talents like Bobby Charlton and Denis Law. Charlton has no doubt of Best's genius: 'He had skill, speed, he was deceptively strong, he could tackle like a defender – and he could score goals out of nothing.'

Best was 17 when he made his United debut, in September 1963 against West Bromwich Albion. Less than a year later, he was a Northern Ireland international.

His country made it to the World Cup finals in 1982 and 1986, but never when Best was in his prime. As in his last days at United, his international role was often to carry a mediocre team. But Best at his best was something special. In 1966-7, he was at the heart of the United team that won the League title for the second time in three seasons. A year later, he was feted throughout Europe. United ended Busby's quest for the European Cup, bringing the trophy to England for the first time after a 4-1 win over Benfica at Wembley, and Best was the star. Player of the Year in Europe, England's Footballer of the Year and First Division top scorer with 28 goals, he was irresistible.

Next season, United's successful team started breaking up. Best shouldered a huge responsibility. He kept scoring, kept providing magic moments, but the pressure – combined with his off-field problems – finally got to him. In his time at Old Trafford he had scored 137 League goals in 361 appearances. Best played his final game for United at QPR on New Year's Day, 1974 – then left the game for 21 months before attempting a comeback with Fulham.

At Craven Cottage he enjoyed some days that inspired great memories. But his inspiration was no longer consistent. He drifted through clubs in Britain and America before hanging up his boots in 1982. He was dogged by a series of broken relationships and drink-related problems, although he now seems to have found stability in his life. However, his legion of fans would prefer to remember him in his glory days with United.

Born:
Belfast, 22.5.46
Clubs:
Manchester United 63-75, Fulham 76-78, Los Angeles Aztecs 76-78, Fort Lauderdale Strikers 78-79, Hibernian 79-81, San Jose Earthquakes 80-81, Bournemouth 82
Club honours:
English League Championship 64/5, 66/7; European Cup 68
International Honours:
37 (9) Northern Ireland caps

Danny **Blanchflower**

The proud captain of Spurs and Northern Ireland

Danny Blanchflower was not physically a big man, but his influence on 1950s and early 1960s British football was immense. Intellectual, articulate and loquacious – and on occasion forthright and argumentative – he was a revolutionary thinker about the game and, with manager Bill Nicholson, was the inspiration behind the great Spurs 'double' team.

He was a clever and cultivated right-half, and an effortless playmaker with a natural ability to dictate and alter the speed and direction of play, slowing the game down when required, speeding it up when needed. His distribution was immaculate and his presence was dominant.

Born in Belfast, he made his professional debut with Irish side Glentoran in 1946 and was transferred to Barnsley in 1949 for £6,500 .Two years later, he moved on to Aston Villa for £15,000 and his travelling came to an end in 1954 when, disillusioned with Villa's lack of ambition, he joined Spurs for £30,000. The Glory Glory Days were about to begin.

Nicholson was putting together a team which was to be without equal in the era, and the side was to be created around the stylish and visionary Blanchflower, who insisted that the 'double' of League and FA Cup was attainable. At the beginning of the 1960s, playing alongside John White, Dave Mackay and Cliff Jones, Blanchflower and Spurs were unstoppable, and they became the first twentieth-century team to win the Double, in 1961. The next year they again won the FA Cup, helped to their 3-1 win over Burnley by a

Blanchflower penalty, sending the keeper the wrong way.

Also in 1962, Spurs reached the semi-final of the European Cup against Benfica. In one of the most exciting games ever seen at White Hart Lane, Spurs came back from a 3-1 first leg deficit and an early goal conceded in the second leg to score two goals, one coming almost inevitably from a Blanchflower penalty, and they hit the woodwork three times but just failed to get the third. The following year, they reached the final of the European Cup Winners Cup, mostly without an injured Blanchflower, but he was back for the big game and, helped by pain-killing injections, he inspired Spurs to a 5-1 drubbing of Atletico Madrid.

Blanchflower's talents had been recognised by Northern Ireland and he received his first cap in 1949 against Scotland. He gained a total of 56 caps, and his proudest moment was in the 1958 World Cup finals when he captained the team to the quarter-finals, only to be beaten 4-0 by a Just Fontaine-inspired France.

By 1964 the Spurs team was beginning to disintegrate and Blanchflower, at the age of 37 and suffering from a chronic knee injury, decided to retire. He moved into a successful career in broadcasting and journalism, and a rather less successful career in management and, in 1974 when Nicholson resigned, he was unsuccessfully touted as Spurs manager.

Blanchflower died in 1993, the victim of a debilitating illness, a sad end for a complicated, often perverse but authentic football genius.

Born:
Belfast, 10.2.26
Clubs:
Glentoran 45-49, Barnsley 49-51, Aston Villa 51-54, Tottenham Hotspur 54-64
Club honours:
League Championship 60/1; FA Cup 61, 62; European Cup Winners Cup 63
International honours:
56 (2) Northern Ireland caps
Individual honours:
Footballer of the Year 58, 61

Billy Bremner

The battling leader of Leeds and Scotland

Small, brave and determined, with a temper to match his red hair, Billy Bremner was an inspiring leader of men. Never one to admit defeat, and possessing abundant skill and an ability to score goals when it really mattered, Bremner was the driving force behind Leeds United's rise from obscurity to English domination, and the midfield general of Scotland in the 1960s and 1970s.

A boy from Stirling, he was coaxed away from his Celtic aspirations by Leeds, and made his first team debut in 1960 against Chelsea. During 1960-61, at the age of 19, he played 31 League matches for the club and, although originally an inside-forward, by the mid-1960s he had developed into a right-half, becoming the heir apparent to Bobby Collins (and assuming his captaincy).

The astute purchase by manager Don Revie of Johnny Giles from Manchester United in 1963 united Bremner's passion and commitment with Giles' touch and vision, and the partnership formed the creative engine of the great Leeds side of the era.

Bremner powered Leeds to League Cup victory in 1968 and, in 1968-69 to the first League Championship in their history, going 28 games without defeat. In 1970, a Bremner left-foot screamer past Manchester United's Alex Stepney put Leeds into the FA Cup final, although they lost out to Chelsea in a final replay. The same year, a brilliant Bremner goal in the European Cup semi-final was not enough to prevent Celtic going through 3-1 to the final. In 1970, he was named Footballer of the Year.

In 1972 Bremner led Leeds to FA Cup final victory in a boring 1-0 victory over Arsenal and to the final the next year when they were defeated by unfancied Sunderland. However, what was then regarded as an aging Leeds team won the League title again in 1973-74, but the club's supremacy was fading,

Bremner was first capped by Scotland in 1965 against Spain and went on to achieve 54 caps for his country. His most notable games were in the 1967 3-2 humiliation of England at Wembley and in the 1974 World Cup finals when captain Bremner's Scotland unluckily failed to qualify, without losing a game. Had Bremner put away a good chance with the score 0-0 against Brazil, however, the story may have been different.

Bremner was a provocative and fiery player, evidenced by his punch-up with Keegan in the 1974 Charity Shield, when both players were sent off – the first British footballers to be dismissed at Wembley.

Also, his off-the-pitch behaviour could occasionally be less then acceptable and, as a result of a nightclub incident in Copenhagen, after a European Championship qualifier, he was banned for life by the Scottish FA, a ban later rescinded.

He moved to Hull City in 1976 and, shortly afterward, became manager of Doncaster Rovers. He came back to Leeds in the mid-1980s for an unhappy and unsuccessful spell as manager, and died of a heart attack in 1997.

Born:
Stirling, 9.12.42
Clubs:
Leeds United 60-76, Hull City 76-78
Club honours:
English League Championship 68/9, 73/4; FA Cup 72; League Cup 68; Fairs Cup 68, 71
International honours:
54 (3) Scotland caps
Individual honours:
Football Writers' Player of the Year 70

Raich Carter

The maestro with only 13 caps

There was over 13 years between Raich Carter's first international and his last, yet incredibly he won only 13 caps. This is partly because of a nine-year gap for the Second World War. In an era of great inside-forwards, he built a reputation as one of the best.

A Schoolboy international, he was signed by Leicester, who inexplicably allowed him to return home to Sunderland, where he made his debut in 1932, aged 19. The following season he was a regular for the Wearsiders, and won his first cap, helping beat Scotland 3-1. But in their next match England lost 2-1 to Hungary (only the third-ever England defeat by a 'foreign' team) and he was dropped.

However, Carter was playing brilliantly for Sunderland, where he inspired a mid-table team of players older than himself to second place in 1934-35 and to the League Championship in 1935-36. He won his third cap in a 3-0 defeat of Germany, and was made Sunderland captain.

Carter was only 5ft 8in and wore his black hair greased back, with the common centre parting of the day. He was such an immaculate, unhurried player that it was said (falsely) that he combed his hair during matches. He operated from around the centre circle, commanding the play with the imperiousness of his namesake, Horatio, Lord Nelson. He was not short of confidence, and believed he could do anything he wanted on the pitch. He certainly had uncanny positional sense, brilliant control and the vision to make defence-splitting passes. The supreme midfield general,

he could also score, as 216 goals in 451 League appearances testify. His Sunderland predecessor, Charlie Buchan, called him 'the finest inside-forward of his generation'.

In 1936-37 he won the last three of his pre-war caps, and led Sunderland to Wembley to win the FA Cup, scoring in a 3-1 win over Preston. He got married that morning, and the Queen (now the Queen Mother) told him the Cup was a fine wedding present. Next day the Carters visited the Queen at Windsor Castle.

During the war he played alongside Stanley Matthews for the RAF and England – some regard Carter as the best partner Matthews had. He and the mercurial Irish international Peter Doherty were stationed at Loughborough and 'guested' for Derby County. At the end of the war, Derby were surprisingly able to buy Carter and Doherty from Sunderland and Manchester City respectively, and the two inside-forwards were, for a season, invincible together. County won the first post-war FA Cup beating Charlton 4-1.

Carter played in the first seven internationals after the war (only Lawton and Matthews also played for England pre and post-war) but was now a silver-haired 34-year-old. He went to Hull City in 1947-48 as player-manager, and took them up into the Second Division in the following season. He left Hull in 1952, and had a brief spell with Cork Athletic, winning an Irish Cup winners' medal. From 1953 to 1966 he managed successively Leeds United, Mansfield Town and Middlesbrough before drifting out of football. He died in October 1994.

Born:
Sunderland, 21.12.13
Clubs:
Sunderland 32-39, Derby County 45-48, Hull City 48-52, Cork Athletic (Republic of Ireland) 52-53
Club honours:
League Championship 35/6, FA Cup 37, 46, FA of Ireland Cup 52/3
International honours:
13 (7) England caps

John Charles

The Gentle Giant of Leeds United and Juventus

Although it is commonplace to see top players move seamlessly from attacking to midfield positions, it is rare indeed for a centre-forward at the highest level to perform equally effectively as a centre-back. John Charles, however, had this unique ability and he was probably the finest all-round footballer to have come out of the British Isles.

A tall, powerfully built Welshman, unbeatable in the air and with surprisingly delicate touch and control, Charles signed for Second Division Leeds United on his 16th birthday in 1947 and was blooded in the first team in 1949. Starting his career as a centre-half, by 1952-53 he was playing up front for Leeds, scoring 26 goals that season and 42 the next, a Leeds record.

Leeds were promoted in 1955-56 thanks

mainly to Charles' goal-scoring prowess, and in their first season in First Division he scored 38 goals to confirm his and Leeds' arrival at the top. He had scored 151 goals in 297 games, but his career was to change direction.

Umberto Agnelli, the Juventus president, was looking for a striker for his goal-starved team, and offered Leeds £65,000 for Charles – a huge fee and a record for a British player – which Leeds could not refuse. In June 1957 he joined the Turin club and, in spite of concerns about his ability to break down the defensive Italian system, he was an immediate success.

Playing alongside the Argentinian inside-forward Omar Sivori, he was adored by the Juventus fans, who christened him Il Buon Gigante – The Gentle Giant – and he was in a

free-scoring mood. In the five seasons he spent at Turin, he won three Serie A Championships, two Italian Cups and scored 93 goals in 150 League games.

His international career was equally successful. He earned his first cap as the youngest player ever to play for Wales, at the age of 18 years, 71 days in 1950 (a record since overtaken by Ryan Giggs and then Ryan Green), and was made captain of his country in 1957. To illustrate the man's versatility, the season he broke Leeds' goal-scoring record, he played a game for Wales at centre-half. Probably his proudest moment was in leading Wales to the quarter-final of the 1958 World Cup in Sweden, where they were eliminated by a Pele goal, although unfortunately Charles himself could not play in that match due to injury. He gained a total of 38 caps, his last in 1965.

Don Revie re-signed Charles for Leeds in 1962, but his pace had gone and he was sold on to Roma for £65,000 the same year. He joined Cardiff City in 1963, and in 1966 moved into coaching with Hereford Town.

Born:
Swansea, 27.12.31
Clubs:
Leeds United 49-57, Juventus 57-62, Leeds United 62, Roma 62-63, Cardiff City 63- 65
Club honours:
Italian Championship 57/8, 59/60, 60/1; Italian Cup 59, 60
International honours:
38 (15) Wales caps

Bobby Charlton

The legend of Manchester United and England

Born:
Ashington, Northumberland, 11.10.37
Clubs:
Manchester United 54-73, Preston North End 74-75
Club honours:
League Championship 56/7, 64/5, 66/7; FA Cup 63; European Cup 68
International honours:
106 (49) England caps, World Cup 66
Individual honours:
European Footballer of the Year 66, Footballer of the Year 66, OBE 69, CBE 74, knighted 94

Probably England's best-ever footballer, and internationally the most famous of them all, Charlton was a delight to watch. A graceful, powerful player with a deceptive body swerve, he possessed an explosive shot with either foot. He had great pace and acceleration, was a sweet passer of the ball over distance and could conjure goals out of nothing.

He was also an adaptable player, playing in most of the forward positions in his career. Starting as an attacking inside-forward, he then moved to the left wing, finally adopting the deep-lying centre-forward role where his craft, guile and close control allowed him the space to create and finish.

Charlton, whose mother was the cousin of Newcastle's famous Jackie Milburn, was a schoolboy prodigy, signed for Manchester United in 1954, marking his first-team debut at the age of 18 against Charlton in 1956 with two goals. A key member of the exuberant 'Busby Babes', he survived the 1958 Munich air crash, making his international debut against Scotland two months later and scoring in England's 4-0 victory at Hampden.

Teaming up with Denis Law, Pat Crerand and latterly George Best, Charlton was at the heart of the United team which won the FA Cup in 1963, and the League in 1964-65, pipping Leeds on goal average, and 1966-67, and was captain of the team which won the European Cup at Wembley in 1968. Charlton scored twice in the emotional 4-1 extra time victory over Benfica.

His greatest international moment came in 1966, when along with his brother Jack who was a centre-half with Leeds United, he was in England's World Cup winning team at Wembley. Two goals from Bobby had finished off Eusebio's Portugal in the semi, and that year he was named both the English and European Footballer of the Year.

He had been in the 1958 World Cup squad, and had played in the 1962 tournament, and his last game for England was in the 1970 finals in Mexico, when he was substituted by Alf Ramsey against West Germany in the quarter-final. He was dropped for England's next game, and that was that. He holds the record number of goals scored – 49 – for England.

Manchester United were by now an aging team and Charlton's long and illustrious career with the club was over. Relegated to the reserves in August 1972 he decided to retire at the end of that season.

In his 16 years in the first team at Old Trafford he made 606 league appearances and scored 199 League goals, and his heroic status with the fans was underlined by the crowd of over 60,000 who turned up for his testimonial against Celtic in 1972.

He briefly became player/manager of Preston North End in 1974-75 but a boardroom dispute led to his departure. He came back to United in 1984 as a member of the board, where his presence continues to act as a talisman to the young players and fans.

15

Kenny Dalglish

King Kenny of Parkhead and Anfield

Born:
Glasgow, 4.3.51
Clubs:
Celtic 67-77, Liverpool 77-89
Club honours:
Scottish League Championship 71/2, 72/3, 73/4; Scottish Premier Division 76/7; Scottish Cup 72, 74, 75, 77; Scottish League Cup 75; Football League Championship 76/7, 79/80, 81/2, 82/3, 83/4, 85/6; FA Cup 86; League Cup 81, 82, 83, 84; European Cup 78, 81, 84
International honours:
102 (30) Scotland caps
Individual honours:
Footballer of the Year 79, 83; MBE 85

When 17-year-old substitute Kenneth Mathieson Dalglish trotted onto the pitch at Hamilton in a League Cup game in 1968, there was no inkling among the few watching Celtic supporters that they were seeing the debut of a superstar. By the time he left the club in 1977, however, he had become a Celtic legend and, in his subsequent Liverpool career, his status as footballing god was confirmed.

He was a tenacious and determined inside-forward. Possessing acute awareness, tight control, a gift for shielding the ball and a sonar-like ability to find teammates, he was unselfish, well-balanced and a strong tackler when required. His heading wasn't up to much but he compensated by his anticipation and quick thinking, and his innate tactical intelligence made him a master at exploiting the crowded

penalty area. Most of all, though, he loved playing football. And, of course, he scored goals.

A Rangers supporter as a boy, Dalglish was a first-team regular by season 1971-72, and was the star of Jock Stein's all-conquering side. Within six years, he had collected four League, four Scottish Cup and one League Cup winners' medals, including three 'double' years, the third being his last season 1976-77. When he left Parkhead, to the dismay of the Celtic faithful, he had played 204 League games and collected 112 League goals for the 'Bhoys'.

Moving to Liverpool as replacement for Kevin Keegan for a then British record transfer fee of £440,000, Dalglish demonstrated the value of Liverpool's investment by netting 30 goals in his first Anfield season, including the winner, a

clever chip over the goalkeeper, in the European Cup final against Bruges. Playing alongside Hansen, Souness and Rush, Dalglish was the creative, goalscoring hub of a resurgent Liverpool side which went on to win two more European Cups, six League Championships, one FA Cup and four League Cups. He was the Kop favourite, and the banners proclaimed 'King Kenny' and 'Kenny's From Heaven'.

He received his first Scottish cap against Belgium in 1971, and went on to gather another 101, a Scottish record. However, although he played some fine games for his country, the general Scottish view is that the national team never saw the best of his talents. That said, very few Scottish fans will forget his strike against Belgium in the 1982 European Championship qualifier or the surge of hope (quickly dashed by Johnny Rep) generated by his and Archie Gemmill's goals against Holland in the 1978 World Cup finals. He played in two other World Cups – in 1974 and 1982 – but he paraded his talent to little effect.

He took over as player/manager of Liverpool under the worst possible circumstances the day after the Heysel Stadium disaster in 1985 and he was still in charge at the time of the horror of Hillsborough in 1989. He subsequently managed Blackburn Rovers to the Premier League title, and then ran Newcastle United.

A publicly taciturn but privately charming man, Dalglish demonstrated dignity and courage both on and off the pitch. This exhilarating footballer mightily deserved the many plaudits and honours he received in his career.

'Dixie' Dean

The Everton striker with the all-time English goal record

If William Ralph 'Dixie' Dean were playing today, he would be worth millions. With his strength, skill, mental resilience, leadership abilities and goal-scoring talents, he would be perfectly suited to today's pressurised and demanding game.

Although he was only 5ft 10in, his heading ability was awesome – nearly half his goals came from headers, powered in with force and accuracy – and he was two-footed with good acceleration, as well as being a wily exponent of the body-charge, a perfectly legal tactic in those days. In his heyday in the 1920s and 1930s, his achievements dwarfed those of his contemporaries and he set a goalscoring record in 1928 which, more than 70 years later, still stands.

A Birkenhead lad, Dean joined his local club Tranmere Rovers in 1924. After only one season, his unerring ability to find the back of the net alerted most of England's senior clubs. He elected for Everton, for a transfer fee of £3000, where he was to become the superstar of Goodison Park.

A coincident change in the offside law, from three to only two defenders between the attacker and the goal, could not have been more timely for Dean, and the goals followed.

In spite of fracturing his skull in a road accident in 1926, when he was unconscious for nearly two days, by 1927-28 Dean was back on song. In that season he set his goal-scoring record of 60 goals, overtaking Middlesbrough's George Camsell's record of

Born:
Birkenhead, 21.2.06
Clubs:
Tranmere Rovers 23-25, Everton 25-37, Notts County 38, Sligo Rovers 39
Club honours:
League Championship 27/8, 31/2; FA Cup 33
International honours:
16 (18) England caps

59 the previous season, and Everton won the League. Dean's tally included seven hat-tricks. In the final game of the season against Arsenal, he needed three goals to reach the record and scored two in the first eight minutes. In the last few minutes, his head connected with an Alec Troup cross and the ball was in the net. Even the Arsenal fans cheered.

Catastrophically for Toffees fans, Everton were relegated in 1929-30, for the first time in their long history, but they bounced back the following season, thanks to Dean's 39 goals in the Second Division. The first season back, 1931-32, he scored another 44 and Everton won the League again. In 1933, they beat Manchester City 3-0 in the FA Cup final, Dean scoring with another powerful header, this time off the back of his head.

By 1936 Dean had passed Steve Bloomer's League record of 352 goals and, in 1938 with a young Tommy Lawton pushing for Everton's centre-forward spot, he moved to Notts County where injuries ended his England career. A short sojourn with Sligo Rovers followed. He retired with the proud total of 379 goals in 437 games.

Although one of the most prolific goalscorers in his country's history, he only played 16 games for England, securing his first cap in 1927 against Wales. However, he did score 18 goals.

He died, probably where he would have wished, watching a game at Goodison in 1980.

Tom **Finney**

The Preston Plumber and flying English winger

Born:
Preston, 5.4.22
Clubs:
Preston North End 37-60
Club honours:
Second Division Championship 51
International honours:
76 (30) England caps
Individual honours:
Footballer of the Year 54, 57; knighted 97

In the immediate post-Second World War years, England dominated the international football scene, fielding players of the quality of Stan Matthews, Stan Mortensen and Wilf Mannion. However, arguably the most complete and effective of them all was Tom Finney.

Of no great height, and wiry in frame, Finney was nonetheless versatility personified. Possessed of an orthodox winger's speed and trickiness, he was also two-footed (and played on both wings), courageous in the tackle, an immaculate header of the ball and an expert finisher.

He made his League debut in 1946 for his home club of Preston North End – the 'Old Invincibles', a club with a fine tradition but one which had fallen on less glamorous times – and was to stay there for the rest of his career. This explains why, in spite of gaining 76 caps for England, he never won a major honour, other than the Second Division Championship.

The closest he came was in 1953, when Preston were pipped to the First Division title by Arsenal on goal average and the following year when a disappointing Finney and his team were beaten in the Cup final by West Bromwich Albion. However, he averaged 13 goals a season for the club, playing in all five forward positions, and was a constant inspiration to his teammates.

He was awarded his first England cap against Northern Ireland in 1946, scoring on his debut, and in 1948 scored two goals in England's defeat of Italy. England were all-powerful, but the come-uppance was around the corner. Defeated in the 1950 World Cup by Spain and by 'no-hoper' USA, humiliated three years later by Hungary 6-3 and 7-1 and knocked out by Uruguay in the 1954 tournament, Finney and England were in disarray.

However, six months later, England defeated World Champions West Germany 3-1. Finney went on to score 30 international goals for his country.

Finney's contribution to English football was recognised in 1954 when he was voted Footballer of the Year, an award he was to receive again in 1957. In 1956 he moved to centre-forward for Preston and was a revelation, scoring 22 goals that season and 26 the next, and he also played in the centre-forward position three times for England.

In 1958 he played in his third World Cup but was injured in the first game against the Soviet Union and was out of the tournament. Increasing injury problems led to his retirement from the game in 1960, returning only to play for Distillery in a European Cup tie.

Currently president of Preston North End, a role Finney combines with his plumbing business, he was honoured with a knighthood in 1997, a fitting honour for a player who was never booked, never sent off and who played nearly 500 games and scored over 200 goals for his club.

Paul **Gascoigne**

Gazza's turbulent career

Born:
Gateshead, 27.5.67
Clubs:
Newcastle United 85-88, Tottenham Hotspur 88-92, Lazio 92-95, Rangers 95-98, Middlesbrough 98-
Club honours:
FA Cup 91; Scottish Premier League Championship 95/6, 96/7; Scottish Cup 96; Scottish League Cup 97
International honours:
 57 (10) England caps
Individual honours:
Scottish Footballer of the Year 96

A hyperactive, podgy but prodigiously gifted footballer, 'Gazza' was the football story of the 1990s. His childish and often self-destructive antics were the stuff of tabloid headlines, but they could not obscure his moments of sheer footballing genius nor his standing as the best English midfield player of the decade.

He had tight control and intricate dribbling skills, with the strength and balance to hold off tackles, twisting and feinting his way through defences. He could find his teammates with inch-perfect passes, possessed a powerful and accurate shot and could turn a game with a flick of the ball or a sudden, unforeseen lay-off. If he only had the temperament to handle his talent, he could have been the greatest of them all.

An irrepressible Geordie lad, he made his debut for Newcastle United at the age of 17, quickly gathering a fanatical local support. In 1988 Terry Venables paid £2 million, a British record, to bring the young star to Spurs, and Gascoigne scored in his first home game against Arsenal. It was largely through Gascoigne that Spurs reached the 1991 Cup final, the midfielder scoring superb goals against Portsmouth and Notts County and a marvellous free-kick from 35 yards against Arsenal in the semi-final. Already set for a big money move to Lazio, Gascoigne committed an ugly foul in the final on Nottingham Forest's Gary Charles, badly damaged his own cruciate ligament and was out of football for a year.

He gained his first cap as a substitute against Denmark in 1988 and had a memorable 1990 World Cup finals, his expertly taken free-kick in the last minute of extra time allowing David Platt to score against Belgium and England to progress to the quarter-final against Cameroon. A tearful Gazza left the pitch as West Germany knocked out England on penalties in the semi-final.

He had a turbulent time at Lazio, not helped by his injury and by breaking his leg in April 1994, and never really settled into the team. He was brought back to British football by Rangers and he repaid the high transfer fee of £4.3 million by scoring 14 League goals in 1995-96, putting Rangers on course for the Premier title.

At the end of the season he was voted Scotland's Player of the Year. In the European Championships that summer he scored one of the goals of the tournament, completely outfoxing Scotland's Colin Hendry and goalie Andy Goram with a flick and volley, to put England 2-0 up.

His eccentric behaviour and often outrageous acts, such as playing an imaginary Orange flute against Celtic, were proving too much for Rangers, and he was sold to Middlesbrough for nearly £3.5 million in 1998 where, at the time of writing, he is attempting a rehabilitation of his talents under the guiding hand of Bryan Robson.

However, his self-confidence was dealt a nasty blow in the summer of 1998 when he was omitted from Hoddle's England squad for the World Cup finals, and it would appear that his international career is now over.

Jimmy Greaves

The top division's top goalscorer

Jimmy Greaves was the greatest marksman English soccer has ever seen. All his 357 goals were scored in the top flight, and nobody has ever scored more. He made a point of scoring on his first appearance for each club at every level of football.

The son of a London tube driver, he joined Chelsea at 15 and made his debut against Spurs as a 17-year-old. A series of photos shows him beating four players, two still on the ground after missed tackles as he slots the ball into goal. A bemused Danny Blanchflower spoke of his 'uncanny deceptiveness'.

Greaves was only a slim 5ft 8in, and with his baggy shorts looked like a boy playing with men. His balance was superb, and there seemed something magic about the way he picked his way past baffled opponents tackling thin air.

Allied to this uncanny dribbling, he was deadly near goal. According to Jimmy Hill, it was all temperament – he was 'no more excited in front of goal than he was cleaning his teeth in the morning'.

Greaves was at his most prolific in his four seasons with Chelsea. His total of 41 First Division goals in 1960-61 is unapproached in post-war football. This total included six hat-tricks, also a post-war record. Greaves often went on to four or five with Chelsea, most memorably netting five in a 6-2 win over Billy Wright's Championship-winning Wolves side (a sixth was marginally disallowed).

In 1960 Greaves became the youngest player (20 years and nine months) to score 100 League goals. To escape the maximum wage for footballers in England, he engineered a transfer to AC Milan. In what he called a 'sick joke' the maximum wage was immediately abolished, and after only ten League games (nine goals) he returned to Spurs. Bill Nicholson paid £99,999 for him, to avoid him become Britain's first £100,000 player.

Having scored four in his last match for Chelsea, Greaves netted three in his first for Spurs. He topped their scoring list in each of his nine seasons with them, and altogether topped the First Division list six times (three consecutively). He rarely blasted the ball in, and rarely scored with his head. He was the master of placement, and hardly ever failed in one-to-one situations with the goalkeeper.

Greaves got England's only goal on his international debut in 1959, and in one spell of five matches in 1960-61 netted 11, including two hat-tricks, one in a 9-3 defeat of Scotland.

A spell of hepatitis in November 1965 knocked a fraction off his pace, and he was never quite the same, but he remained an England player and played in the first three matches of the World Cup finals in 1966. But then he lost his place through injury, and was not recalled when fit for the final. Bitterly disappointed, he declined to attend training sessions if he wasn't going to play, and was not selected again. His 44 international goals place him third on England's list, just behind Bobby Charlton and Gary Lineker, who each played far more games than Greaves.

On retirement, he did some motor racing, fought back from alcoholism, and enjoyed a long run with Ian St John on a popular football programme, 'The Saint and Greavsie'.

Born:
East Ham, London, 20.2.40.
Clubs:
Chelsea 57-61, AC Milan 61, Tottenham Hotspur 61-70, West Ham United 70-71
Club honours:
FA Cup 62, 66, European Cup Winners Cup 63
International honours:
57 (44) England caps

Johnny Haynes

The £100 per week one-club one-man show

Born:
Edmonton, London, 17.10.34
Clubs:
Fulham 52-70
International honours:
56 (18) England caps

Many footballers have been noted for the astuteness and accuracy of their passing, But none excelled Johnny Haynes, in many minds the greatest passer of a ball there was. Haynes was outstanding from an early age, and the first to represent England at all five levels: Schoolboy, Youth, Under-23, B and Senior. Dave Mackay, who was on the losing side, remembers with awe how Haynes orchestrated an 8-2 thrashing of Scotland in a Wembley schoolboy international in 1950. He could have signed immediately for Spurs, but chose Fulham because his schoolboy colleague Tosh Chamberlain had signed for them the year before.

Haynes made his debut on Boxing Day 1952, aged 18. Fulham were in the Second Division where Haynes was to spend half his career. He soon became the fulcrum of the side, wearing the inside-left's No 10 shirt and operating mostly in the region around the centre circle. Fulham's strategy was for the defence to pass the ball to Haynes, who was always available. Haynes' job was to set up attacks with defence-splitting passes.

His passing was superlative. Haynes knew more angles than a geometry teacher. He carried in his head a picture of the whole field, as if he were looking down from above. If he received a ball facing his own goal, he could turn and instantly play a perfectly weighted ball inside the full-back for a winger to run on to, or a ball so angled as to bisect central defenders and fall into the path of the centre-forward.

Before he was 20, Haynes was playing for England, and at Fulham bossing one of the best forward lines in the whole country. Charlie Mitten, Bobby Robson, Bedford Jezzard and Arthur Stevens (the only non-international) were his partners. So dominant and perfectionist was Haynes that he was impatient with colleagues' errors, and showed it by exaggerated body language. Later, with Tosh Chamberlain and Jimmy Hill as partners, Haynes' gestures became regular crowd entertainment.

Fulham's defence was always poor, but they reached the FA Cup semi-final in 1958, losing to Manchester United 5-3 in a replay. Next season they were promoted. Haynes was ready to seek his fortune in Italy, but the abolition of the maximum wage came just in time to keep him in England. Tommy Trinder, Fulham's chairman, immediately made him England's first £100 per week footballer.

Haynes was made England captain in 1959 and they won six successive games in 1960-61, scoring 40 goals (nine against Scotland, for whom Dave Mackay was again playing). In August 1962, soon after he had led England in the World Cup finals in Chile, he was told he would never play again after a car accident in Blackpool. He returned after a year but never regained his England place, despite a big newspaper campaign in his favour.

In 1964, when Spurs' John White was killed by lightning, manager Bill Nicholson unsuccessfully offered Fulham £90,000 for Haynes, which would have been a record between British clubs. Fulham remained unable to surround Haynes with players of comparable calibre, and in each of his last two seasons Fulham were relegated. He won no domestic honours, but moving to South Africa he helped Durban City win a League title. After that he looked after his business interests and lived in Scotland.

Glenn **Hoddle**

The hero of White Hart Lane

Born:
Hayes, Middlesex, 27.10.57
Clubs:
Tottenham Hotspur 75-87,
Monaco 87-91, Swindon Town
91-93, Chelsea 93-95
Club honours:
FA Cup 81, 82; UEFA Cup 84;
French Championship 87/8
International honours:
53 (8) England caps

Glenn Hoddle was an enigma, a curious and unpredictable blend of the brilliant and the indifferent. Sometimes he would turn it on – a stylish and exceptionally gifted midfielder with a delicate touch, mastery of the long pass and powerful long-range shooting power. At other times, he would fade away and drift out of games as if he was uninterested. He also never relished the defensive aspect of his duties and this, coupled with his inconsistency, denied him the number of international appearances his talent deserved.

He was, however, a firm favourite at White Hart Lane. He signed professional forms in 1975 and, in his second full season Spurs were relegated to the Second Division, bouncing back again in 1978-79. In November 1979 he was awarded his first England cap against Bulgaria where he marked his arrival with a 20-yard volleyed goal.

In 1981, Spurs won the FA Cup in a replay against Manchester City – the occasion of the famous Villa solo goal – and they won the Cup again the following season, again needing a replay against QPR. Hoddle scored in both games, hitting a deflected shot in extra time through Tony Currie's legs in the first encounter, with the replay decided by his sixth-minute penalty. Hoddle was on top of his game at this point in his career, his Argentinian teammate Ardiles commenting that Hoddle was one of the best players in the world.

Hoddle was also gaining experience in Europe, and his delicate shot 10 minutes from time was enough to eliminate Eintracht Frankfurt from the quarter-finals of the European Cup Winners Cup in 1982. Spurs were knocked out in the semis by Barcelona. It was a different story in the 1984 UEFA Cup where Spurs won the trophy, beating holders Anderlecht on penalties.

At the international level, he was highly regarded by opponents (and idolised by a youthful Dennis Bergkamp), with Platini stating that, had Hoddle been a Frenchman, he would have won 150 caps. In the event, he settled for a respectable 53. He made a couple of appearances in the 1982 World Cup finals and played in 1986, and his final game for his country was in the 3-1 defeat by the USSR, ending England's disastrous 1988 European Championships. While many had argued that the England team should be built around Hoddle's creative and often visionary playmaking skills, manager Bobby Robson was not convinced of Hoddle's reliability and willingness to tackle back. And he picked the team.

In 1987, after Spurs lost the FA Cup final 3-2 to a battling Coventry side, Hoddle left the club and signed for Monaco in the French League for a fee of £750,000. In 1987-88, he helped his new club to the French Championship, playing under current Arsenal manager Arsene Wenger.

In 1991 he became player/manager of Swindon, then performed the same role for Chelsea, taking over responsibility for the English national team in 1996. His much-publicised statement on disabled people led to his departure from the job in February 1999.

Alex James

The Wee Wizard of 1930s Arsenal

Short, pugnacious, self-confident to the point of cockiness, an intelligent reader of the game and an excellent passer, Alex James was the first in a line of distinctively Scottish midfielders – Bremner and Strachan spring immediately to mind. James, however, had true footballing genius, surpassing them all, and deserves to be considered as one of the genuine legends of British football.

Born near Glasgow at the turn of the century, James began his career in 1922 at Raith Rovers as an aggressive, attacking inside-forward and moved south to Preston in 1925. He scored 53 League goals in his four years at Preston, and was bought in 1929 by Herbert Chapman, manager of Arsenal, who was looking for a playmaking replacement for the retired Charlie Buchan. In his eight seasons at Highbury, James was to fill this role to perfection.

Arsenal's revolutionary new 'WM' formation required a creative, deep-lying inside-forward to collect the ball from the defenders and feed it to the two wingers and the centre-forward. Arsenal had the predatory players – Hulme and Bastin the attacking wingers, Jack and Lambert, the centre-forward – to score the goals, and link man James had the guile, close control and effortless dominance of the midfield to supply them.

James took a while to settle in at Highbury but his and Arsenal's great era began in 1930 when they played then mighty Huddersfield Town at Wembley in the FA Cup final, the famous 'Graf Zeppelin Final'. James scored the first, from a quickly taken free-kick, made the

other, and Arsenal had won the Cup for the first time in their history.

With his trademark long shorts flapping around his knees, and his shuffling gait, James did not always look the part, but he was the

very heart of that great side which, orchestrated by himself, won the FA Cup again in 1936 and won the League four times between 1931 and 1936. Although by then no great goalscorer (it was said that the corner flag was more at risk from a James shot than was the back of the net); he did put away 26 League goals in his time at Highbury, including a 20-minute hat-trick against Sheffield Wednesday in 1935, much to the incredulity of his teammates.

Strangely enough for such a sublime footballer, he was only capped eight times. Whether this was because his forceful personality and individualism annoyed the selectors or because he was based in England is difficult to say. However, he did play in the 1928 'Wembley Wizards' team which thrashed England 5-1, and he will be ever remembered for this in Scotland.

His last League game was against Bolton and he retired from football and Arsenal in 1937. He died from cancer in 1953, his passing marked by an obituary in *The Times*.

Born:
Mossend, Lanarkshire, 14.9.01
Clubs:
Raith Rovers 22-25, Preston North End 25-29, Arsenal 29-37
Club honours:
League Championship 30/1, 32/3, 33/4, 34/5; FA Cup 30, 36
International honours:
8 (4) Scotland caps

Kevin Keegan

The Mighty Mouse of Liverpool and Hamburg

Born:
Armthorpe, Doncaster, 14.2.51
Clubs:
Scunthorpe United 68-71,
Liverpool 71-77, SV
Hamburg 77-80, Southampton 80-82, Newcastle
United 82-84
Club honours:
League Championship 72/3, 75/6, 76/7; FA Cup 74;
UEFA Cup 73, 76;
European Cup 77; German Championship 78/9
International honours:
63 (21) England caps
Individual honours:
European Footballer of the Year 78, 79; Footballer
of the Year 76

Although not one of the most naturally gifted players of the era, nonetheless Kevin Keegan was a huge influence on British and European football in the 1970s.

Small, strong and tireless, the indefatigable Keegan was a creator and a goalscorer, with a work rate and commitment second to none. Surprisingly powerful in the air, and possessing a wicked shot, he scored some crucially important goals and also served as an effective and selfless fetcher and provider for his teammates.

Turning professional with Scunthorpe in 1968, Keegan's abilities were soon noticed by

Bill Shankly and he was signed by Liverpool in 1971. He scored in his first game for Liverpool, and the following season he was establishing himself at the core of the team, which won the League title and the UEFA Cup. That season Keegan collected 22 goals including two in the first leg of the UEFA final against Borussia Monchengladbach.

In 1974, Liverpool beat Newcastle in the FA Cup final where he scored two in Liverpool's 3-0 victory, and the club again won the League and the UEFA Cup in 1976 against Bruges, Keegan scoring in both legs of the final. That year, he was voted Footballer of the Year.

His glorious swansong for Liverpool was in the 1977 European Cup final against Borussia. Playing at his elusive and impish best,

Keegan was scythed down in the penalty box by a frustrated Berti Vogts and Phil Neal converted the penalty, sealing a 3-1 victory for Liverpool. In the summer, to the deep disappointment of the Kop, Keegan left Liverpool for SV Hamburg for a record £500,000. He had played 230 games and scored 68 goals for the Reds.

First capped by his country against Wales in 1972, he collected 63 caps (31 as captain) and his last game was as a substitute against Spain in the 1982 World Cup finals. New manager Bobby Robson dropped Keegan for the European Championship qualifying game against Denmark that autumn, and a hurt Keegan announced that his international career was over.

Keegan returned to English football in 1980 with, to general astonishment, Southampton where he teamed up with Mick Channon and manager Lawrie McMenemy, and his final move was to Newcastle in 1982. Back in top form, and perhaps with one eye on Robson, Keegan scored on his debut and his goals helped Newcastle to gain promotion at the end of the season. He retired in 1984, and returned to the game in 1992 as Newcastle manager, subsequently taking over at Fulham. In 1999 he was appointed England's team coach.

Twice European Footballer of the Year, and recipient of international respect and affection, Keegan is proof that a lustrous football career can be achieved as much by hard work, determination and complete self-belief as by dazzling virtuosity.

Denis Law

The exuberant hitman for Manchester United and Scotland

Arm raised triumphantly aloft, shirt fluttering around the wiry frame, broad grin beneath the shock of blond hair – who else but the irrepressible Denis Law, the showman and ruthless finisher who was one of the most potent and exciting attacking forwards in British football in the 1960s?

Law had a God-given talent for the game of football. He was a superb entertainer, a player capable of enthralling the crowds with his teasing unpredictability and his audacious personality. He was cocky, brave and abundantly skilful, his ability in the air was breathtaking, and his sheer enjoyment of the game was obvious and infectious.

Although he had a fiery and highly strung temperament, this was an essential part of his explosive artistry and he flourished in the hothouse atmosphere of the big game.

A skinny, seemingly frail Aberdonian teenager who signed pro at Huddersfield Town in 1957, his goals and potential led to him joining Manchester City in 1960 for a British record fee of £55,000. His ambition and taste for the exotic took him to Torino the following year to team up with Joe Baker for another record £100,000 (records followed Law around), but he walked out of the Italian club in 1962 to join Manchester United (for £116,000, yet another record...), where he became a key member of one of the great British sides.

Playing alongside Crerand, Best and Charlton, he was in his goalscoring element. In the 1963 Cup final he scored the first and was involved

Born:
Aberdeen, 24.2.40
Clubs:
Huddersfield Town 57-60, Manchester City 60-61, Torino 61-62, Manchester United 62-73, Manchester City 73-74
Club honours:
League Championship 64/5, 66/7; FA Cup 63
International honours:
55 (30) Scotland caps
Individual honours:
European Footballer of the Year 64

in the other two goals which won the Cup for United. That year, he also scored for the Rest of the World against England. With 'The Lawman' in unstoppable net-finding form, United won the League in 1964-65 and 1966-67 and he scored four hat-tricks in United's European campaigns. Unfortunately, he missed United's greatest triumph – the 1968 European Cup final – due to an injured knee.

By the early 1970s, United were in decline and, when Tommy Docherty took over as manager, Law was deemed surplus to requirements, and went across town to Manchester City on a free transfer. In his ten years at Old Trafford, he had been the king of the Stretford End and had scored 236 goals in 399 appearances for the Reds.

He remained a United man in spirit, and few can forget the dejection on his face as he walked slowly away from his backheel which sent United into the Second Division in 1974.

Starting his international career in 1958 at the age of 18, the youngest Scot to have represented his country since 1899, he went on to gain 55 caps, scoring 30 goals, equalled only by Dalglish. He played in one World Cup finals tournament, in 1974, but his greatest Scottish moment was when he and Slim Jim Baxter, in a display of impudence and outrageous trickery, routed England 3-2 at Wembley in 1967.

He retired in 1974, stating: 'I always wanted to call it a day when I was still on top', and his departure left football a duller game.

Gary Lineker

The clean-cut but deadly finisher for Barcelona and Spurs

Despite his boyish grin, affable manner and boy-next-door charm, Gary Lineker was a lethal predator around the penalty boxes of Europe in the 1980s.

His explosive acceleration, understanding of space and ability to be in the right place at the right time led to him scoring a feast of goals. Although not quite an out-and-out poacher, he rarely dropped back to find the ball, preferring instead to make himself available to the through ball from midfield which he generally dispatched with lightning speed and accuracy.

His career began at Leicester City in 1978 and the club see-sawed between the First and Second Divisions, Lineker's 26 goals securing them promotion in 1983. An £800,000 move to Everton followed, and in 1985-86 Lineker scored 30 League goals, and was voted PFA and Football Writers' Player of the Year. Also in 1986, his *annus mirabilis*, he scored six goals for England in the World Cup finals – including a hat-trick against Poland – and he was awarded the Golden Boot.

In the summer of that year he was transferred to Barcelona, then run by Terry Venables and he initially fitted in well at the Nou Camp. The arrival of Cruyff as manager, and his insistence that Lineker play on the right wing, unsettled the striker and, although he helped Barca to a Cup Winners Cup victory in 1989, Venables bought him back to England and Spurs in the summer of 1989.

In his first season at White Hart Lane he scored 24 League goals and, in 1991 Spurs

Born:
Leicester, 30.11.60
Clubs:
Leicester City 78-85, Everton 85-86, Barcelona 86-89, Tottenham Hotspur 89-92, Grampus Eight 92-94
Club honours:
European Cup Winners Cup 89, FA Cup 91, Spanish Cup 88
International honours:
80 (48) England caps
Individual honours:
PFA Player of the Year 86; Football Writers' Player of the Year 86, 92; World Cup Golden Boot 86

reached the FA Cup final where, in spite of a disallowed goal and a penalty miss by Lineker, they won the Cup. The following season, after a strong start, only Lineker's 28 League goals kept the club in the top division.

At Italia 90, facing humiliation against Cameroon in the quarter-final, England were rescued by Lineker's two penalty goals, the second in extra time after he had been pulled down. In the semi-final, trailing 1-0 to West Germany, England were granted a temporary reprieve by Lineker's 80th minute strike, but were eliminated on penalties. A successful West End play – 'An Evening with Gary Lineker' – celebrated his Italian exploits.

After captain Lineker's volley against Poland secured England's entry into the 1992 European Championships, Graham Taylor's team disappointed in the tournament, the low point for Lineker being his substitution by Alan Smith in the last game against Sweden. He had hoped to at least equal Charlton's record of 49 international goals, but he left English football one short of this target.

In 1992, Lineker drew a crowd of nearly 35,000 for his last game for Spurs, moving thereafter to Grampus Eight in the Japanese League. He returned two years later to a journalism and broadcasting career.

Nat **Lofthouse**

The fearless 'Lion of Vienna'

Born:
Bolton, 27.8.25
Club:
Bolton Wanderers 46-61
Club honours:
FA Cup 58
International honours:
33 (30) England caps
Individual honours:
Footballer of the Year 1953

Nat Lofthouse was an old-fashioned footballer. Born in Bolton, he played his whole career for his home club, became assistant trainer, coach, manager, backroom influence and finally President. Moreover, he was what is called an 'old-fashioned' centre-forward. His whole career was played in the maximum wage era, which ended the year he retired. He was not dissatisfied. He said: 'For me, football is pleasure with pay'.

Lofthouse went to the same school, Castle Hill in Bolton, as his hero and a former England centre-forward, Tommy Lawton. He first played for Bolton in March 1941, when 15 years old, scoring twice. His first 95 goals do not appear in his record, as they were scored in wartime seasons, when Nat spent eight hours working down the pit before matches.

In 1946, when the FA Cup resumed, Lofthouse was signed full-time by Bolton on the maximum wage of £10 per week. He played in the home Cup-tie against Stanley Matthews' Stoke which resulted in the Burnden disaster and 33 deaths.

Lofthouse was a typical bustling centre-forward of the type that England loved. He was a superb header of the ball and packed a terrific shot. Fearless, he spearheaded the forward line with strength and verve.

Nat's first cap came in 1950, when he scored both goals in a 2-2 draw with Yugoslavia. He soon became a regular and a regular scorer. His greatest game came in Vienna in May 1952. Before a partisan crowd of 65,000 in the Prater Stadium, a fierce match was tied 2-2 with nine minutes left when Lofthouse broke

clear from the halfway line. As the Austrian keeper advanced, Nat slid the ball home for his second goal before a crunching collision with the keeper, which led to him being stretchered off. But it was the winner, and Lofthouse earned the title 'Lion of Vienna'.

Lofthouse was named 'Footballer of the Year' the following season, when he scored in every round of the FA Cup, including the final. But in those pre-substitute days Bolton lost a man after 20 minutes through injury, and also lost a 3-1 lead when Blackpool scored twice in the last two minutes to win 4-3. It was the 'Matthews Final'.

However Lofthouse won his Cup-winners medal in 1958, when again Bolton had all the crowd against them. Their opponents were the post-Munich Manchester United. Bolton won 2-0, with Lofthouse scoring both goals. He played a blinder throughout, but in scoring his second goal he barged the United goalie, Munich hero Harry Gregg, into the net. It was a perfectly fair goal but many, particularly non-football fans, hated him for it. It is a great pity, because Lofthouse was one of the fairest and most sporting men who ever played the game.

His England career had ended the year before, and he played only one more full season before an ankle injury forced his retirement. He scored 256 League goals in 452 appearances. At the time he was England's top scorer with 30 goals in only 33 matches, a remarkable ratio, and he still stands fourth as the century ends.

Stanley Matthews

The mesmerising right-winger for Stoke and Blackpool

Born:
Hanley, Stoke-on-Trent, 1.2.15
Clubs:
Stoke City 30-47, Blackpool 47-61, Stoke City 61-65
Club honours:
FA Cup Winner 53
International honours:
54 (11) England caps
Individual honours:
Footballer of the Year 48, 63; European Footballer of the Year 56; CBE 56; Knighted 65

If one man can be said to have been the master of English wing-play, then it is surely Stanley Matthews. With a top-class career lasting over 30 years, Matthews was the indisputable king of the right touchline, with his sublime feinting and dummying skills, acceleration and pin-point crossing. The 'Wizard of Dribble' was aptly named.

He joined his local club Stoke City in 1930 on leaving school, and they were promoted to First Division at the end of season 1932-33. He made over 250 appearances for the club, scoring over 50 goals, and was idolised by the fans who, in 1947, were dismayed when Stoke sold him to Blackpool for £11,500.

In 1948, he and Blackpool reached the FA Cup final but were beaten by Manchester United, who scored three in the last 20 minutes. Nevertheless, he was voted the first Footballer of the Year. A provider *par excellence*, he was not a great goalscorer and he went three years without scoring from 1949 to 1952, churlish though it may be to mention this. His greatest moment came in 1953 when his speed, trickery and accurate distribution overcame a Bolton 3-1 lead in the Cup final, and Blackpool won 4-3. The game is still remembered as the 'Matthews Cup final'. He made 379 League appearances for Blackpool, scoring 17 goals.

He was awarded his first cap in 1934, scoring in a game against Wales, and inspired England to some memorable victories, notably the 1948 4-0 defeat of Italy, the 1955 7-2 rout of Scotland (when he made all seven goals) and the 1956 4-2 victory against Brazil. He played in the 1950 and 1954 World Cup finals, and received the last of his 54 caps in 1957. He was named the first European Footballer of the Year in 1956.

His lifelong attention to fitness and diet gave him the stamina of men half his age, and at the age of 46 he re-signed for Stoke City in 1961 for £3,500, and helped them to promotion in 1962-63, scoring in the last game against Luton to ensure their First Division place. Such was his charisma that, on his first home appearance, the crowd was 35,000 compared to 8,000 the previous game. He was voted Footballer of the Year for a second time in 1963 and retired in 1965 at the age of 50, the oldest player ever to have appeared in the top division.

He received a benefit game from Stoke in 1965, in which appeared such legendary players as Masopust, Yashin, Di Stefano and Puskas, a mark of the affection and respect in which he was internationally held. Already a CBE, he was knighted in 1965, an honour applauded by a grateful nation.

Bobby Moore

The Hammers skipper who led England to World Cup glory

Born:
Barking, Essex, 12.4 41
Clubs:
West Ham United 58-74, Fulham
74-77, Seattle Sounders 76, San
Antonio Thunder 78
Club honours:
FA Cup 64; European Cup Winners
Cup 65
International honours:
108 (2) England caps, World Cup 66
Individual honours:
Footballer of the Year 64; OBE 67

Characterised by a seemingly effortless authority, elegance and skill, Bobby Moore was the best defender in Britain in the 1960s and early 1970s.

Although far from being the fastest player in the game, he compensated for this with his great anticipation and vision, and his tackling was clean, incisive and perfectly timed. His unruffled and often diffident manner concealed a sharp, aware football brain, exemplified by his sliderule pass to Geoff Hurst for England's fourth goal in the 1966 World Cup final, when it may have been easier to hoof the ball into the stand.

Barking-born Moore made his first-team debut, at the expense of Malcolm Allison, for West Ham in 1958 at the age of 17. Playing at left-half (in spite of the fact he was predominantly right-footed), he received his first England cap in 1962 against Peru, and he was appointed captain of the national side by Alf Ramsey the following year.

In the 1964 Cup final, West Ham scrambled their way to a 3-2 victory against Preston North End, with Moore turning in a lacklustre performance, and in 1965 they were back at Wembley, this time facing TSV Munich 1860 in the European Cup Winners Cup final. The Hammers, captained by Moore and fielding a young Martin Peters, played brilliantly to win the trophy 2-0. However, his greatest achievement was just a year ahead. In July 1966, England, led by Moore, won the World Cup, beating West Germany 4-2, and

Moore's career was at its zenith. Three consecutive Wembley final victories was a remarkable achievement for the inspirational and tireless Moore.

In 1970 England again reached the World Cup finals in Mexico. Despite being unsettled by a trumped-up jewellery theft charge in Bogota days before the first game against Romania, Moore, and the England team, turned in a magnificent and unforgettable performance in the group stage against the Brazil of Pele, Jairzinho *et al*, but were eliminated by West Germany in the quarter-final. England failed to qualify for the 1974 World Cup finals, partly due to a rare error by Moore in Poland, and he collected the last of his 108 caps against Italy in 1973, a record only beaten by Peter Shilton.

Meanwhile, he was becoming increasingly restless at West Ham andwas frequently in disagreement with manager Ron Greenwood. Moore wanted to win a League Championship but, in spite of interest from some of the bigger clubs, he stayed at West Ham until 1974 when, surprisingly, he moved to Fulham, for whom he played in the 1975 Cup final – against West Ham, who won 2-0 – and he ended his playing days in America.

In March 1977 he retired from the English game and began a disappointing managerial career with Oxford City and Southend. In 1993 he died, tragically, of cancer at the age of 51. A saddened Pele commented: 'The world has lost one of its greatest players and a great gentleman.'

Bryan Robson

Captain Marvel of Manchester United and England

Had Bryan Robson not been quite so injury-prone, he would have added significantly to his remarkable collection of 90 England caps. Courageous almost to the point of foolhardiness, aggression was a central part of his game and of his make-up as a footballer, and he suffered the consequences of this.

However, he was much more than simply a strong, tough player. A dominating presence in midfield, he was fast, skilful and an accurate passer and header of the ball. Possessing a fierce shot, he scored well over a hundred League goals in his career, many of them coming from surging, last-minute runs into the penalty box. And, as captain of his club and country, he was an inspiring figure to his teammates.

Starting his career in 1971 at West Bromwich Albion, his susceptibility to injuries became ominously obvious in 1976 when he broke his leg three times that season. He moved to Manchester United in 1981, having made nearly 200 appearances for the 'Baggies', for a British record £1.5 million ('not for sale at any price' said the West Brom chairman). It was at United that he established himself as the finest British midfield player of the 1980s.

Assuming the club captaincy from Ray Wilkins, Robson led his team to three FA Cup victories in 1983, 1985 and 1990, scoring twice in the first Wembley triumph against Brighton, and to the club's record ten League victories in succession in 1983-84. Robson's determination and ability to read and control the game were crucial factors in the success of the 'Red Devils', and this was recognised by the fans

Born:
Chester-le-Street, Durham, 11.1.57
Clubs:
West Bromwich Albion 71-81, Manchester United 81-94, Middlesbrough 94-98
Club honours:
Premier League Championship 92/3, 93/4; FA Cup 83, 85, 90; European Cup Winners Cup 91
International honours:
90 (26) England caps

who chaired him off the pitch after the 3-0 victory over Barcelona in the 1984 European Cup Winners Cup quarter-final at Old Trafford. Seven years later, with Robson at the helm, United won the trophy, the club's first European success for 23 years, again beating Barcelona in the final in Rotterdam.

He was first capped by England in 1980 against Ireland, and in the 1982 World Cup finals, he scored the fastest goal ever in the tournament, within 27 seconds in the 3-1 victory over France. Again taking over from Wilkins the captaincy, this time of his country, Robson played two games in the 1986 finals, but dislocated his shoulder in the 0-0 draw with Morocco and was out of the competition. He played in the European Championships in 1988, and received his last cap for England against Turkey in 1991.

In 1992-93 United won the inaugural Premier League Championship, and a proud Robson paraded the trophy with Steve Bruce after the last home game of the season. Fittingly, Robson scored in the final game against Wimbledon. United won the title again the following season but Robson was in and out of the team, and was absent for the 1994 FA Cup final.

He left the club in the close season to join Middlesbrough as player-manager, and almost immediately took 'Boro back into the top flight. He had made nearly 450 appearances for United. Although he had offers from other Premier sides, he could not face the prospect of playing against United, an indication of the pride and affection he felt for his old club.

Graeme **Souness**

The hard-tackling midfielder of Liverpool and Scotland

Born:
Edinburgh, 6.5.53
Clubs:
Tottenham Hotspur 68-73, Middlesbrough 73-78, Liverpool 78-84, Sampdoria 84-86, Glasgow Rangers 86-89
Club honours:
League Championship 78/9, 79/80, 81/2, 82/3, 83/4; League Cup 81, 82, 83, 84; European Cup 78, 81, 84; Italian Cup 85; Scottish Premier League 86/7, 88/9; Scottish League Cup 87, 88, 89
International honours:
54 (3) Scotland caps

His controversial career as a manager cannot dim memories of Graeme Souness's marvellous accomplishments as a player.

The finest Scottish midfielder of the 1980s, Souness was an uncompromising footballer. He was a tough and often ferocious tackler who took no prisoners on the pitch, but he was also a wonderfully perceptive passer who controlled the speed and tempo of the game. He had a fierce, accurate shot, and he dominated games as much by force of his single-minded personality as by his tenacity and vision.

Arriving as a teenager at Spurs in 1968, Souness didn't manage to break into the first team and was transferred to Middlesbrough in 1973, helping them to the Second Division Championship in 1974. Bob Paisley took him to Liverpool in 1978 for a record fee (between two English clubs) of £352,000 and four months later he was on hand to slip the ball through to Dalglish for the winning goal in the European Cup final.

His subsequent Anfield career was a glorious one. He was the mainstay and the midfield supremo of the team which won five League titles, three European Cups and four successive League Cups between 1977-78 and 1983-84.

As captain of that great side, Souness led by example. His aggressive and often intimidating style of play was complemented by the sweetness of his distribution, and he could score goals, as Everton found out in the 1984 Milk Cup final replay when a Souness shot from the edge of the area proved to be the decider.

His midfield mastery of AS Roma in the 1984 European Cup final led to his departure to Sampdoria for £650,000 in the close season. He had played 352 games for the Reds and scored 56 goals. He spent two successful seasons in Genoa, helping his club to the Italian Cup, and returned to British football in 1986, joining Rangers as player/ manager.

The same year, he played his last international match for Scotland in the 2-1 defeat by West Germany in Mexico. He had played 54 times for his country, many of them as captain, and appeared in three World Cup finals.

His time at Rangers was a stormy one. In his first League game, Souness was sent off at Hibs, and had his marching orders on a further two occasions in his first year. However, under Souness Rangers won their first League title for nine years, and won it twice more in his charge. He was the first Rangers manager to sign a Catholic (Mo Johnston) and he packed his squad with experienced English players, something of an innovation in Scottish football.

He left Rangers in 1991, amid some acrimony, to move to Liverpool as manager, and his subsequent managerial career has been a chequered one, including spells at Galatasaray and Benfica.

Billy Wright

The unflappable centre-half for Wolves and England

William Ambrose Wright may not have caught the eye as much as some of his flashier contemporaries but he was the most consistent and effective defender of the 1950s.

As captain of Wolverhampton Wanderers and England he was fit, dependable and preferred to lead by example rather than by words. He was an intelligent reader of the game, strong in the tackle and, for such a relatively short man, he was a fine header of the ball.

He was signed by Wolves manager Major Frank Buckley and made his debut in 1941 in a home win over Notts County. A PT instructor during the Second World War, Wright made his international debut against Northern Ireland in 1946 and, on the retirement of Stan Cullis in 1947, he was made Wolves team captain, a position he held for 12 seasons.

New manager Cullis was turning Wolves into one of the most feared sides of the 1950s and Wright was to be the backbone of the team. In the next two seasons Wright missed only ten games, and in 1949 Wolves won the FA Cup. Through disciplinarian Cullis' training methods and under Wright's on-pitch direction, Wolves developed a fast, powerful, long-ball game which swept them to the club's first League title in 1953-54.

Originally a defensive right-half, Wright moved to centre-back and inspired Wolves to further League titles in 1957-58 and

Born:
Ironbridge, Shropshire, 6.2.24
Club:
Wolverhampton Wanderers 41-59
Club honours:
League Championship 53/4, 57/8, 58/9; FA Cup 49
International honours:
105 (3) England caps
Individual honours:
Footballer of the Year 52, CBE 60

1958-59. Wright's reliability, strength and fitness ensured that he was virtually ever-present throughout the 1950s, and he was the figurehead of that great team.

At the international level, Wright played in three World Cups – 1950, 1954 and 1958 – and, in 1959 against Scotland, he became the first English player to reach 100 caps. He went on to make a total of 105 appearances for England, 90 of them as captain, a proud record but one which included the 1-0 defeat by USA in 1950 and the crushing of England by the Puskas-inspired Hungarians in 1953.

At the end of the 1958-59 season Wright played his last game for Wolves, helping his team beat Leicester 3-0 at home, and he was awarded the CBE shortly thereafter. He had made 491 appearances for the club.

Clean-cut, articulate and modest, he was the model sportsman of the age, and his marriage to singing star Joy Beverley, of the popular Beverley Sisters, had cemented Wright's position in the affection of the public.

In 1962 he took over as manager of Arsenal but he was not particularly successful and he left the club in 1966 to move into sports journalism and broadcasting.

He rejoined Wolves in 1990 as a director and was welcomed back to Wolverhampton by thousands of his fans. He died of cancer in September 1994.

Florian Albert

Albert the Great of Goodison Park

Everton fans know about classy footballers. In the 1960s they worshipped a blond-haired centre-forward named Alex Young, who inspired a television play, 'The Golden Vision'. In the 1966 World Cup, when Hungary played all their group matches at Goodison Park, the fans found his dark-haired equivalent. Florian Albert was so brilliant and so graceful that they chanted his name, and made him a cult figure.

Things hadn't gone smoothly for Albert in his footballing life. Born in 1941, he moved to Budapest when he was 11 years old. At this time Hungary had the finest football team the world had seen, robbed of the 1954 World Cup only by injury and bad luck. Their defeat in the final was their first for 30 matches. Then Soviet tanks rolled into Hungary to crush the 1956 revolution, at a time when the national team was playing abroad. Many of the great team – among them Puskas, Czibor, Kocsis – stayed away, and built new careers with clubs like Real Madrid and Barcelona.

It was in this year that Albert made his pro debut for Ferencvaros. In 1959, after being top scorer in the European Youth Championship, he made his international debut in a 3-2 victory over Sweden. He was hailed as the man around whom Hungary would build a new world-beating side. The expectations at first were too heavy for his 18-year-old shoulders. Then a hat-trick against Yugoslavia and goals in defeats of West Germany and England restored his reputation and from then on he was Hungary's king-pin.

Albert was a complete centre-forward. He had

Born:
Hercegszanto, Hungary 15.9.41
Clubs:
Ferencvaros 56-74
Club honours:
Hungarian League Championship 62/3, 63/4, 66/7, 67/8, Hungarian Cup 72, 74, Fairs (UEFA) Cup 65
International honours:
75 (31) Hungary caps
Individual honours:
European Footballer of the Year 67

pace and vision, could draw defenders, create space and release colleagues with perceptive and subtle passing. He could dribble at speed and he could score goals with either foot. He ran the whole show, and did it with such natural style that he was an inspiration to his team-mates. His only drawback was that he was so gifted that sometimes he didn't pay too much attention to training. And he became so important to Ferencvaros that he gained more power among the management than a footballer should, and this caused some resentment among other players at the club.

He excelled in the 1962 World Cup, scoring a dazzling solo winner in Hungary's first group match with England, and netting a hat-trick in a 6-1 demolition of Bulgaria. But Hungary went out 1-0 to the surprise team Czechoslovakia in the quarter-finals when a disputed offside went against them.

Albert's virtuosity at Goodison in 1966 reached a peak when, in a great match, Hungary beat Brazil, the winners of the previous two World Cups, 3-1. One impressed Everton fan was reported as saying: 'If I went home and found Albert in bed with my wife I'd make him a cup of coffee....' Again Hungary went out in the quarter-final when defensive errors lost them the match with their oppressors, the Soviet Union, 2-1.

All Albert's club football was for Ferencvaros, with whom he won many honours and was League top scorer for three seasons. He retired from international football in 1971 but played on for three more years for Ferencvaros.

Roberto **Baggio**

The Little Prince of the Azzurri

Born:
Caldogno, Italy, 18.2.67
Clubs:
Vicenza 82-85, Fiorentina 85-90,
Juventus 90-95, AC Milan 95-97,
Bologna 97-98, Inter Milan 98-
Club honours:
Italian League Championship
94/5, 95/6; Italian Cup 95; UEFA
Cup 93
International honours:
55 (27) Italy caps
Individual honours:
World and European Footballer
of the Year 93

Slight, unassuming and a Buddhist, Roberto Baggio is an unusual figure to be the idol of a generation of Italian football fans. However, this veteran of three World Cups, and in his time the best player in the world, belies his appearance and manner and has demonstrated marvellous technique and goalscoring skills in Serie A and on the world stage.

A native of Northern Italy, Baggio began his career with his local club in the Italian Third Division and moved in 1985 to Fiorentina where he gained his first international cap in 1988. By the time he left in 1990, he had become the superstar of Italian football, his departure to Juventus for a world record £8 million provoking two days of street riots in

Florence. Shortly after his transfer, he joined the Italian squad for the 1990 World Cup where, although not picked for the early stages, his electric performances with Schillaci in later matches, notably his brilliant individual goal against Czechoslovakia, were the highlights of the tournament.

Baggio settled quickly in Turin and scored 14 goals in 33 League games in his first season with the 'Old Lady'. Over the next four seasons with the club he found the net regularly and,

in 1993-94, he finished with 17 goals in 32 League games. His scoring helped Juventus to win the UEFA Cup in 1993 and the Serie A title in 1995, and his talents were recognised in 1993 when he was awarded World and European Footballer of the Year.

At the 1994 World Cup in the USA, Italy under coach Arrigo Sacchi reached the final inspired by some excellent goals from the 'Divine Ponytail' Baggio who, along with the Brazilian Romario, was one of the players of the tournament. However, he carried a thigh injury into the Rose Bowl Stadium and was largely anonymous, apart from missing a penalty in the shoot-out, which handed the game and the World Cup to Brazil.

Back at Juventus, the emergence of the striking talents of a young Del Piero meant that Baggio's role and influence at the club were on the wane and it was no surprise when, in 1995, he moved to AC Milan. Unfortunately, he was used by coach Capello as a substitute and ultimately, with the arrival of Sacchi, with whom Baggio had had certain disagreements, he was on the move again, this time to Bologna. His period in the relative doldrums was now behind him and he finished the 1997-98 season with 22 goals.

In the 1998 World Cup finals, Cesare Maldini tended to prefer Del Piero to Baggio, although Baggio did score two goals in the tournament, and a penalty in the quarter-final shoot-out against France. In 1998, he moved yet again, this time to Inter Milan, where he seems set to enjoy a deserved Indian summer.

Marco **Van Basten**

The Dutch centre-forward who dominated the 1980s

Born:
Utrecht, Holland, 31.10.64
Clubs:
Ajax 82-87, AC Milan 87-95
Club honours:
Dutch Championship 81/2, 82/3, 84/5; Dutch Cup 83, 86, 87; European Cup Winners Cup 87; Italian Championship 87/8, 91/2, 92/3; European Cup 89, 90; World Club Championship 89, 90
International honours:
58 (24) Holland caps, European Championship 88
Individual honours:
Dutch Footballer of the Year 88, 89; World Footballer of the Year 88, 92; European Footballer of the Year 88, 89, 92

Marco Van Basten was one of the most exciting strikers of the modern era. Elegant and strong, equally proficient with either foot, powerful in the air and highly mobile, the Dutchman was a prolific goalscorer for his clubs and his country. However, he was injury-prone and the close and often brutal attention of defenders, unable to match his speed and his skill, led to his early retirement from the game.

Spotted by Ajax as a teenager, he joined the club at the age of 18, coming on as a substitute for Cruyff in his first senior game. From 1982 until 1987, his goals rejuvenated the Dutch club, which was emerging from an unaccustomedly fallow period, and Ajax lifted three Championships, three Dutch Cups and the European Cup Winners Cup, the latter with a winning goal from Van Basten, his last game for Ajax. He had scored 128 League goals in 133 games, and was awarded the European Golden Boot in 1986 for notching up 37 goals that season.

In 1987 he joined the Berlusconi-funded AC Milan, for the give-away fee of £1.5 million, and teamed up with fellow Dutchmen Ruud Gullit and Frank Rijkaard, under coach Arrigo Sacchi. The great days were back at the San Siro. The following year the club won the Serie

A title and in 1989 and 1990 they won the European Cup.

1988 was Van Basten's year. He was awarded European and World Footballer of the Year and his goals helped Holland to win the European Championship. He scored a hat-trick against England, two goals against West Germany and a sensational volley.against USSR in the final, regarded as one of the best goals ever scored.The Dutch were back as masters of Europe and Van Basten was top striker in the tournament.

In 1989 and 1992 he again achieved the status of European Footballer of the Year, a three-time honour to equal his mentor Cruyff and Michel Platini.

Holland and Van Basten under-performed at Italia 90, and were defeated by Denmark in the 1992 European Championships semi-final when Van Basten uncharacteristically missed a penalty in the shoot-out, but Van Basten was back on the goal trail at AC Milan, and was again named World Footballer of the Year.

Van Basten scored 13 goals in 15 matches at the beginning of the 1992-93 season, but his injuries were increasingly sidelining him. His last competitive game was in the 1993 European Cup final against Marseille, where an obviously unfit Van Basten could do nothing about his team's 1-0 defeat. He had scored 90 goals in 147 games for Milan. He retired from the game at the age of 30, a decade of heavy and clumsy tackles prematurely ending a remarkable career.

Franz **Beckenbauer**

'Der Kaiser', the majestic sweeper of Bayern Munich and West Germany

Born:
Munich, 11.9.45
Clubs:
Bayern Munich 64-77, New York Cosmos 77-80,
SV Hamburg 80-82, New York Cosmos 83
Club honours:
German League Championship 68/9, 71/2, 72/3, 73/4;
German Cup 66, 67, 69, 71; European Cup 74, 75, 76;
European Cup Winners Cup 67; North American
League Championship 76/7, 77/8, 79/80
International honours:
103 (14) West Germany caps, World Cup 74,
European Championship 72
Individual honours:
European Footballer of the Year 72, 76; West
German Footballer of the Year 66, 68, 74, 76

Striding imperiously up the pitch, ball under close control, eyes searching for the gap in the defence, a sudden defence-splitting pass...this was the trademark of Franz Beckenbauer, the gifted architect of Bayern Munich and West Germany's successes in the late 1960s and 70s.

Turning the traditional, defensive role of the sweeper on its head, Beckenbauer pioneered the attacking sweeper system, which he and his teammates used to brilliant effect. Defence swiftly became attack and opposing midfield and defence were caught out in a single movement. However, only a player with the elegance, pace, vision and distribution of Beckenbauer could have perfected this role.

Beckenbauer made his debut for Bayern Munich on the left wing in 1964 and for his country in 1965 in a successful World Cup qualifier against Sweden. In reaching the 1966 final Beckenbauer scored four goals, including one against Russia which completely deceived the veteran keeper Lev Yashin. West Germany lost in the final to England, 4-2, Beckenbauer having the thankless task of marking Charlton.

Beckenbauer was now captain of Bayern and led them to two German Cup victories in 1966 and 1967, the European Cup Winners Cup, beating Rangers 1-0 and the German League in 1969. West Germany won their three games in the qualifying rounds for the 1970 World Cup and, in the quarter-final, met England who went 2-0 up. A Beckenbauer shot sneaked under goalie Bonetti, and inspired Germany into winning the game 3-2. The Germans were, however, eliminated in the next round by Italy.

Now also captain of his country, 'Der Kaiser' Beckenbauer became the fulcrum of an exciting West German team, centred around him as sweeper, and they won the European Championship in 1972, beating the USSR in the final. The same year Beckenbauer was named European Footballer of the Year.

The next four years were to be astonishingly successful for Beckenbauer. Under his captaincy, Bayern won three straight German League titles and three successive European Cups, as well as the World Clubs Cup, and Beckenbauer, with such celebrated international teammates as Muller and Sepp Maier, reigned supreme.

The peak of his international career was as German captain in the 1974 World Cup final when he inspired his team to a 2-1 victory over the sparkling Dutch team of Cruyff, Neeskens, Rep *et al*, coming back to win from being a goal down in the second minute. In 1976 he was again awarded the title of European Footballer of the Year.

In 1977 he was lured to the North American Soccer League to play for New York Cosmos, winning the Soccer Bowl three times in four years. He finished his career with a brief season at Hamburg and another with Cosmos, and retired in 1984 to become manager of his national team. In 1990, West Germany beat Argentina in the World Cup final which, although a deeply disappointing game, meant that Beckenbauer is the only man to captain and manage a World Cup-winning team. He is currently club president at Bayern.

Dennis **Bergkamp**

The Ice Man of Arsenal and Holland

Born:
Amsterdam, 10.5.69
Clubs:
Ajax 81-93, Inter Milan 93-95, Arsenal 95-
Club honours:
Dutch Championship 89/90; Dutch Cup 87, 93; UEFA Cup 92, 94; European Cup Winners Cup 87; Premier League Championship 97/8; FA Cup 98
International honours:
68 (36) Holland caps
Individual honours:
Footballer of the Year 98, Dutch Player of the Year 92, 93

The goal was stunning. Level against Argentina in the 1998 World Cup quarter-final, Holland had to do something. In the last minute, a long, high pass from Frank De Boer found Dennis Bergkamp. He trapped the ball, flicked it in the air and smashed it past the keeper, the whole movement executed in a blur of control, delicacy and brilliance. Goal of the tournament it certainly was, and a contender for goal of the century.

All football fans treasure moments like this and Bergkamp does not disappoint. Ever alert, always on the move, his sudden changes of pace and direction, guile and awareness of space deceive and torment opposing defences. His mastery of the ball, and his bewildering feints and shimmies, set up teammates for goal, and his shooting can be sublime. Neither an out-and-out striker nor an attacking midfielder, Bergkamp prefers to control the space in the 'hole', a deep-lying forward who manipulates and organises his team and who can, and does, burst forward to score some memorable goals.

Named after Denis Law, Bergkamp was a member of the famed Ajax youth team side by the age of 12. Promoted by the returning Cruyff, he was in the first team at 17 and he didn't waste the opportunity. He was a perfect replacement for Van Basten, scoring 103 League goals in his seven years with Ajax, helping the club to win the Cup Winners and UEFA Cups and gaining his first Dutch cap against Italy in 1990. His performance in the 1992 European Championship was of the highest class, and all the big clubs came after Bergkamp.

Going to Inter in 1992, against Cruyff's advice, the Dutchman's career faltered. Frozen out by many of his superstar colleagues, a situation not aided by his natural off-pitch diffidence, and unable to gain a regular first-team slot, his three years at Milan resulted in only 52 appearances and 11 goals. 'I learned a lot in Italy', said Bergkamp ambiguously, but his surprise £7.5 million move to Arsenal in the summer of 1995 rejuvenated the player.

Although he didn't score in his first six League games, two stunning goals against Southampton at Highbury kick-started his Arsenal career and the fans' love affair with Dennis. Forging an attacking partnership with Ian Wright, he scored and created goals and was the Gunners' inspiration the following season when, under Arsene Wenger, the team finished third in the League. In season 1997-98, Bergkamp won PFA Player of the Year and Arsenal won the 'double'. He was in sensational form, scoring 22 goals for the Gunners, and even securing the top three slots on Match of the Day's 'Goal of the Month' competition.

In season 1998-99, Arsenal narrowly failed to win the League, and Bergkamp, tired after his World Cup exertions and carrying an injury, had a good season if slightly below his own high standards. He signed a new contract with Arsenal, so the North Bank will sing 'Walking in a Bergkamp Wonderland' into the new century.

Liam **Brady**

The midfield general who missed the biggest campaigns

Born:
Dublin 13.2.56
Clubs:
Arsenal 73-80, Juventus 80-82, Sampdoria 82-84,
Inter Milan 84-86, Ascoli 86-87, West Ham 87-90
Club honours:
FA Cup 79, runner-up 78, 80, Italian League
Championship 80/1, 81/2
International honours:
72 (9) Republic of Ireland caps
Individual honours:
Irish Player of the Year 76, PFA Player of the Year 79

Liam Brady's devotion to football has been absolute, ever since the day he was expelled from school for captaining the Irish Schoolboys against Wales rather than play in a Gaelic football match. For an outstanding footballer whose international career lasted nearly 16 years, he was unlucky in his small number of honours, and in never being able to show his skills in the final stages of the World Cup or European Championships.

Brady's uncle Frank had played for Ireland 30 years before Liam was born in 1956, and two older brothers played over 450 English League games between them for QPR and Millwall.

After captaining Ireland's schoolboys, Liam was an apprentice with Arsenal, signing pro forms as a 17-year-old in 1973, and making his debut almost immediately against Birmingham. A year later the Republic of Ireland's player-manager,

Johnny Giles, picked Liam for a European Championship qualifier against the Soviet Union. In a major upset the Republic beat the Soviets 3-1, but failed by a point to reach the finals. Brady became a regular in the side.

Arsenal at first thought 'Chippy' Brady was too small and tried unsuccessfully to beef him up. But he did not need brawn. He played in the old inside-left position, an attacking midfielder. His assets were his vision and control and his ability to penetrate defences with imaginative passing. Despite his lack of bulk he could shoot with power, too, and scored a goal roughly every six matches.

Brady became Arsenal's playmaker, and took

them from a mid-to-lower table side to title challengers by the end of the 1970s, climaxed by four Cup finals. Unfortunately Arsenal won only one, the FA Cup final of 1979, when Brady fashioned the last-minute winner against Manchester United. Then in 1980, to the disappointment of Arsenal's supporters, Brady decided to play in Italy, joining Juventus for £600,000. In his two seasons with them Juve won the Serie A title, after which Brady played for Sampdoria, Inter Milan and Ascoli, before returning to London and West Ham in 1987.

Brady's international career continued successfully with all of these clubs, and in 1985, when he scored against England at Wembley, he became the youngest player to reach 50 caps for the Republic. He was also made captain. But the appointment of Jack Charlton as Ireland's manager in 1986 signalled the beginning of the end. Charlton preferred tough-tackling midfielders who transferred the ball hard and high to the penalty area.

Nevertheless, Brady helped get the Republic to the 1988 European Championship finals (where they beat England) but unfortunately a bad knee injury prevented him playing in the final stages. He won only five more caps, retiring in fury when Charlton took him off after only 35 minutes of a match with West Germany in 1990. His 72 caps was an Irish record.

A year later he was appointed manager of Celtic but in two years failed to reverse the ailing club's fortunes, and resigned. It was a similar story at Brighton and he is now head of youth development with Arsenal.

Eric Cantona

The philosopher/poet and Manchester United superstar

The brooding, enigmatic presence of Eric Cantona loomed large over English football in the 1990s.

This emotionally complex, enormously talented Frenchman was a player with delicacy, vision and often breathtaking skill, and he had the ability to change games with a sudden flick or a thundering shot. He was also capable of outrageous behaviour and shocking antics. You never knew what Cantona was going to do next, and that's what made him such an exciting and mesmeric player.

Bought from Auxerre by Marseille in 1988 for £2 million, Cantona then led a peripatetic existence around French football, pausing only to be suspended yet again for various disciplinary reasons. On trial with Sheffield Wednesday, he was lured to Leeds for £900,000 in 1992 and, playing with Gordon Strachan, he inspired Leeds to their first League title for nearly 20 years. According to Strachan in the Leeds official history, Cantona's talent was that 'he does simple things brilliantly', but he could also do difficult things brilliantly, as his Charity Shield hat-trick in 1992 against Liverpool demonstrated.

To the dismay of the Elland Road fans, he was sold to Manchester United that year for £1.2 million, the most astute signing of Alex Ferguson's long managerial career. In his first full season for United, the club won the Premier League. In 1993-94, they won the 'double', with Cantona majestic throughout the campaign, although he was sent off twice in four days in March. He scored two virtually

Born:
Marseilles, 24.5.66
Clubs:
Auxerre 81-88, Marseille 88-91, Nimes 91-92, Leeds United 92, Manchester United 92-97
Club honours:
French League Championship 88/9; French Cup 90; Premier League Championship 91/2, 92/3, 93/4, 95/6, 96/7; FA Cup 94, 96
International honours:
45 (19) France caps
Individual honours:
Football Writers' Player of the Year 96

identical penalties in the Cup final, beating Chelsea 4-0. 'Ooh! Aah! Cantona!' was the Stretford End chant throughout that season, as the fans paid homage to their great playmaker.

It all went wrong for Cantona in 1994-95. Sent off at Crystal Palace in January, on his way to the tunnel he reacted to a torrent of abuse from a spectator with a spectacular kung-fu kick, and the incident provoked sensational headlines. Suspended and fined by his club and the FA, his season was over.

He was back to his imperious best in 1995-96, scoring on his first game back at Old Trafford, a penalty against Liverpool. His sublime skills, passing and reading of the game seemed to have been reinvigorated by his long lay-off, and United won the 'double' again. An otherwise drab FA Cup final against Liverpool was lit up by Cantona's instinctive, match-winning volleyed goal from a David James clearance.

In 1996 Cantona was voted Player of the Year – the first overseas footballer to receive the honour – and he had gained three League title medals with United. After a shaky start, United collected the Premier Championship in 1996-97, but at the end of the season Cantona stunned his fans with the announcement of his immediate retirement.

He has now embarked on an acting career, although his devoted supporters always saw him as a film star. He has simply moved his proud and immensely captivating talent from one great stage to another.

Johan **Cruyff**

The Total Footballer and master of Ajax, Barcelona and Holland

Born:
Amsterdam, Holland, 25.4.47
Clubs:
Ajax 64-73, Barcelona 73-78,
Los Angeles Aztecs 79,
Washington Diplomats 80-81,
Levante 81, Ajax 81-83,
Feyenoord 83-84
Club honours:
Dutch League Championship
65/6, 66/7, 67/8, 69/70, 71/2,
72/3, 81/2, 83/4; Dutch Cup
67, 70, 71, 72, 84; Spanish
League Championship 73/4;
Spanish Cup 78; European Cup
71, 72, 73
International honours:
48 (33) Holland caps
Individual honours:
European Footballer of the
Year 71, 73, 74

Long-limbed and graceful, with electric pace and majestic touch and vision, Cruyff epitomised Dutch football in its glorious period of dominance in the 1970s.

Born in Amsterdam in 1947, Cruyff began playing for Ajax's junior teams at the age of ten. His skilful forward play and eye for goal did not go unnoticed at Ajax, and at 17 he was handed a professional contract and a place in the first team. The young striker immediately adjusted to senior football and marked his first appearance with a goal.

Cruyff's debut-scoring exploits continued when, as a 19-year-old, he earned his first cap for the Dutch national team, grabbing a late equaliser in a 2-2 draw against Hungary. By the early 1970s, Cruyff had matured into one of the world's top players and in 1971 he was named European Footballer of the Year – he would win the award again in 1973 and 1974.

Further European glory followed for Cruyff, and in 1971 Ajax won their first of three successive European Cups. The 1972 final brought Johan's greatest moment in the competition, when he scored both goals in a 2-0 win over Inter Milan. Victory in the 1973 European Cup final, however, was his last contribution to Ajax's 1970s success and shortly afterwards he left his native Amsterdam to join Barcelona for a world record fee of £922,000.

When Cruyff arrived at the Nou Camp, Barcelona were in a slump, but by the end of the season the Catalans were champions. After his first Spanish season, Cruyff was chosen to captain the Dutch team in the 1974 World Cup finals. The skilful 'total football' of their skipper and his team-mates made them among the favourites for the tournament.

Cruyff was at the peak of his game during the 1974 tournament and his intelligent and innovative play was instrumental in Holland's progress to the final. However, a thrilling match in Munich ended in defeat for Holland at the hands of West Germany. It was Cruyff's first and last World Cup. By the time the next tournament came around in 1978 the Dutch master, at the age of 31, had retired from international football.

Cruyff's international retirement coincided with his decision to leave Europe to play in the USA. But after three seasons in America he was on his way back to Spain to play for Levante, before returning to Ajax where he won two more League titles. A contract dispute, however, saw him quit Ajax to join rivals Feyenoord as player-coach. It was the beginning of a managerial career with Ajax and Barcelona that would bring almost as much success as in his playing days.

Eusebio (da Silva Ferreira)

The Black Pearl of Benfica

Born:
Lourenco Marques, Mozambique, 25.1.42
Clubs:
Benfica 61-75, Rhode Island, Boston Minutemen, Monterrey, Toronto Metros, Beira-Mar, Las Vegas Quicksilvers, Beira-Mar, New Jersey Americans
Club honours:
Portuguese Championship 60/1, 62/3, 63/4, 64/5, 66/7, 67/8, 68/9, 70/1, 71/2, 72/3; Portuguese Cup 62, 64, 69, 70, 72; European Cup 62; North American League Championship 75/6
International honours:
64 (41) Portugal caps
Individual honours:
European Footballer of the Year 65; World Cup Golden Boot 66

Muscular and with a thunderbolt right-foot shot, Eusebio was the greatest goalscorer Portugal has ever known. Born in the Portuguese colony of Mozambique, he began his football with his local team at 16, having already been a junior sprint champion and a good basketball player. This team, Sporting, was a nursery of Portugal's Sporting Lisbon, who summoned him for a trial at 19, but he was intercepted at the airport by Benfica officials who lured the young striker to the Stadium of Light.

Very soon, Eusebio made his first-team debut for Benfica. His spectacular goals made him a fans' favourite and he was nicknamed the 'Black Pearl'. In Eusebio's first season, Benfica were crowned Portuguese Champions – a feat they repeated another nine times before 1974.

Eusebio was top scorer in Portugal in seven of these seasons, and in 1968 and 1973 was top scorer in Europe. International recognition also came early to Eusebio, and he earned his first cap for Portugal in 1961.

During the early 1960s, Benfica established themselves as a major force in European football. In 1961 Eusebio played his first European Cup match as the Portuguese Champions set out to defend the trophy they had won against Barcelona. They reached the final where two goals in three minutes from Eusebio ensured victory over a Real Madrid side that included Di Stefano and Puskas. The following season, Benfica again progressed to the European Cup final, but on this occasion they were defeated by AC Milan, despite a goal from Eusebio.

In 1963 Eusebio was in the Rest of the World side against England at Wembley, and in 1965, he was named European Footballer of the Year and Benfica were again runners-up in the European Cup. A year later, he was able to display his talents to the biggest possible soccer audience, as Portugal travelled to England for the 1966 World Cup. Three Eusebio goals in the group stage eased Portugal's passage to a seemingly easy quarter-final tie with North Korea. The Koreans, however, failed to appreciate their status as soccer minnows and promptly sped into a 3-0 lead. Eusebio, though, was not ready for an embarrassing elimination and inspired his team to a 5-3 victory with four goals. Portugal fell at the penultimate hurdle, going out to hosts England, but Eusebio had scored an amazing nine goals to end up as the tournament's top scorer.

In 1968 Eusebio made his last appearance in a European Cup final when Benfica took on Manchester United at Wembley. With the score at 1-1, he had a chance to score a late winner but was denied by a fine reflex save from Alex Stepney. The game went into extra time and United ran out comfortable victors. Eusebio's total of 46 European Cup goals was second only to the 49 of Di Stefano.

In 1975 Eusebio crossed the Atlantic to play in America for the last few years of his career. He had scored 317 goals in 291 League games for Benfica and 41 goals in 64 games for Portugal. Although Eusebio did return to Benfica as a coach in 1977, it was as a scorer of spectacular goals that he will be best remembered.

Just **Fontaine**

More than just a goalscorer

Born:
Marrakech, Morocco, 18.8.33
Clubs:
USM Casablanca (Morocco) 50-53, Nice 53-56, Reims 56-61
Club honours:
French Cup 54, 58, French League Championship 55/6, 57/8, 59/60
International honours:
20 (27) France caps

Luck played a large part in the career of Just Fontaine. In the 1958 World Cup finals he seized his chance when a team-mate was injured and netted 13 goals, a record for a single tournament. But before he could add to this total in subsequent World Cups he had been forced out of the game through a fractured leg.

Fontaine was born in Marrakech, Morocco, of a French father and Spanish mother. He loved football and played for his local club, AC Marrakech, as a centre-forward before joining USM Casablanca when 17. He was spotted by the French side Nice and signed for them in 1953, making an immediate impression. As a 20-year-old he was picked for the French Under-23 team and scored a hat-trick in an 8-0 win over Luxembourg. But he was considered too young for the 1954 World Cup and waited till 1956 for his senior debut.

He was not tall, but he was muscular and strong. He had good ball control and awareness. Above all, he had supreme confidence, the striker's instinct to anticipate openings and the speed off the mark and mobility to convert them into goals.

In 1956 Reims paid a record French transfer fee for him as a replacement for the legendary Raymond Kopa who, after playing for Reims in the first European Cup final, was bought by their conquerors, Real Madrid.

Fontaine had a great year in 1958. Reims did the French 'double' and Fontaine went to Sweden for the World Cup. He expected to be a reserve, and said: 'I am centre-forward until Kopa comes'. Kopa was a late arrival, having helped Real win their third consecutive European Cup. But on the eve of the finals Kopa's expected strike partner, Fontaine's club team-mate Rene Bliard, was injured and Fontaine played.

Fontaine immediately struck up a great partnership with Kopa, and netted three times in France's 7-3 defeat of Paraguay. He got both French goals as they lost 3-2 to Yugoslavia, and he and Kopa both scored as Scotland were beaten 2-1. Two more goals in a quarter-final 4-0 defeat of Northern Ireland and another in a 5-2 semi-final defeat by Brazil meant that he had scored in every match. He had one match to come – the third place play-off with West Germany. Fontaine netted four in a 6-3 win to take his total to 13, still the highest for a single finals tournament, and only one fewer than Gerd Muller's overall record.

Fontaine helped Reims to the European Cup final in 1959 but they lost to Kopa's Real Madrid. But Reims then bought Kopa back to restore their exciting partnership and the Championship was duly won. But late in the season, on 20 March 1960, Fontaine suffered a double fracture of his leg playing at Sochaux. He fought back and in December returned to the French team. It was his last appearance. His leg was broken again on 1 January 1961 and he was forced to retire at only 27. He became a sports writer, president of the French players' union, and – for two matches in 1967 – French team manager.

Garrincha

The Little Bird of Brazil

(Manuel Francisco dos Santos)

Born:
Pau Grande, Brazil, 28.10.33
Clubs:
Pau Grande 47-53, Botafogo 53 - 66, Corinthians, Barranquilla, Flamengo, Bangu, Red Star Paris, Portuguesa, Olaria
Club honours:
Rio Championship 56/7, 60/1, 61/2
International honours:
50 (12) Brazil caps, World Cup 58, 62

Despite his apparent handicap and his many off-the-field problems, Garrincha remains unsurpassed as the greatest winger ever.

Physically damaged by childhood polio – one leg bent inwards, the other curved outwards and shorter – he was a dazzlingly quick and dangerous winger, a brilliant dribbler and a master of the powerful long-range and 'banana' shots. He was also, for such a small man, a surprisingly effective header of the ball.

Born into poverty near Rio de Janeiro, Garrincha (the name means 'little songbird')

began his career with his local club and in 1953 signed for Botafogo where he was to play 580 games and score 232 goals. He remained with the club until 1966 when he was transferred to Corinthians of Sao Paulo. Although he won several Rio de Janeiro League titles with Botafogo, at the time there was no national Brazilian League. However, it is for his performances in World Cup finals that he is internationally remembered.

He made his international debut against Chile in 1955. In the 1958 finals in Sweden, he missed the first two games and his teammates petitioned manager Feola to

include him in the next game. Garrincha played alongside the 17-year-old Pele and the team was transformed. Garrincha created the first two Brazilian goals in the final and Brazil won the Cup.

In the 1962 tournament in Chile, Pele was injured after the second match and played no further part in the competition. By default, Garrincha took over the centre-forward role and he created havoc in opposing defences. He scored two goals in the quarter-final defeat of England, the second a beautifully placed 25-yard shot, and two more in the semi-final victory over Chile, a game in which he became only the second player to be sent off at this late stage.

A personal intercession by the president of Brazil ensured Garrincha's presence at the final, where he collected his second World Cup winner's medal as Brazil beat Czechoslovakia 3-1. In 1966, Garrincha was not completely fit, and Brazil, with Pele cynically hacked off the pitch by Portugal, exited at the first round.

Garrincha gained 50 Brazilian caps in his career and was on the losing side in only one World Cup finals match of the 11 he played, against Hungary in 1966. Brazil never lost with him and Pele playing together.

After 1966, Garrincha played for several other clubs in Europe and South America and then retired. His lifelong over-indulgence in alcohol tragically led to his death at the age of 49 in January 1983 from alcohol poisoning.

Ruud **Gullit**

The dreadlocked star of Holland and Milan

In appearance more a rock star than a hugely talented footballing athlete, the flamboyant and charismatic Ruud Gullit has enjoyed success at the highest levels of the game. Dreadlocks flying behind him, his strong and surging runs, accurate passing and instinctive awareness of space prompted AC Milan and Holland into achieving some of their greatest triumphs.

Born in Amsterdam to Surinamese parents, the 16-year-old was taken on by Haarlem in 1979 and he gained his first international cap against Switzerland in 1981 on his 19th birthday. In 1982, he moved to Feyenoord, playing mainly as a sweeper in a side which included Johan Cruyff, and in 1983-84 helped the team capture the Dutch Championship and Cup.

Transferred to PSV Eindhoven in 1985, he began to take on more of a midfield attacking role, and in 1985-86 and 1986-87 PSV won the Dutch Championship, Gullit being twice voted Dutch Footballer of the Year. In 1987, AC Milan paid a world record £6 million to secure his services, and Gullit was awarded European and World Footballer of the Year.

The best was yet to come for the intelligent and extravagantly gifted Dutchman. The following season, Milan won the Serie A title and, in 1989 and 1990, playing alongside fellow Dutchmen Frank Rijkaard and Marco Van Basten, for whom Gullit was a master provider, he led Milan to two successive European Cup victories and two World Club Championships.

In 1988, however, he suffered a serious knee injury which was to plague him for the next

Born:
Amsterdam, Holland, 1.9.62
Clubs:
Haarlem 79-82, Feyenoord 82-85, PSV Eindhoven 85-87, AC Milan 87-93, AC Milan 94, Sampdoria 94-95, Chelsea 95-98
Club honours:
Dutch Championship 83/4, 85/6, 86/7; Dutch Cup 84; Italian Championship 87/8, 91/2, 92/3; Italian Cup 94; European Cup 89, 90
International honours:
65 (16) Holland caps, European Championship 88
Individual honours:
European Footballer of the Year 87; World Footballer of the Year 87, 89; Dutch Footballer of the Year 86, 87

three years. Milan again won the Italian Championship in 1991-92 and 1992-93, the year Gullit left to join Sampdoria, with whom he won the Italian Cup in 1994.

At the international level, Gullit was the inspiration behind Holland's 1988 2-0 European Championship final victory over the Soviet Union, scoring a fine header from Van Basten's headed cross, and he also played in the 1990 World Cup finals, the Dutch reaching the second round before being knocked out by West Germany. In the 1992 European Championships, Holland were narrowly beaten in a penalty shoot-out by Denmark in the semi-finals.

A proud man, possessed of great self-belief and strong opinions, Gullit is an articulate and vocal analyst of the game. This, combined with a degree of stubbornness, led to him walking out of the Dutch camp three weeks before the 1994 World Cup finals in the USA after a series of arguments with his manager Advocaat. He did not play in the tournament.

That same year he moved back to Milan for a short period, before rejoining Sampdoria. In 1995 a free transfer took him, rather surprisingly, to Chelsea, where he was playmaker under manager Glenn Hoddle before taking over Hoddle's role, leading Chelsea to FA Cup victory in 1997.

He left Chelsea in 1998 and is currently managing Newcastle United whom he took to the 1999 FA Cup Final.

Jairzinho

A Christmas present for Brazil

Born:
Caxias, Brazil, 25.12.44
Clubs:
Botafogo 61-71, Marseille
71-73, Cruzeiro 73-76,
Portuguesa 76-78
Club honours:
Rio de Janeiro League
Championship 62/3, 66/7,
67/8; Copa Libertadores
(South American Club
Cup) 76
International honours:
87 (37) Brazil caps, World
Cup 70

The baby born Jair Ventura Filho on Christmas Day 1944 became one of Brazil's greatest footballers. Jair was the name of a World Cup hero of 1950, so when the young prodigy began to play he took the name Jairzinho. Jairzinho's own personal hero was the Brazilian right-winger Garrincha, and their careers overlapped. They played in the same side together in one match of the World Cup finals of 1966. Soon afterwards Jairzinho took over the right-wing spot from his fellow-great for both Botafogo and Brazil.

As a boy, the football-mad Jairzinho used to sneak into the Botafogo ground to watch the players train. He signed as an amateur for the club in 1961, and won a gold medal at the Pan-American Games. He turned professional in 1962, when Garrincha suffered a bad leg

injury, and that year helped win the Rio de Janeiro Championship (one of Brazil's two regional titles). The following year he made his debut for Brazil.

He was just taking over completely in club and national teams from Garrincha in 1967 when he, too, suffered a leg injury – a double fracture. For the next three years he struggled to establish a regular place in the strong Brazilian team, his quick temper and niggling injuries not being to his advantage. However when the 1970 World Cup finals began, manager Mario Zagalo made him his first choice on the wing. He scored twice in a 4-1 defeat of Czechoslovakia, his second goal coming after a run which took him past four opponents. He said Zagalo's faith in him had given him the confidence he needed.

Jairzinho's assets as a winger were strength, speed, superb ball control, directness and an ability to shoot hard and straight. He would have liked to have led the attack, but Pele and Tostao were established in the centre in 1970, and Jairzinho and Rivelino (on the left) had to settle for being crackshot goalscoring wingers. Rivelino was Brazil's free-kick expert, and in the World Cup match against Czechoslovakia in 1970, Jairzinho helped him score the equaliser by joining the opposition wall, becoming one of the first players to employ this now common tactic.

As the 1970 tournament progressed, Jairzinho scored the only goal to beat England and another in the 3-2 defeat of Romania. Goals in the quarter- and semi-finals meant that Jairzinho came to the final with the prospect of becoming the first man to score in every round, including the final. Twenty minutes from the end he accepted the chance when Pele nodded down a cross to him and made history with his seventh goal.

Jairzinho's brilliance encouraged the French club Marseille to buy him in 1971, but he didn't settle down in Europe and after some disciplinary problems returned to Brazil to play for Cruzeiro, with whom he won the Copa Libertadores (the South American version of the European Cup) in 1976. He scored 14 goals in 13 matches. He also scored twice more for Brazil in World Cup finals, playing seven matches in 1974.

In 1976 Jairzinho went to Venezuela to end his career with the Caracas club Portuguesa, his 1970 World Cup scoring feat still unique.

Paolo Maldini

The classy defender for Milan and Italy

Born:
Milan, 26.6.68
Club: AC Milan 85-
Club honours:
Italian League Championship 87/8, 91/2, 92/3, 93/4, 95/6, 98/9; Italian League Super Cup 88, 92, 93, 94; European Cup 89, 90, 94
International honours:
101 (6) Italy caps
Individual honours:
World Soccer Player of the Year 94

A Nike ad a few years ago summed it up neatly – 'Stoppage time. When a striker meets Paolo Maldini.'

The best defender in the world, Maldini is probably also one of the most versatile. A strong, impassable left-back, he is equally effective in the centre of defence. With his close ball control and his skilful distribution, he often moves forward, initiating moves and setting up attacks, and his heading ability from corners and free-kicks throws opposing defences into disarray. Unusually for an Italian footballer, he has spent his entire career with one club, AC Milan, and this stylish and devastatingly effective footballer has become synonymous with the team.

Son of Cesare Maldini, ex-AC Milan sweeper, European Cup winner and manager of Italy's 1998 World Cup team, the Juventus-supporting young Paolo joined Milan as a left-winger, but made his debut as a left-back against Udinese at the age of 16 in 1985. Since then, the left-back position has been his. Tutored by Franco Baresi and Mario Tassotti, his play soon caught the eye of the Italian coach Vicini, and he came off the bench in a friendly against Yugoslavia at the age of 19 to gain his first international cap.

His consistency, defensive abilities and surging runs were an essential component of the great Milan team of the late 1980s and Maldini picked up two European Cup Winner's medals in 1989 and 1990, with another to come in 1994 in Milan's crushing 4-0 defeat of Barcelona. In 1990 and 1994 he played for Italy in the World Cup finals, losing in the final in 1994 to Brazil on penalties.

Taking over as Italian captain from Baresi, who retired in 1995, Maldini led his team to European Championship finals in 1966 in England where they beat Russia 2-1 with the flying winger Kanchelskis in a constant battle of wits with the authoritative Maldini, lost to the Czech Republic 2-1 in a thrilling game, drew with Germany but failed to qualify for the semis. Maldini was one of the players of the tournament. Father and son both led their country to France for the 1998 World Cup finals, losing in the quarter-finals to France on penalties.

In 1998-99 AC Milan won the Italian League, giving Maldini six League Championship medals in 14 virtually unbroken seasons with the club. Still only 31 years old, he has made over 400 appearances for Milan with plenty more to come.

With 101 caps to his credit, this peerless player will go down on record as the greatest all-round footballer in Italian history.

Diego Maradona

The little Argentinian with the magic feet

There are some who argue that Maradona, the brilliant orchestrator of the Argentine team, was a better footballer than Pele, who thrived on the all-round genius of Brazil. The debate continues, but there is no dispute that Diego was to the 1980s what Pele was to the 1960s – simply the best player on the planet.

A child footballing star who played for Argentinos Juniors at the age of 15, Maradona developed into a prodigiously talented footballer, a provider and finisher with exquisite control, intricate dribbling skills and surging pace. He could turn defences in the tightest of spaces, creating passes for teammates or setting off on mazy runs past hapless defenders, and his left-foot was lethal near goal.

Leaving Argentina for Barcelona in 1982 for a world transfer record of £3 million, Maradona was hacked and bruised by Spanish defences until Terry Venables sold him to Napoli in 1984. The little superstar had found his stage and his audience. Relishing the mass adulation of the southern Italian support, Maradona virtually single-handedly transformed the club's fortunes and brought them the Italian 'double' in 1986-87 and the UEFA Cup in 1989.

Internationally, he had been deeply upset at being dropped from Menotti's 1978 World Cup squad ('too young', opined the chain-smoking manager), but he appeared in 1982, when Argentina had a bad tournament and Maradona was sent off against Brazil. However, in 1986 he was the player of the finals. Although hated by English fans for the 'hand of God' incident in the quarter-finals, the rest of the world adored him for his amazing goal four minutes later, and for his virtual repeat of this in the semis against Belgium. His pass to Burruchaga in the final for the winning goal over West Germany, confirmed his elevation to the status of world's best player.

By 1990 an overweight and unfit Maradona captained Argentina to the final but lost to West Germany in a dreadful match. In the same year his relationship with Napoli was disintegrating under allegations about his sleazy private life and criminal connections. In 1991 he was banned for 15 months for failing a drugs test. He left Napoli in 1992 and spent a disastrous few months with Seville, before heading back home to join Newell's Old Boys.

A surprisingly trimmed-down and energetic Maradona arrived in the USA in 1994 for the World Cup finals and all the old skills appeared to be back. To the sadness of many, however, he again failed a drugs test and was sent home by the Argentinian authorities. He moved to Boca Juniors in 1995 and retired in 1997 on his 37th birthday.

The reasons for Maradona's fall from grace have been well documented. The physical, emotional and commercial pressures and expectations were too much for a vulnerable and immature man, and it is to be hoped that the glittering career of this troubled genius will be remembered for the football and not for anything else.

Born:
Buenos Aires, 30.10.60
Clubs:
Argentinos Juniors 76-80, Boca Juniors 80-82, Barcelona 82-84, Napoli 84-92, Seville 92-93, Newell's Old Boys 93-95, Boca Juniors 95-97
Club honours:
Argentinian Championship 80/1; Spanish Cup 83; Italian League Championship 86/7, 89/90; Italian Cup 87; UEFA Cup 89
International honours:
91 (34) Argentina caps, World Cup 86, runner-up 90
Individual honours:
South American Player of the Year 79, 80

Lothar **Matthaus**

Germany's Captain Courageous

Bayern Munich's libero Matthaus is the most-capped German player in history. A skilful midfield player, he is also an incisive tackler and a tough ball-winner and is, alongside Stefan Effenberg, the fulcrum of the Bayern team. He has played in five World Cup finals and three European Nations tournaments, and his influential presence as captain inspired West Germany to win the 1990 World Cup.

Matthaus spent five seasons with Borussia Moenchengladbach before moving to Bayern in 1984 for £650,000. As midfield general, he led the club to three German League titles, and he went to Inter Milan in 1988 for £2.4 million, where his experience and determination helped the club to lift the Italian League title in 1989 and the UEFA Cup in 1991, with a 2-1 aggregate win over Roma.

He was in the squad for the 1982 World Cup, making two appearances as substitute, and was back in 1986 where, in the final, he marked Maradona and gave away the foul which led to Argentina's first goal and ultimate victory. However, his and West Germany's triumph in 1990, in an admittedly tedious 1-0 victory over Argentina in the final, led to Matthaus being awarded Player of the Tournament and European Player of the Year.

After sitting out the 1992 European Championship finals due to a knee injury, he played in the World Cup finals in 1994, where Germany was bundled out by Stoichkov's Bulgaria, and he was again injured in a game against Albania in December that year. Matthaus' single-mindedness and tendency to

unhelpful public pronouncements irritated several teammates, notably Jurgen Klinsmann, and his increasingly personal disagreements with Klinsmann and manager Berti Vogts resulted in him being dropped from the German team. 'He will never play in the German national team again', said Berti Vogts in May 1996.

Moving back to Bayern in 1992, Matthaus got the club back on the winning trail with a 5-1 aggregate victory over Bordeaux in 1996 in the UEFA Cup final and two more German League titles in 1994 and 1997. He missed out in the 1966 European Championships but, to the surprise of many, was recalled to the German team for the 1998 World Cup finals, the absence through injury of Sammer and Thorn forcing Vogts to pick Matthaus, even though it was something of a personal climbdown for the manager. He played in four games in the tournament, including Germany's 3-0 elimination by Croatia in the quarter-finals.

In 1999, Bayern played Manchester United in the European Cup final in Barcelona. After United's dramatic last-minute 2-1 victory, with Matthaus having been substituted in the second half, he threw away his runner-up medal in disgust. He knows that the greatest prize in club football has almost certainly eluded him and that, at the age of 38, his career is nearly over.

A great servant to his country for nearly 20 years, Matthaus has no reason to think himself a failure.

Born:
Erlangen, Germany, 21.3.61
Clubs:
FC Herzogenaurach 78-79, Borussia Moenchengladbach 79-84, Bayern Munich 84-88, Inter Milan 88-92, Bayern Munich 92-
Club honours:
German League Championship 84/5, 85/6, 86/7, 93/4, 96/7; German Cup 86; Italian League Championship 88/9; UEFA Cup 91, 96
International honours:
136 (22) W. Germany/Germany caps, World Cup 90
Individual honours:
Player of Tournament World Cup 90, World Footballer of the Year 91, European Footballer of the Year 90, German Footballer of the Year 90

Gerd Muller

The bomber who rarely missed the target

Gerd Muller had to prove he was a great striker the hard way – by getting goals. Few believed that the short (5ft 7in), slightly overweight player with the short legs and thick thighs could ever make a centre-forward. When the president of his first senior club, Bayern Munich, suggested to coach 'Tschik' Cajkovski that he sign him, the coach replied: 'I don't want that elephant among my thoroughbreds'. Luckily for Bayern, the president insisted.

Muller played with his local club, TSV Nordlingen, between the ages of 15 and 17 before he was taken to Munich. He was slow in a sprint and had to overcome being called 'Der Dicker' – the fat fellow. But his physique was to prove a great asset. Much of his power was packed into those imposing thighs. In conjunction with his low centre of gravity, this made it very difficult to knock him out of his stride or to dispossess him. His leg power not only got him off the mark quicker than his opponents, but also got him into the air fast and, despite his shortness, he was an effective scorer with his head.

Muller rarely operated outside the penalty area. The German manager, Helmut Schon, called him his 'scorer of little goals'. 'His reflexes and his reading of any situation are remarkable', he said. 'Maybe the ball will slip from the goalkeeper's hands for just a second. That is long enough for a man with Muller's reflexes.' Because he did not tackle or track back into midfield, or play much part in the build-up of moves, some at Bayern Munich at first thought him a luxury. But 365

Born:
Zinsen, Bavaria, West Germany, 3.11.45
Clubs:
TSV Nordlingen 60-63, Bayern Munich 63-79, Fort Lauderdale Strikers (USA) 79-82
Club honours:
German Championship 67/8, 70/1, 71/2, 72/3, German Cup 67, 68, 69 71, European Cup Winners Cup 67, European Cup 74, 75, 76
International honours:
62 (68), World Cup 74
Individual honours:
West German Footballer of the Year 67, 69, European Footballer of the Year 70

goals in only 427 League matches show what a part he played. It was the same with West Germany, where Muller's goals (68) actually exceeded his games (62), making him perhaps the deadliest striker of all time. His nickname soon became 'Der Bomber'.

Muller made his international debut in 1966. West Germany already had a great centre-forward in Uwe Seeler, the idol of the fans. Seeler played 21 games in four World Cup finals, being on the field (including extra time) for 33 hours, a World Cup record. Seeler's last World Cup, 1970, was Muller's first.

The young pretender and the old favourite seemed set to feud, but manager Schon's remedy, to make them share a hotel room for five weeks, worked. Muller netted ten goals and Seeler three as West Germany reached the semi-finals. Muller scored four more goals in the 1974 finals, his total of 14 finals goals establishing his own World Cup record.

Muller announced his retirement from international football after scoring the winning goal in the 1974 Final. He was only 29, and continued to play for Bayern for another five seasons, by which time he was laden with club and international honours, including three European Cup winners medals. At 34, he then wound down in the USA, playing three seasons with Fort Lauderdale Strikers and adding a final 38 goals to his total by way of a PS.

Pele

The King of Football

(Edson Arantes do Nascimento)
Born:
Tres Coracoes, Brazil, 23.10.40
Clubs:
Santos 56-74, New York Cosmos 75-77
Club honours:
Paulista League 55/6, 57/8, 59/60, 60/1, 61/2, 63/4, 64/5, 66/7, 67/8, 68/9, 72/3; Brazilian Cup 61, 62, 63, 64, 65; USA League Championship 76/7
International honours:
91 (77) Brazil caps, World Cup 58, 62, 70
Individual honours:
South American Footballer of the Year 73

If the essence of a sport can be embodied in one towering, supreme practitioner – such as Ali in boxing and Michael Jordan in basketball – then there is only one figure who personifies the glorious spirit of football. Pele.

The unique legend, and the player against whom all others are judged, Pele had it all. Strength, speed, astonishing skills, breathtaking ball control, gravity-defying heading ability, a ferocious shot and the audacity to attempt the near-impossible, these were all part of his stunning repertoire.

A precocious footballer as a child, Pele joined Santos at the age of 16 in 1956 and, at the age of 17, arrived with the Brazil squad at the 1958 World Cup finals in Sweden. Coming into the team during the group stage, he scored against Wales, devastated France with a hat-trick in the semis, and scored two against Sweden in the final, one of which was an exquisite overhead lob and volley. A tearful, teenage footballer left the pitch a superstar.

In 1962 in Chile, Pele played in the first game against Mexico, scoring a brilliant individual goal, but he was injured in the next game and out of the tournament. Garrincha took over his role, and Brazil were champions for the second time. England in 1966 was no better for Pele. Defeated by Hungary, and with Pele kicked around the park by a cynical and brutal Portugal and again withdrawing from the competition, Brazil were eliminated at the group stage.

The Brazilian team which assembled in Mexico for the 1970 World Cup finals was arguably the best football side the world has ever seen. Rivelino, Jairzinho, Tostao, with Pele the heart of the team, were unstoppable. Storming their way through the competition – including a titanic 1-0 victory over Bobby Moore and England – their flair, dazzling talents and brilliant teamwork took them to the final against Italy.

Pele scored a jackknife header and made two more, a nonchalant, perfectly weighted lay-off to his right setting up Carlos Alberto's thunderbolt fourth goal. Italy were dismissed 4-1, Brazil were again champions of the world, and they secured permanent possession of the Jules Rimet trophy.

Soon after this, Pele retired from international football but continued to play for Santos, winning the South American Player of the Year in 1973. On his retirement in 1974, Santos removed the number 10 shirt from the line-up, a tribute to the greatness of the man who wore it. In 1975 Pele was tempted out of retirement by a $4.5 million deal with New York Cosmos, and remained in the USA for three seasons.

He retired for good in 1977 to take up a role as Brazil's sporting ambassador, and he is currently Brazil's Minister for Sport.

Michel **Platini**

The idol of Juventus and France

Born:
Jouef, France, 21.6.55
Clubs:
Nancy 72-79, St Etienne 79-82, Juventus 82-87
Club honours:
French Cup 78; French League 81; Italian League Championship 83/4, 85/6; Italian Cup 83; European Cup 85; European Cup Winners Cup 84
International honours:
72 (41) France caps, European Championship 84
Individual honours:
European Footballer of the Year 83, 84, 85; Knight of the Legion d'Honneur 87

Platini was the finest footballer France has ever produced. A graceful, elegant player, he was an expert passer of the ball, a quick and intelligent reader of the game and a master at wrong-footing and deceiving opponents. Technically a midfielder, he was also an accomplished finisher and spot kick-taker and he scored many important goals for his club and country.

He started his career with Nancy in 1972, scoring 98 goals for the club until his departure for St Etienne in 1979. In 1980/1, assisted by Platini's 20 League goals, 'The Greens' won the league, and the following year he crossed the Alps to join Juventus. He took a while to adjust to the Italian League's robust defending but,

playing alongside Boniek, Cabrini and Tardelli, he soon settled in and his 16 League goals that season took Juve to the European Cup final, losing to Hamburg. That season 'Il Francese' was named European Footballer of the Year. However, 1984 was the year of Platini, a year which ensured his presence in the pantheon of all-time greats. He became the hero of the Juventus fans by helping the club to the League title and the Cup Winners Cup, beating Porto 2-1, and he ended up top scorer in the League.

He had played in the 1978 and 1982 World Cup finals, making his international debut in 1976, but in 1984 he took France to new

heights. In the European Championships, partnered by Giresse and Tigana, he steered France to the trophy, scoring nine goals in the process including a hat-trick against Yugoslavia, the last-gasp, extra-time winner against Portugal in the semis, and a free-kick goal in the final to help France to a 2-0 victory over Spain. Player of the tournament, he unsurprisingly became European Footballer of the Year for the second year running.

In 1985, he was yet again top scorer in the League, picked up the European Cup after the Heysel disaster and was awarded European Footballer of the Year for the third time. In the 1986 World Cup finals, an apparently unfit Platini struggled through the group stage, but he was back on form against Italy where his goal and his tireless running and passing inspired the 'Blues' to a 2-0 victory. There then followed a penalty shoot-out victory over Brazil, although Platini missed his kick, but a defeat by West Germany in the semis ended France's participation.

After a home match against Brescia in May 1987, Platini announced his retirement and the same year he collected his 72nd and last international cap against Iceland. He took over as manager of the French national team and more recently was involved in the organisation of the 1998 World Cup.

Platini was a true French sporting idol, his sheer technical brilliance and obvious love of the game serving as an example to a generation of French school kids, one of whom, Zidane, took over his mantle.

Ferenc Puskas

The Galloping Major of Honved, Hungary and Real Madrid

Stocky, short and overweight he may have been, but in the 1950s and early 1960s Ferenc Puskas was one of the finest forwards in the world. Indeed, many still regard him as one of the greatest players ever to have graced the game.

Blessed with a lethal, deadly accurate left-foot shot, Puskas also possessed sharp acceleration and a sublime artistry with the ball, which made him feared by defences throughout the continent.

He made his debut at the age of 16 for Kispest in his native Hungary, gained his first cap at 18 and won an Olympic Gold Medal in 1952. Known as the 'Galloping Major', after his army rank created when Kispest became Honved, the team of the Hungarian Army, he captained Hungary in their devastating 6-3 victory over a reeling England side at Wembley in 1953, and scored a memorable goal when he rolled the ball back with the sole of his foot, swivelled and snapped an unstoppable shot past Gil Merrick, the England goalie. The 'Mighty Magyars' repeated England's humiliation later that year with a 7-1 crushing in Budapest.

In his international career with Hungary, Puskas accumulated a total of 84 caps, scoring 83 goals in the process.

Remaining in Western Europe after the Hungarian revolution of 1956, Puskas searched around for a team and was eventually taken on by Real Madrid in 1958 where he was to form a lethal strike force with the Argentinian Alfredo Di Stefano and the Spanish winger Gento. The Spanish fans christened him 'Canoncito' – the little cannon. Madrid were dominant in Europe, winning the European Cup five times in a row between 1956 and 1960, culminating in the 'game of the century' against Eintracht Frankfurt at Hampden Park in the 1960 final when – with Puskas making his first appearance in the final – Madrid won 7-3,

Puskas claiming four goals, the only player ever to score this many in a final. Inspired by Puskas and Di Stefano, Real won the Spanish Championship five times running from 1961 to 1965, and again reached the European Cup final in 1962 when Puskas scored another three in their 5-3 defeat by Benfica. He netted 35 goals in 38 European Cup matches for Madrid and was also capped by Spain four times.

Although they won the European Cup again in 1966, Real Madrid's period of dominance was nearing an end, and Puskas retired in 1966 to concentrate on what was to prove rather a lacklustre coaching career, although he took the Greek outsiders Panathinaikos to a Wembley European Cup final in 1971, beating Everton and Red Star Belgrade. They lost the final 2-0 to Ajax, but Puskas was a hero in Greece. Touchingly, his defection was forgiven by Hungary in 1993 when he was asked to take over the national team for the World Cup qualifiers.

Born:
Budapest, 2.4.27
Clubs:
Kispest/Honved 43-56, Real Madrid 58-66
Club honours:
Hungarian Championship 49/50, 51/2, 53/4, 54/5; Spanish Championship 60/1, 61/2, 62/3, 63/4, 64/5; Spanish Cup 62; European Cup 60
International honours:
84 (83) Hungary caps, 4 Spain caps

Paolo **Rossi**

From crock through corruption to glory

Born:
Prato, Tuscany, Italy, 23.9.56
Clubs:
Juventus 72-75, Como 75-76, Lanerossi Vicenza 76-79, Perugia 79-80, Juventus 81-85, AC Milan 85-86, Verona 86-87
Club honours:
Italian Championship 81/2, Italian Cup 83, European Cup Winners Cup 84, European Cup 85
International honours:
48 (20) Italy caps, World Cup 82
Individual honours:
European Footballer of the Year 82

Paolo Rossi's career had more ups and downs than a streamlined yo-yo. It could have ended in injury and ignominy before he was 25, but when he finally called it a day at 30 he was an Italian national hero and recognised as one of football's great strikers.

As a youngster, he quickly built up such a big reputation as an attacking right-winger, that the giant Turin club Juventus signed him when he was 16. The young Rossi however underwent so many cartilage operations that it was thought he would never make the grade, and at 19, before he had made a League appearance for the club, he was loaned to Como, and later to the Serie B club Lanerossi Vicenza. It could have been the end.

The Vicenza coach, Battista Fabbri, recognised his potential, however, and converted him to centre-forward, where he proved fast, courageous and very difficult to mark. Rossi became the leading Serie B scorer in his first season in the role and Vicenza were promoted. He made his debut for Italy in 1977 and was selected for the 1978 World Cup. Only 21, he scored Italy's equaliser in their 2-1 win over France, the first goal in a 3-1 defeat of Hungary, and helped Bettega get the only goal of the game against the hosts and eventual winners, Argentina. Rossi then scored one of the tournament's best goals, in a 1-0 defeat of

Austria, after a brilliant back-heel in a build-up with Causio. Italy eventually lost 2-1 to Brazil in the third-place match.

In the meantime, Vicenza had bought Rossi from Juventus, who now wanted to buy him back, but were beaten to his signature by Perugia. There, in 1980, he was convicted with several other players of fixing a match against Avellino in a betting and bribes scandal. He was banned from football for three years, reduced to two years on appeal.

Juventus gave Rossi some hope by buying him during his suspension for a knockdown £600,000 and he played three games for them at the end of the 1981-82 season. Amazingly, after three matches in two years, he was selected for Italy's 1982 World Cup squad in Spain. Italy scraped through the group phase, and in their fifth match Rossi came to life. Italy needed to beat Brazil to reach the semi-final, and Rossi was superb, scoring a hat-trick in a 3-2 win. It was regarded as the best match of the tournament. Rossi then scored both goals in a 2-0 semi-final defeat of Poland, and with delirious Italian fans shouting 'Forza Paolo' he netted the first in the final against West Germany, his sixth consecutive goal for Italy, enough to win him the Golden Boot as the tournament's highest scorer. Italy won the World Cup with a 3-1 win, and Rossi was European Footballer of the Year. Sadly, his injuries soon caught up with him, and despite moving to AC Milan and Verona he was forced to hang up his boots. He became a pundit and fronted a PR company which was involved in World Cup 90, held in Italy.

Socrates

The Brazilian midfield medic

Socrates had an appropriate name. Like the Ancient Greek philosopher he believed that truth came from knowledge, and would not become a footballer before he had completed his training as a doctor. On the field he carried with him an air of philosophic detachment from the hurry and scurry about him, and always seemed calm and composed in his play.

His full name was Socrates Brasileiro Sampaio de Sousa Vieira de Oliveira. He was not particularly interested in football until, at the age of 16, he watched the great Brazilian side led by Pele win the World Cup in 1970. He became a great fan of Pele and his club Santos, and when he joined his local team Botafogo, as an amateur at 22, he tried to play like Pele at centre-forward. But he was playing mainly for recreation and fitness, while continuing his medical studies.

In 1978 Corinthians of Sao Paulo offered him a contract as a professional, and Socrates, now a doctor of medicine, decided to give it a go. Socrates dropped back to midfield and his stylish and polished displays helped Corinthians to win the Sao Paulo championship (one of Brazil's two regional divisions) in his first year. The same year he made his debut for Brazil in a 2-2 draw with Argentina.

By 1982 Socrates was captain of Brazil, and in that year's World Cup he was influential in Brazil reverting to the brilliant attacking football that he had so admired as a 16-year-old. Brazil had in the meantime been trying to play tighter, more cautious football in the European style. Socrates became a world star almost overnight

Born:
Belem, Brazil, 19.2.54
Clubs:
Botafogo 76-78, Corinthians 78-84, Fiorentina 84-85, Flamengo 85-87, Santos 88-90
Club honours:
Sao Paulo Championship 78/9, 81/2, 82/3
International honours:
60 (22) Brazil caps
Individual honours:
South American Player of the Year 83

following Brazil's first match, when he scored a brilliant equaliser 15 minutes from time against the Soviet Union. Picking up a misplaced Soviet pass, he neatly side-stepped two defenders before hitting home a superb shot from outside the area. Brazil won 2-1, and then scored four goals against both Scotland and New Zealand to win their group with comfort. In the next round they easily beat Argentina, and needed only to draw against Italy to reach the semi-final. Socrates raced through for another brilliant solo goal but, with the score 2-2, Brazil continued to attack and conceded the winner

through defensive errors. Italy won the Cup, but Brazil were arguably the best team in it.

In 1984 Socrates was signed by the Italian club Fiorentina for £2.3 million, but his thoughtful style did not impress, and when he broke an ankle in training he decided to return to Brazil and the Flamengo Club.

In the 1986 World Cup, Brazil were favourites and Socrates notched the only goal in their opening match with Spain. Brazil cruised through to the semi-finals but then lost to France on penalties in one of the best matches of the tournament. Socrates, whose air of calm extended to taking penalties from a two-step walking approach (he had already scored one against Poland), missed the first penalty.

Soon after the World Cup, Socrates, now 33, suffered a back injury and retired. But the late starter now found he missed the game, and in 1988 he made a comeback with Santos. It didn't last and he retired to take up politics.

Alfredo Di Stefano

The playmaker and goal-scoring genius of Real Madrid

There are many seasoned football watchers who would nominate Alfredo Di Stefano as the world's greatest ever all-round football player.

Although apparently a deep-lying centre-forward, with a phenomenal, free-scoring goal record, his balance, vision and passing skills were those of a midfielder, and his overall contribution to team play was unselfish and inspirational.

Born in Argentina to Italian parents, he began his professional career with River Plate, making his first-team debut on the right wing at the age of 16. In 1947, a players' strike in Argentina led to his joining Millionaros of Bogota, where he stayed for six years, scoring 259 League goals in 292 games and winning four League titles. At this point he was the finest player in South America.

In 1953, after orchestrating a Millionaros victory in a friendly against Real Madrid, he was lured away by the Spanish team and, in his first game for the then dormant Real, he scored four in a 5-0 hammering of Barcelona. The next season, boasting players of the quality of Di Stefano, Gento and Rial, Real Madrid won the Spanish League, a trophy they were to collect a further seven times under the direction of the maestro Di Stefano, the 'Blond Arrow' of Madrid.

However, it is for his performances in the European Cup that Di Stefano is most fondly remembered. Between 1956 and 1960, Real scaled the heights of European football five

Born:
Buenos Aires, Argentina, 4.7.26
Clubs:
River Plate 43-47, Millionaros Bogota 47-53, Real Madrid 53-64, Espanyol 64-66
Club honours:
Argentine Championship 46/7; Copa America 47; Colombian Championship 48/9, 50/1, 51/2, 52/3; Spanish Championship 53/4, 54/5, 56/7, 57/8, 60/1, 61/2, 62/3, 63/4; Spanish Cup 1962; European Cup 56, 57, 58, 59, 60
International honours:
7 (7) Argentina caps, 2 Colombia caps, 31 (23) Spain caps
Individual honours:
European Footballer of the Year 57, 59; Spanish Player of the Year 57, 59, 60, 62, 64

times in succession, with Di Stefano scoring in every final, a unique record. His power, close ball control and peerless distribution were at the heart of these triumphs, and his hat-trick against Eintracht Frankfurt in the 1960 final served only to underline his glittering all-round abilities. Also during this period he was twice awarded European Footballer of the Year, in 1957 and 1959.

Despite collecting 40 international caps for three countries, Di Stefano never played in the World Cup finals. He was selected for Spain in 1962, but was ruled out by injury (although some commentators suggested that a dispute with manager Helenio Herrera was a more probable reason for his non-appearance).

Real Madrid's European dominance began to fade in the early 1960s and, although they reached the final again in 1962, where a defence-splitting pass from di Stefano to Puskas set up the first goal in the latter's hat-trick, they were beaten 5-3 by Benfica. Di Stefano played in one further final – a defeat by Inter in 1964. In his 56 European games, he scored 49 goals, an achievement to date unequalled.

The 1964 final was his last major game for Real, and he moved to Espanyol on a free transfer at the age of 38. He stayed there for two seasons, scoring 11 League goals in 37 games, and retired in 1966 to embark on a successful managerial career with Boca Juniors, Sporting Lisbon, River Plate, Valencia and, appropriately, Real Madrid.

Lev Yashin

The Black Panther of the Soviet Union

Born:
Moscow, 22.10.29
Clubs:
Moscow Dynamo 49-70
Club honours:
Soviet League 53/4, 54/5, 56/7, 58/9, 62/3; USSR Cup 53, 67, 70
International honours:
78 Soviet Union caps
Individual honours:
European Footballer of the Year 63, Order of Lenin 60

As popular and respected off the pitch as he was dominant and impregnable on it, Lev Yashin was an excellent sportsman and, by common consent, the greatest goalkeeper in the history of football.

Rescued from a Moscow tool factory by Moscow Dynamo in 1950, he started his career as a goaltender in the Dynamo ice hockey team, making his first-team debut in the football team in 1951. He established himself as regular first-team keeper in 1953 and, by now wearing his distinctive all-black strip, he gained his first cap in 1954 in a 7-0 defeat of Sweden. With Yashin in goal, the Soviets won the Olympic gold in 1956 and in the 1958 World Cup finals, they knocked out England in the group play-off, losing to hosts Sweden in the quarter-final.

In 1960, Yashin's acrobatics helped the Soviet Union win the inaugural European Championships (then the European Nations Cup), beating Yugoslavia 2-1. They reached the World Cup finals again in 1962, but Yashin, uncharacteristically, was completely off form. He let in a goal from a corner against Colombia and, in the quarter-finals, could not hold two fairly innocuous long-range shots from Chile. The Soviets were out, and Yashin was devastated.

He was, however, in marvellous form for his club and helped Dynamo to five League Championships between 1954 and 1963. Also in 1963 he played in goal for The Rest of the World, with the likes of Puskas, Di Stefano and Baxter, against England in a match to mark the centenary of the Football Association. Yashin was outstanding, although England won 2-1. In that year he was voted European Footballer of the Year, the only goalkeeper ever to have achieved that honour.

After finishing runners-up to Spain in the 1964 European Championships, the Soviets qualified for their third consecutive World Cup finals in England. They topped their qualifying group, beat Hungary in the quarter-finals and faced West Germany in the semi-final. In an ugly and bad-tempered match, the Germans won 2-1, with Yashin being blamed by some observers for the decisive goal, scored by Beckenbauer. Although he had played well in the tournament, and had won the affections of the British public, that goal may have been the final factor in his eventual decision to retire, which he did in 1970.

Yashin made 326 League appearances for Dynamo, a club record, and played for the Soviet Union 78 times. In his career he kept a total of 270 clean sheets. He received the Order of Lenin in 1960, and he was awarded a testimonial in 1971 in front of a packed Lenin Stadium.

A knee injury led to his leg being amputated in 1986 and he died in 1991. The world of football mourned the passing of a legend.

Zinedine Zidane

'Zizou', the World Cup winner for France

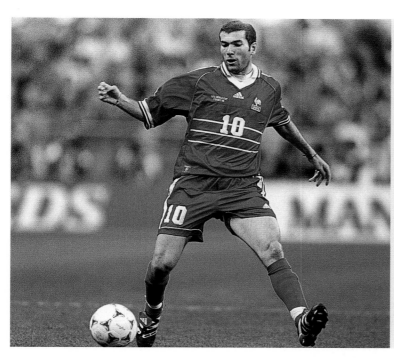

Born:
23.6.72, Marseille
Clubs:
AS Cannes 88-92,
Bordeaux 92-96,
Juventus 1996-
Club honours:
Italian League
Championship 96/7,
97/8
**International
honours:**
44 (11) France caps,
World Cup 98
Individual honours:
French Player of the
Year 96, European
Footballer of the Year
98, World Footballer of
the Year 98

two successive European Cup finals in 1997 and 1998.

Juventus' attempt to reach a third final was halted by Manchester United in April 1999 at the second leg of the semi-final stage. In spite of providing a sparkling performance at Old Trafford, a lacklustre Zidane, and an equally unimpressive Juventus, gave away a two-goal lead after ten minutes to go down 3-2 in Turin.

He made his debut for France against the Czech Republic in 1994, spectacularly scoring two goals in 16 minutes, and he is now the mainstay of the national side. Although he had a poor Euro 96, he was a massive influence in the 1998 World Cup finals. France qualified top at the group stage, although Zidane was sent off for stamping on an opponent in the Saudi Arabia game, a surprising and uncharacteristic act of folly for such a normally fair player.

With his two headed goals in the final against Brazil, Zinedine Zidane brought the World Cup home to an ecstatic France in 1998. Petit added a third, the country celebrated, and Zidane and his victorious colleagues became national heroes, their images flashed onto the Arc de Triomphe.

The heir to Platini in the French team and at Juventus, Zidane is a technical player of great sophistication and, for such a big man, he possesses a surprisingly delicate touch. Constantly probing defences, and delivering passes with pinpoint accuracy, he is at the heart of the side, often seemingly languid in

movement but with sharp acceleration and deadly finishing when required. He is the finest French playmaker of his generation and, at 27 at the turn of the century, he is at his footballing peak.

The son of Algerian immigrants, Zidane grew up in Marseille and made his professional debut for Cannes in 1988. He moved to Bordeaux in 1992 and reached the UEFA Cup final with them in 1996, losing to Bayern Munich. He was voted France's Player of the Year in 1996, and was transferred that year to Serie A and Juventus, where his tireless and astute midfield play took the club to

France then narrowly beat Paraguay and squeezed through to the semi-final against Croatia by beating Italy on penalties, with Zidane running the game and scoring in the shoot-out. A 2-1 victory over the Croats ensured Zidane's place in the final and in the history of French football.

As a result of his performance in the finals, and recognising his crucial contribution to Juventus, Zidane was named not only European Footballer of the year but also FIFA World Footballer of the Year in 1998. There is a lot more yet to come from this modest but extravagantly gifted player.

Matt **Busby**

The man who created Manchester United

By the time Matt Busby retired from Manchester United in 1969, he had become the most lauded manager in the history of British football. Twenty-four years earlier, he had taken over a failing club, with no ground nor money, and during that period he created three of the greatest post-war English football sides.

Busby was a powerful and determined personality, with a love of football, and a deep desire to win. He was also a risk-taker and an innovator who combined his respect for tradition with an urge to experiment. And he was a motivator extraordinaire. During his reign he became the embodiment of the club, and latterly that became something of a problem. But he was brilliantly successful.

He spent his playing days as a wing-half with Manchester City and Liverpool, and joined Manchester United from his wartime sergeant-major posting in 1945. Having few assets to play with, he used his experience and tactical nous to develop the existing players into a team which won the FA Cup in 1948 and the League in 1951-52, their first League win in 41 years.

In 1952, he conceived the 'Busby Babes', bringing into an aging side teenagers like Edwards, Pegg and Viollet and by 1956 his team won the League title by a massive 11 points from Blackpool. The next year they won it again, and reached the semi-final of the European Cup, defeated 5-3 on aggregate by Real Madrid. His home-grown 'Babes' were set to conquer England and Europe but the tragedy of the Munich air crash in 1958 on the

Born:
Orbiston, Lanarkshire, 26.05.09
Club:
Manchester United 45-69
Club honours:
League Championship 51/2, 55/6, 56/7, 64/5, 66/7; FA Cup 48, 63; European Cup 68
Individual honours:
Knighted 69

way back from playing Red Star Belgrade put paid to Busby's hopes, and nearly his life. He had to rebuild again and he and his coach Jimmy Murphy set to work.

Busby's shrewd purchases of Law in 1962 and Crerand in 1963 laid the foundation for the great United team of the 1960s. Although they were nearly relegated in 1962-63, they won the FA Cup that season and, with Munich survivor Charlton and newly arrived Belfast boy George Best in the team, they won the League in 1964-65 and 1966-67.

From the start of his United career Busby had realised the importance of European football and had gone into the first competition in the face of opposition from the Football League. United's marvellous 5-1 victory in Lisbon over Benfica in 1966 had merely whetted Busby's ambition for the European Cup, and Bill Foulkes' unlikely goal against

Real Madrid in 1968 put Busby one game away from his dream.

United's 4-1 victory over Benfica in May 1968 to win the European Cup was Busby's greatest moment and expiated his guilt over the Munich crash. With nothing left to achieve in his career, he became general manager the following year.

However, he was still the dominant presence at the club, and the next two managers – McGuinness and O'Farrell – were ousted, partially at his instigation, with United not achieving success again until the arrival of Docherty. Busby was appointed president of the club in 1980 and died in January 1994. Although allegations have recently been made concerning Busby's parsimony and insensitivity to some of his players, these should not be allowed to detract from what he achieved at Manchester United.

Herbert **Chapman**

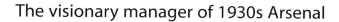

The visionary manager of 1930s Arsenal

Born:
Kiveton Park, South Yorkshire, 19.1.1878
Clubs:
Northampton Town 07-12, Leeds City 12-19,
Huddersfield Town 21-25, Arsenal 25-34
Club honours:
League Championship 23/4, 24/5, 30/1, 32/3; FA
Cup 22, 30

It is no exaggeration to claim Herbert Chapman as the father of modern English football. His vision, foresight and tactical understanding not only propelled two old clubs from the doldrums to the heights of English football, but also laid the foundation for the modern game.

An intelligent, well-educated Yorkshireman, he had an undistinguished playing career and he took over as player/manager at Northampton Town in 1907. He moved to Leeds City in 1912, and the club was closed down in 1919 after allegations of illegal payments to players.

Chapman resurfaced in 1921 as manager of Huddersfield Town.

By the time he left Huddersfield in 1925, they had won two League titles, the FA Cup and were to win a third League title in a row in 1925-26, a club which had never before won anything in its history. His powers of motivation, innovative methods and belief in discipline, allied to the lessons learnt in a long career in the game, turned Huddersfield into one of the most feared clubs in the country.

Attracted by the challenge of Arsenal, an under-performing club with no major silverware to its credit, and by the then princely salary of £2,000 per year, Chapman joined the club in 1925 and set about putting his ideas into action. With the change in the offside rule from three defenders behind the ball to two, the goals started flowing in English football. How best to capitalise on this?

Persuaded by his newly acquired captain Charlie Buchan, Chapman created a system where the 'stopper' centre-half pulled back level with the full-backs, the inside-forwards dropped back into midfield, and the wingers, intent on goal, cut inside full-backs, rather than dribbling down the wing and crossing from the corner flag. The system was based on containment and counter-attack. However, to perfect this formation, Chapman needed the right players.

In 1926 he signed Herbie Roberts, the original 'stopper' centre-half, and in 1928 signed the star English forward David Jack from Bolton

and, in the most inspired move of all, the brilliant Alex James from Preston, switching him from a forward position to midfield playmaker. The acquisition of Cliff 'Boy' Bastin and Eddie Hapgood, and the moving of George Male from the wing to right-back, completed his line-up. Starting with their FA Cup victory over Huddersfield in 1930, Arsenal swiftly became the team of the 1930s. Inspired by the genius of James and the goalscoring of Jack, Bastin and Hulme, Chapman's team won five League titles and two FA Cups between 1930 and 1938.

Chapman, however, was not to live to see all their triumphs. Catching a cold at a reserve game in early January 1934, he died of pneumonia at the age of 55. His death shocked Arsenal fans and English football.

Chapman was an original thinker and a master tactician, with a natural authority and confidence in his judgements. As Bastin observed: 'he should have been Prime Minister.' Something of a showman, his persuasive powers were legendary, and his revolutionary suggestions to improve the game – such as floodlights, numbers on shirts and a white ball – are now commonplace, although disregarded at the time. An instinctive flair for publicity – such as having the Gillespie Road tube station renamed Arsenal – did much to change the image of the rather staid old club, and he created modern Arsenal.

A Jacob Epstein bust of Chapman stands in the entrance to the East Stand at Highbury, lest anyone forget this.

Brian Clough

The eccentric and outspoken boss of Derby and Forest

Born:
Middlesbrough, 21.3.35
Clubs:
Hartlepool United 65-67, Derby County 67-73, Brighton and Hove Albion 73-74, Leeds United 74, Nottingham Forest 75-93
Club honours:
League Championship 71/2, 77/8; League Cup 78, 79, 89, 90; European Cup 79, 80

Cloughie – 'Old Big 'Ead' – never did anything by halves. A larger-than-life, egotistic and totally unpredictable figure, he was also one of the most effective and shrewd of all the post-Second World War managers. His blunt, abrasive and often dictatorial manner masked a deep understanding of football and an intuitive ability to motivate players, and he could coax out of apparently average footballers performances worthy of the highest level of the game.

A prolific and aggressive goalscorer for Middlesbrough and Sunderland – scoring 251 goals in 274 league appearances until serious injury ended his career – he took on his first managerial role in 1965 at Hartlepool, where he teamed up with his long-term coaching partner, Peter Taylor, and where he became the youngest manager in the Football League.

The pair moved to Derby in 1967, where Clough set about building the unfashionable

club into a team which won the cliffhanging First Division title in 1971-72. Bizarrely, they were on post-season holiday in Majorca when news reached them that Liverpool had drawn, Leeds had lost and dDerby were champions. However, after a public dispute in 1973 with Derby chairman Sam Longson, they went to Brighton, with whom they also managed to fall out after one season. Clough had firm opinions on football, and was not afraid to voice them.

In July 1974, Clough went to Leeds to succeed Don Revie, a strange choice after his public criticism of the Leeds team. He immediately encountered strong resistance from the experienced players to his authoritarian attitudes and methods, and he left after only 44 days in charge, the victim of a players' revolt. As Eddie Gray said: 'As far as the players were concerned, Clough just didn't exist.'

He teamed up again with Peter Taylor and took over at Nottingham Forest, whom he guided

into the First Division in 1976-77, winning the First Division title and the League Cup the following season. His astute signing of Peter Shilton that year, and his capture of Trevor Francis for the British record transfer fee of £1 million in 1979, gave him a team, including Kenny Burns and John Robertson, which won the European Cup in 1979, Francis scoring with a header to beat Malmo 1-0. The following year Clough did it again, his team disposing of Dynamo Berlin and Ajax on their way to another European Cup final, where a Robertson goal against Hamburg ensured the retaining of the trophy. As Cloughie said: 'absolutely marvellous'.

In 1982 a bitter and acrimonious dispute with Peter Taylor led to Taylor joining Derby, and the pair never spoke again. Many believe that Clough never got over this, and that the split provoked his managerial decline. Whatever the reason, Forest stuttered through the 1980s, enlivened only by two League Cup victories in 1989 and 1990, and Clough retired, to emotional scenes at the City Ground in 1993.

He was never far from the headlines. Whether it was hauling fans off the pitch in 1989 (and being fined £5000 by the FA), his practical and sincere support for the striking miners or his wisecracks ('There are more hooligans in the House of Commons than at a football match'), his often outrageous actions and pronouncements ensured controversy.

Dogged by allegations of 'bungs' and excessive drinking, Clough's reputation has recently dipped, although the memories of his many achievements in football will never diminish.

Alex **Ferguson**

The man who brought the 'treble' to Old Trafford

Born:
Govan, Glasgow, 31.12.41
Clubs:
East Stirling 75-76, St Mirren 76-78,
Aberdeen 78-86, Manchester United 86-
Club honours:
Scottish Premier Championship 79/80, 83/4,
84/5; Scottish Cup 82, 83, 84, 86; Scottish
League Cup 86; English Premier
Championship 92/3, 93/4, 95/6, 96/7, 98/9; FA
Cup 90, 94, 96, 99; League Cup 92; European
Cup 99; European Cup Winners Cup 83, 91
International honours:
Scotland caretaker manager 85-86, 5 games
Individual honours:
Knighted 99

'It is the greatest night of my life. It is a fairytale.' With these words, Alex Ferguson finally laid the ghost of Sir Matt Busby as his players celebrated the fantastic European Cup final victory over Bayern Munich in May 1999. He had just achieved the 'treble', the others being the FA Cup and the Premiership title, and his career was at its zenith. However, it had been a long journey.

A competitive, driven man, with a short fuse and an iron determination to win, Ferguson is by some way the most successful manager of his generation. His understanding of tactics and strategy, as well as psychological gamesmanship, has been honed in his long and varied career as player and manager, as has his close and protective relationship with his players. An obsessively hard worker and perfectionist, he expects the same from those around him and he rewards loyalty with loyalty.

A playing career which included a two-year spell as centre-forward at Ibrox was terminated by injury in 1975, and Ferguson took over as manager of East Stirling and then St Mirren, whom he took into the Premier Division. Moving to Aberdeen in 1978, he set his sights on the 'Old Firm'. With players of the quality of Strachan and McLeish, Ferguson turned the club into the leading force in Scottish football, winning, within eight years, three Premier titles, four Cups, one League Cup and, in 1983, the European Cup Winners Cup.

In 1986, as caretaker manager he led Scotland to the 1986 World Cup finals where they were one goal away from going into the second stage. In November of that year, and having resisted job offers from most of the leading English clubs, he succumbed to Manchester United, a club still living in the shadow of Busby. Ferguson immediately started restructuring the scouting and coaching systems and buying in new players, such as Anderson, McClair, Bruce and Hughes, but success seemed far away and Ferguson's future was being called into question. The board, however, stuck with him and were rewarded in 1990 with the FA Cup and the Cup Winners Cup the following year.

Then Ferguson pulled his master stroke. Acquiring Eric Cantona for £1 million from Leeds in November 1992 was seen as good business, but Cantona's impact until he retired in 1997 was incalculable. Cantona was simply sensational, not only in his presence on the park but also in his influence on the talented younger players, such as Scholes, Beckham, Giggs and Butt, and Ferguson was finally beginning to see all his hard work bearing fruit. United won the League that year and, between then and 1998-99 won two 'doubles', two Premier titles and, of course, the 'treble'.

Ferguson's youth policy – 'Fergie's Fledglings' – has been vindicated and the United board were wise to keep faith in him. The conveyor belt of talent from the youth team continues to roll and Ferguson has not only achieved the highest success, he has also laid the framework for the future. It is hard to envisage another British team mounting a serious sustained challenge against United in the foreseeable future, and this is Ferguson's legacy.

Bill Nicholson

Spurs 'double' manager

Born:
Scarborough, 26.1.19
Club:
Tottenham Hotspur 58-74
Club honours:
League Championship 60/1; FA Cup 61, 62, 67;
League Cup 71, 73; European Cup Winners Cup 63;
UEFA Cup 72

An honest, hardworking and dignified manager, Bill Nicholson was never one to seek out the TV cameras and was happier with his players on the training ground than basking in the limelight. He found it difficult to maintain a low profile in 1961, however, when his extravagantly talented Spurs side became the first team in the 20th century to win the 'double' of League and FA Cup, and Nicholson became a national sporting hero.

He was a loyal one-club man, signing professional forms with Spurs in 1937 and, in his right-half position, helping Arthur Rowe's 'push and run' team to the League title. In that year, he achieved his only England cap (Billy Wright owned the position), scoring a goal against Portugal within 19 seconds of the start. He retired in 1955, becoming club coach at White Hart Lane and, after coaching England in the 1958 World Cup, he took over from Jimmy Anderson as manager at the Lane.

By the end of his first day in charge, he had presided over a 10-4 home win against Everton but he nonetheless knew he had to build up his team. He was a clever and incisive player on the transfer market, and he bought Dave Mackay, John White and Les Allen and, with the opinionated but astute Blanchflower, Jones and Norman already at the club, the basis for the 'double' team was in place.

Nicholson was an excellent coach and tactician and, with the motivational Blanchflower leading on the pitch, Spurs were becoming one of the most exciting and attractive teams in the country. As Nicholson said in the Spurs official history: 'I felt in 1960 that I had a side well prepared to do something. You cannot put it into words, it's a feeling you get.' Marshalled by

Blanchflower and Mackay, with White and Jones carving open defences and Smith and Allen rattling in the goals, Tottenham won the League in 1961 at a canter. A 2-0 victory over Leicester in the FA Cup final ensured the 'impossible double' was theirs.

The next year they won the Cup again and Nicholson felt that, but for a tactical disagreement with his players in a League game against Ipswich, they could have repeated the 'double'. He became in 1963 the first British manager to win a European trophy when Spurs defeated Atletico Madrid 5-1 in the European Cup Winners Cup final, but in 1964 the 'double' team were fading and Greaves, bought from AC Milan in 1961, Gilzean, Mullery and Jennings were now regulars.

Spurs won the Cup again in 1967, beating Chelsea 2-1, acquired two League Cups in 1971 and 1973, and clinched the UEFA Cup in 1972, but their League form was erratic. Nicholson was in disagreement with some of his senior players, particularly the high-scoring Martin Chivers, and by 1974, in spite of a deputation from Martin Peters and others to persuade him to stay, he resigned. He was disillusioned and exasperated by the demands of modern footballers, saying: 'I am abused by players. There is no longer respect.'

He returned to the club as managerial consultant in 1976, but a new generation had taken over at White Hart Lane. He was awarded a testimonial in 1986, and was presented with a silver plaque by Alan Sugar in 1996, marking his 60th year of association with Spurs.

Bob Paisley

The quiet man behind Liverpool's triumphs

Born:
Hetton-le-Hole, County Durham, 23.1.19
Clubs:
Liverpool 74-83
Club honours:
League Championship 75/6, 76/7, 78/9, 79/80, 81/2, 82/3; League Cup 81, 82, 83; UEFA Cup 75/6; European Cup 77, 78, 81
Individual honours:
OBE 77

Bob Paisley did not fit the stereotype of a 1970s football manager. In an age seemingly typified by extrovert, voluble, champagne-swilling bosses, ever watchful for the TV soundbite, the self-effacing, almost shy Paisley took a back seat, concerned more about his players than the promotion of his image. And he won more than the lot of them.

In fact, Paisley was the most successful British manager ever. Although he inherited from Bill Shankly one of the finest English teams, he refined and modelled Liverpool into a team which conquered Europe.

A bricklayer from County Durham, Paisley joined Liverpool in 1939 as a wing-half. Playing alongside the great Billy Liddell, he won a League Championship medal in 1947, and retired as a player in 1954, staying with Liverpool on the training staff and studying physiotherapy.

Between the arrival of Shankly in 1959 and his departure, Paisley was an integral member of the famous Boot Room at Anfield, advising

Shanks on injuries, fitness and general tactics and, when he was offered the manager's job in 1974, he didn't want it and he told the players and club as much. But he took it, anyway, and history records this as the correct decision.

Within the space of ten years, Paisley and Liverpool won 13 major trophies. Although taking over from a legend could not have been easy, Paisley rode out the initial pressure and expectations of the club and the fans and delivered more than anyone had hoped. He took the club to their first-ever European Cup final victory in 1977, defeating Borussia Moenchengladbach 3-1 in Rome ('the last time I was here I was in a tank', said the ever-phlegmatic Bob), and two more European Cups, becoming the first English manager to

claim this illustrious hat-trick. To this glittering prize he added six League titles, the UEFA Cup and three League Cups in succession from 1981 to 1983.

Although the nucleus of the side was there in 1974, it was Paisley who brought in Dalglish, Souness and Hansen, the backbone of Liverpool's triumphs. A canny and astute judge of footballing talent, he followed in Shankly's footsteps by buying from the lower divisions young players such as Phil Neal from Northampton Town. He lured Terry McDermott from Newcastle and, in the most inspired gamble of all, acquired for £300,000 a young Fourth Division centre-forward named Ian Rush. He also re-energised Ray Kennedy's career by moving him from attack to midfield.

An intensely loyal Liverpool man, he demanded the same from his players, and he could be stubborn and ruthless when required, for instance dropping the evergreen Ian Callaghan from the 1977 FA Cup final line-up. He also instilled the importance of consistency, application and, above all, teamwork, which became the hallmark of the club.

When Liverpool won the League Cup in 1983, captain Souness ushered Paisley, who had earlier announced his imminent retirement, up the Wembley steps to take the trophy, and an embarrassed though delighted Paisley saluted the fans. He retired in May 1983.

He was given a seat on the Liverpool board in 1985 and died in 1996. As 1990s manager Roy Evans said: 'Nobody has served this club better.'

Alf **Ramsey**

The autocratic World Cup winner

Born:
Dagenham, Essex, 22.1.20
Clubs:
Ipswich 55-63, Birmingham City 74-75
Club honours:
League Championship 61/2
Internationals:
England manager 63-74, 113 games; World Cup 66
Individual honours:
Knighted 67

An aloof, uncommunicative and dour man, Alf Ramsay never quite captured the hearts of the public, and his mutually antagonistic relationship with the media did nothing to improve his image. He did, however, do something which no other England manager has ever done, and English football will fondly remember him for that.

His playing career began at Southampton and he moved to Spurs in 1949 as a classy right-back, playing in the 'push and run' team until 1955. He won 32 caps for England, including appearances in the 1-0 humiliation by the USA and the 6-3 football lesson inflicted by Hungary, and joined Third Division (South) Ipswich Town in 1955 as manager.

His remarkable powers of motivation, his tactical awareness and his ability to blend together players into an effective team led to unfashionable Ipswich winning the Second Division in 1961 and, to the surprise of the football world, taking the First Division title the following year.

He took over from Walter Winterbottom in 1963, becoming the first full-time England manager, with the power to pick the team and the tactics, and started his reign well, including a 2-1 victory over the Rest of the World. However, in 1964 a disastrous England performance in South America against Brazil and a defeat by Argentina shook Ramsey, and he was further disheartened by the way England limped through their 1965 programme, notching up narrow wins and unimpressive draws. But by early 1966, Ramsey was once again confident in his squad, and remained convinced that 'England will win the World Cup in 1966'.

And, of course, he was right. The story of England's triumph in the tournament is told elsewhere in this book, and Ramsey became a hero and was knighted early in 1967. The success of his 'wingless wonders' changed the face of football and led to traditional wingers becoming an increasing rarity in football, a development deplored by many purists.

Ramsey entered the 1970 World Cup finals with probably his strongest-ever team and started off well. However, England came unstuck in the quarter-finals against West Germany when, to protect a 2-1 lead, Ramsey substituted Peters and Charlton and the team fell apart, losing 3-2 in extra time. In 1972, they were again outplayed by West Germany, and were out of the European Championships.

The knives were now out for Ramsey, and only qualification for the 1974 World Cup would keep him in his job. In October 1973, having to beat Poland at Wembley to qualify, they could only draw, kept out by an inspired performance from the Polish goalkeeper Tomaszewski and by Ramsey's unwillingness to introduce substitutions. This was Ramsey's nemesis, and he was fired the following April.

His 1966 heroes – the Charltons, Banks, Moore, Stiles – had departed the national scene and perhaps Ramsey's time had simply come. For all his suspicion of the press and the FA, and his curt and often charmless public pronouncements, in private he had the respect and admiration of many of his players for his coaching knowledge and his loyalty to them.

He managed Birmingham in 1974-75, but retired from football thereafter. He died in April 1999 and every English football ground held one minute's silence in his memory.

Don Revie

The Leeds manager who deserted England

Don Revie's managerial career embraced triumph and disgrace. He created, from nothing, one of the top English clubs of the 1960s and 1970s, but his reputation was destroyed by greed.

An effective centre forward for Manchester City and Sunderland in the 1950s (he was Footballer of the Year in 1955), with six England caps, Revie went to struggling Leeds in 1959. In 1961 he took over as manager, with Leeds facing relegation to the Third Division. A driven, ambitious man, he immediately signed Bobby Collins from Everton and, with Collins acting as Revie's alter ego on the pitch, kept Leeds up. Over the next few years Revie's success in the transfer market, a function of his meticulous attention to detail and his persuasive manner, brought in such players as Lorimer, Gray and Giles. With Bremner, Sprake, Reaney and Hunter emerging from the reserves, the great Leeds team was nearly in place.

They were promoted to the First Division in 1963-64 and by 1974 Leeds had won two League championships, the FA Cup, the League Cup, and two Fairs Cups, and could have achieved much more. Revie produced a team which matched his ambition to win things, but to many it appeared that they didn't much care how they did this.

Leeds were an uncompromising and often cynical side, and in the early years ultra-defensive, but they were also courageous, tough and single-minded. Revie formed the club in his own image, and perhaps his greatest gift was to engender an almost beleaguered

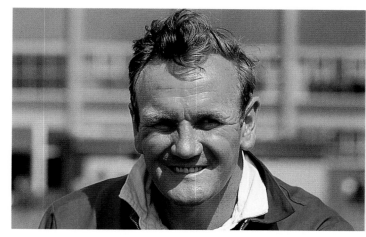

Born:
Middlesbrough, 10.7.27
Club:
Leeds United 61-74
Club honours:
League Championship 68/9, 73/4; FA Cup 72; League Cup 68; UEFA Cup 67/8, 70/1
Internationals:
England manager 74-77, 17 games
Individual honours:
OBE 70

team spirit, an 'us and them' mentality, which saw them through some epic battles. However, he also appreciated skilful football, and some of Leeds' performances, for instance their 7-0 rout of Southampton in 1972, with Lorimer and Clarke scoring at will, underpinned by the intricate and clinical passing of Giles and Bremner, could be breathtaking.

Revie left nothing to chance. He was a man obsessed with tactics and before every game he presented his players with detailed dossiers on the opposition, describing their weaknesses, strengths and vulnerability to set pieces, wing play, high balls and so on. He was single-minded in his determination to create the finest football team in Europe.

All good things come to an end, however, and in 1974 Revie left his aging stars to take over as manager of England. His first eight games in charge resulted in five wins and three draws,

but he had used 27 different players. The suspicion was growing that he was unsure about what he wanted at the international level, and the squad was becoming unsettled. England failed to qualify for the European Championships and the 1978 World Cup, and the saviour had become the villain.

Revie jumped ship in July 1977, and went, without informing the FA, to Dubai to negotiate a £340,000 four-year contract with the UAE. Worse, he tried to secure a pay-off without telling them about his new arrangement. He was given a ten-year ban by the FA, but this was overturned by the High Court in 1979, although the judge criticised Revie's behaviour as a 'sensational and outrageous example of disloyalty'.

Revie then had various jobs overseas, and died in May 1989, the victim of motor neurone disease. He remains a hero at Elland Road.

Bill Shankly

The creator of modern Liverpool

With his contemporaries Stein and Busby, Bill Shankly was one of the last of a breed of Scottish managers. A tough, abrasive man, with a coruscating wit and not a little charisma, he was the architect of the Liverpool side of the 1960s. His single-minded, no-nonsense personality, forged in the coalfields of Central Scotland, drove on the Reds to English and European triumphs, and his managerial reign laid the foundation for the great Liverpool side of the late 1970s and 1980s.

Football was in Shankly's blood. One of five professional footballing brothers, he started his playing career as a right-half at Carlisle and moved to Preston where he won an FA Cup medal in 1938, the year he received the first of his five caps for Scotland, and later played alongside his idol Tom Finney. His managerial career began at Carlisle in 1949 and during the next ten years he managed Grimsby Town, Workington and Huddersfield. In 1959 he joined Liverpool, a declining Second Division club low on ambition and trophies, and he set to work.

He immediately began a clear-out of what he saw as second-rate players and, by 1961, he had brought in Ian St John and Ron Yeats, who were to be the backbone of his team. Liverpool were promoted as Champions the following year. Willie Stevenson and Peter Thompson also arrived at Anfield and in 1964 Liverpool won the League Championship, winning it again in 1966. In between, in 1965, Shankly brought the FA Cup to Liverpool for the first time.

Shankly established the Liverpool tradition of

Born:
Glenbuck, Ayrshire, 2.9.13
Clubs:
Carlisle United 49-51, Grimsby Town 51-53, Workington Town 53-56, Huddersfield 56-59, Liverpool 59-74
Club honours:
League Championship 63/4, 65/6, 72/3; FA Cup 65, 74; UEFA Cup 73
Individual honours:
OBE 74

building and rebuilding sides, continually replacing players to keep the team operating seamlessly and at full throttle. By the late 1960s Larry Lloyd had replaced Ron Yeats and John Toshack had taken over from Roger Hunt, and Shankly's astute transfer market dealings had brought in Emlyn Hughes and Steve Heighway. His £35,000 purchase of Kevin Keegan in 1971 was his canniest move, and a new Liverpool

team was in place for the 1970s. Shankly could be an intimidating figure, a Scottish 'hard man', but he inspired deep affection and respect from the players and fans. His motivational powers were legendary, constantly rubbishing the opposition and nurturing the enthusiasm and self-belief of his team. As Roger Hunt said: 'If you lost a game, you lost to rubbish. If you won, you had beaten a great team.'

As well as being a master of mind games, Shankly's career had made him aware of the crucial importance of fitness and, through fitness and the avoidance of injury, consistency. The passing style of football he introduced meant that injuries were avoidable and, when they did occur, they were immediately treated by physio Bob Paisley. Under his guidance, Liverpool were fast, skilful and, playing as a settled unit, very difficult to stop.

They won the League again in 1973, also that year claiming the UEFA Cup, Shankly's only European victory. After winning the FA Cup in 1974, to the surprise of everyone he announced his retirement at the age of 60. Perhaps that was one of his rare wrong decisions, as afterwards he felt he was treated badly by the club when not given a directorship. A rather embittered Shankly died in September 1981, and Liverpool and football mourned his loss. The Shankly Gates at Anfield – with the message 'You'll never walk alone' – were erected after his death as a tribute to this stubborn, eccentric but passionately dedicated man.

Jock Stein

The Big Man of Celtic and Scotland

In the history of Scottish football, few names are as revered as Jock Stein. A man of vision and integrity, and with a deep pride in his Lanarkshire mining background, Stein was a natural leader with the ability to motivate and manage people to achieve their very best. This, combined with his acute tactical awareness and love of football, made him one of the most successful managers the game has known.

Stein joined Celtic in 1951 where, as a solid centre-half and captain, he led the club to their first 'double' for 40 years, in 1953-54. He left the Bhoys in 1960 to manage Dunfermline and took them to a Scottish Cup final victory (against Celtic) the following year. He enjoyed a brief successful spell at Hibs and, in March 1965, he came back to Celtic as manager. The glory years were about to return to the East End of Glasgow.

In the 13 years he was at the club, he turned Celtic into one of the great European sides. Playing adventurous, attacking football, with the emphasis on speed, skill and exhilarating creativity, Celtic overturned the hegemony of Rangers and ran up an astonishing record of triumphs – ten League titles (nine of them in a row), eight Cups and six League Cups.

Stein's proudest moment, however, was when he took his Lisbon Lions – Murdoch, Johnstone, Auld, Lennox *et al* – to the European Cup final in 1967 against the much-fancied, defensively-minded Inter Milan, and overwhelmed the Italians 2-1 to capture the trophy, the first British side to have done so.

'John, you're immortal', said Bill Shankly after the game.

Stein's team again reached the final in 1970, losing to Feyenoord, and the semi-final in 1972, losing to Inter on penalties, but Celtic were rampant in Scotland, landing the League and Cup 'double' four times between 1970 and 1977, although Stein was absent for season 1975-76 due to a serious car accident which nearly killed him. However, by 1978 Rangers were resurgent, and Stein surplus to requirements. Although he handed over power to his former captain Billy McNeill in a dignified manner, Stein was hurt by Celtic's refusal to make him a director, and he headed south to Leeds United.

Ally Mcleod's resignation as Scottish manager in September 1978 after the Argentina debacle meant that Stein's stay at Elland Road was a brief one, and he was appointed Scottish manager in October that year, having already had a short spell as caretaker manager in 1965/6, when Scotland narrowly failed to qualify for the 1966 World Cup finals.

He led Scotland to the 1982 World Cup finals and failed to qualify for the second stage on goal difference. His last act was to ensure qualification for the 1986 finals by drawing with Wales 1-1 at Ninian Park on 10 September 1985, and his inspired substitution of Davey Cooper for Gordon Strachan changed the game in Scotland's direction. Shortly after the final whistle, Stein suffered a fatal heart attack and died at the ground.

In *The Observer*, Hugh McIlvanney movingly wrote that there were many who 'did not have to go down a pit to know what real darkness was'.

Born:
Burnbank, Lanarkshire, 5.10.22
Clubs:
Dunfermline 60-64, Hibernian 64-65, Glasgow Celtic 65-78, Leeds United 78
Club honours:
Scottish League Championship 65/6, 66/7, 67/8, 68/9, 69/70, 70/1, 71/2, 72/3, 73/4; Scottish Premier League 76/7; Scottish Cup 61, 65, 67, 69, 71, 72, 74, 75, 77; Scottish League Cup 65/6, 66/7, 67/8, 68/9, 69/70, 74/5; European Cup 1967
Internationals:
Scotland manager 78-85, 61 games
Individual honours:
CBE 79

Great Teams

Truly great football teams rarely last for long. Through marvellous skill, self-belief and almost psychic understanding, they flourish, dominate but eventually fade away, usually over a period of just a few years. However, during their brief reigns, they thrill and electrify football fans, and when they are gone they are remembered with awe.

The next 50 pages pay homage to some of the greatest of all – including Brazil of the early 1970s, Real Madrid in the 1950s, and the Bayern Munich of Beckenbauer and Muller – and vividly demonstrate why they will never be forgotten.

Arsenal 1930s

Chapman's team of the decade

Herbert Chapman created the great Arsenal team that dominated the 1930s. But Chapman never lived to see his dream fulfilled.

Few managers build one team that dominates a decade, let alone two. Chapman did it, first with Huddersfield, the side that ruled the mid-1920s, then with the Gunners. It was ironic that when Arsenal advertised for a manager in the summer of 1925, they stipulated the successful candidate shouldn't spend big money in the transfer market. Chapman changed all that. His first master-stroke was bringing Sunderland's great England inside forward Charlie Buchan back to London. Chapman agreed a fee of £2,000, plus £100 for each goal Buchan scored in his first season. Buchan netted 20 and Arsenal finished runners-up, the highest position in their 40-year history.

In 1927, the Gunners reached the FA Cup final for the first time, losing 1-0 to Cardiff, after the ball flicked off keeper Dan Lewis's jersey into the net.

Chapman knew he had to build again. It took time. Right-back and skipper Tom Parker had already arrived from Southampton. So had flying winger Joe Hulme from Blackburn. The changes in the offside law meant the centre-half was now purely a defensive creature. In young Herbert Roberts from Oswestry, Chapman found the ideal stopper. The great man then snapped up England's finest-ever left-back, Eddie Hapgood, from non-League Kettering. He paid a British record fee to Bolton for inside-forward David Jack. He pulled off his greatest coup of all when he signed Alex

Arsenal 1932: (l to r, back) Parker, Jones, Moss, Roberts, John, Black; (l to r, front) manager Chapman, Hulme, Jack, Lambert, James, Bastin, trainer Whittaker

James from Preston. James was the midfield maestro who turned Chapman's vision into reality. Chapman's second greatest coup was signing a young winger from Exeter called Cliff Bastin. 'Boy' Bastin won every honour in the English game by the time he was 20.

Chapman's Arsenal were the most tactically advanced team of their time. They pioneered the WM formation – three at the back, two half-backs and an inside-forward in midfield – supported by another deep-lying inside-forward. The wingers and centre-forward provided the thrust. The formation was perfect for the Gunners. They had the defenders – and the attackers – to make it work.

Most teams in those days used wingers to hug the touchline and put across centres. Chapman used Hulme and Bastin to cut in and strike. 'It's essential to our game that our wingers should come inside and score,' he said. James, the supreme midfield general, was a brilliant provider for their runs.

In 1932-33, Bastin hit 33 League goals from the left wing. Chapman wasn't just a brilliant spotter of talent. He was also a shrewd pyschologist. Bastin wanted to go and play tennis when Chapman travelled to Exeter to meet him. But the teenage winger grew so fed up with Chapman waiting for him that he signed for Arsenal.

Ted Drake; Arsenal's prolific goalscorer who scored 42 League goals in season 1934-35

When Parker retired, Chapman needed a right-back. He decided the ideal replacement was George Male, then a reserve left-half. It was news to Male, but Chapman persuaded him. Said Male: 'Mr Chapman convinced me that not only was I cut out to be a right-back, but I was going to be the best right-back in England.' Chapman was right. Older Arsenal fans still claim Male and Hapgood as the finest pair of full-backs who ever lived.

Chapman chivvied James into being Arsenal's inspiration too. The occasion was an FA Cup replay against Birmingham in 1930. James had been injured. On the weekend before the crunch day, Chapman went to James's house and told him how important he was to Arsenal's cause. James starred in the replay, the Gunners took another step towards Wembley. James went on to become the most famous player in Arsenal's history.

In 1930, Arsenal won the FA Cup for the first time, beating Chapman's old club Huddersfield 2-0. James's quick thinking at a free kick scored the first. Centre-forward Jack Lambert galloped away to hit the second. It was Arsenal's first major trophy – the first of many.

The following year, the Gunners cruised to the title with a record points total. They lost just four games, scored 127 goals – with 38 from Lambert, 31 from Jack and 28 from Bastin – and their critics claimed they were a 'defensive' side!

The following season Arsenal finished runners-up in the League and Cup. Jack Allen's 'over the line' goal, that turned the final against

League Champions: 30/1, 32/3, 33/4, 34/5, 37/8
FA Cup winners: 30, 36

DID YOU KNOW?
Arsenal provided a record seven players for the England team that beat World Cup holders Italy 3-2 at Highbury in 1934 – Frank Moss, George Male, Eddie Hapgood, Wilf Copping, Ray Bowden, Ted Drake and Cliff Bastin.

Newcastle, remains a sore point to this day. Camera footage clearly proved the ball was out of play before Jack Richardson centred for Allen to equalise Bob John's opening goal.

But Arsenal were embarking on a run to rival Chapman's Huddersfield – three championships in a row. It's a tribute to Arsenal's reputation that the Gunners 2-0 defeat by Third Division Walsall in the 1933 FA Cup third round remains one of the biggest shocks in English football history. The Gunners team that day was well below strength. They

were kicked all over the pitch too. But the celebration of the result outside north London says everything about Arsenal's domination of the age.

Chapman died in January 1934. He went to watch a match while he had a cold, which developed into pneumonia. He was only 55.

Director George Allison took the reins. But the powers in the dressing room were Chapman's old assistant Joe Shaw and trainer Tom Whittaker (later another successful Arsenal manager). The Gunners signed greats like Ted Drake, inside-forward Ray Bowden, who replaced Jack, and wing-halves Jack Crayston and Wilf Copping. Their quality ensured that Arsenal carried on winning.

Drake set Arsenal's scoring record with 42 League goals in the third successive championship triumph, of 1934-35. The following season he hit all seven in a 7-1 demolition of Aston Villa. At the end of that season, the Gunners won the FA Cup for the second time – beating Sheffield United 1-0. But the magic was waning. James's retirement in 1937 left a hole too big to fill. Hulme had gone too. England goalkeeper Frank Moss had to retire because of injury. Other clubs had caught up with Arsenal's tactics. Although the Gunners won the title again in 1938, they knew they had to rebuild. Allison signed Wolves midfield star Bryn Jones for a British record £14,000. The war ruined his chances of becoming a Highbury legend – but Arsenal fans had enjoyed enough of them in the 1930s already.

Italy 1934-38

Two World Cups in succession

Italy dominated world football throughout the 1930s. The insular British refused to take part in the World Cup, though England might have made it an interesting contest.

England, based around the great Arsenal club side, drew 1-1 with Italy in Rome before the Italians won the 1934 World Cup, then beat the World Cup holders 3-2 in the 'Battle of Highbury'.

But Italian football in the 1930s wasn't just about sport. It was about politics. Benito Mussolini's Fascist government believed sporting success would boost Italy's prestige around the world. So the country's rulers pumped money into football.

In Vittorio Pozzo, Mussolini found the perfect national team manager. A psychologist, a diplomat, a shrewd builder of teams, Pozzo ideally served his country's ends.

Italy's success began in 1934, when they hosted the second-ever World Cup finals. The Italians had pulled a stroke or two beforehand. Oriundi they were called: Argentinians of Italian descent who could claim Italian citizenship. That's how the Argentinian defender Luisito Monti, the skipper and guide of Pozzo's 1934 team, turned out for Italy. Argentinian attackers Raimundo Orsi and Enrico Guaita became Italians too. Monti's value to his country was seen in the 'Battle of Highbury'. When he went off injured, Italy's discipline departed with him.

In 1934, circumstances favoured Italy. Cup holders Uruguay, incensed by the

ITALY'S ACHIEVEMENTS

World Cup winners: 34, 38
Olympic Champions: 36

ITALY'S WINNING TEAMS

1934: Combi, Monzeglio, Allemandi, Ferraris, Monti, Bertolini, Guaita, Meazza, Schiavo, Ferrari, Orsi
1936: Venturini, Foni, Rava, Baldo, Piccini, Locatelli, Frossi, Marchini, Bertoni, Biagi, Gabriotti
1938: Olivieri, Foni, Rava, Serantoni, Andreolo, Locatelli, Biavati, Meazza, Piola, Ferrari, Colaussi

unwillingness of many European sides to travel to Uruguay in 1930, did not defend the Cup. Argentina sent a weak squad, not wishing any more of their best players to be poached by Italy. They and Brazil went home after the first round, victims of a knock-out system that gave no weight to previous achievements.

Meanwhile, Italy ran up a record 7-1 World Cup win over the USA. The second round was much harder. Reguerio's goal for Spain was a freak, flying in from a hopeful centre. But Italy's response had been pallid. It took Giovanni Ferrari, in the second half, to earn a replay.

Pozzo read the Riot Act at half time that day. He knew his team weren't performing to their potential. A suitably terrified Italian side went out to beat Spain 1-0 in the replay, thanks to Giuseppe Meazza's 12th minute header; then overcame Austria 1-0 in Milan in the semi-final, thanks to Guaita's 18th minute goal

In the final, they met Czechoslovakia. Czechs still talk about that team, of the great goalkeeper Frantisek Planicka, and the forward, Oldrich Nejedly – and the chance they missed.

Antonin Puc gave the Czechs a 71st minute lead. A few minutes later, Frantisek Svoboda hit the post. It was Italy's reprieve. Orsi's 80th minute goal forced extra time. Angelo Schiavo's 95th minute goal won the game for the hosts. Italy were World Champions. Mussolini and his entourage rejoiced. But Pozzo knew he had to rebuild. Too many players – especially the Oriundi – were growing old together. The 1936 Olympic Games in Germany gave him the perfect opportunity.

Italy beat the USA, Japan and Norway (2-1, after extra time) to reach the final. Annibale Frossi scored twice to see off Austria 2-1, again in extra time. Of that line-up, Alfredo 'Papa' Foni, Pietro Rava, and Ugo Locatelli became regulars for the 1938 World Cup finals.

After that 1934 defeat by England at Highbury, Pozzo's squad had to undergo rehabilitation. They'd done that. Now all Italian eyes were focussed on the 1938 World Cup in France Again, the Brits didn't bother to compete.

Pozzo had a way of making players play together. He would put colleagues at each other's throats – often competing for the same position – as room-mates It was a dangerous policy. Pozzo thought it helped them see the sense of working together. He knew when to rant at the players and when to play the father figure. And, as he had shown in the 1934 final –

The Italy team celebrate after beating Hungary 4-2 in the 1938 World Cup Final

when he switched Guaita and Schiavo's positions before the winning goal – his tactical knowledge was immense.

By the time they crossed the border to France for the 1938 World Cup finals, Pozzo had built a new side. Only Giovanni Ferrari and Meazza remained from the 1934 winners. Geraldo Olivieri had taken over from Giampiero Combi and Carlo Ceresoli in goal. Lazio's centre-forward Silvio Piola and Luigi Colaussi from Triestina had become the key strikers. Besides integrating the stars of Italy's Olympic victory, Pozzo had brought in more newcomers – Pietro Serantoni, Michele Andreolo and Amedeo Biavati.

Norway, who'd given Italy a fright in the Olympics, pushed them all the way in the first round in Marseille. Arne Brustad's late equaliser

took Italy to extra time. Not for the last time in the competition, Piola's awesome eye for a goal saw Italy through.

In the second round, Italy beat the hosts France 3-1 at Stade Colombes. Piola did the damage again, with two second-half goals, after Oscar Heisserer had equalised Colaussi's ninth-minute opener. Italy were gathering momentum.

Pozzo couldn't believe Italy's luck in the semi-final. The Brazilians had left out their leading scorer, Leonidas, a victim of team politics. It was said they were saving him for the final.

In the quarter-finals, Brazil had triumphed 2-1 in a replay, over a Czech team missing the injured Planicka and Nejedly. In Marseille, their luck ran out. They held the Italians for 55

minutes. Then Colaussi broke the deadlock. Five minutes later Meazza scored from the spot. Romeu's 87th-minute reply was no more than a consolation.

So to the final: Italy v Hungary. The Hungarian danger man was Gyorgy Sarosi, the Magyars' creative force. The Italians did their best to kick him out of the match. Pozzo was a pragmatist when the World Cup was at stake.

Colaussi prodded Italy into a fifth-minute lead. Pal Titkos levelled two minutes later. Piola restored Italy's lead. Colaussi made it 3-1. With 20 minutes left, Sarosi escaped the hackers at his heels to give Hungary hope. But eight minutes from time, Biavati made a chance and Piola tucked it away. Italy had won their second World Cup.

Hungary 1952-56

The Magical Magyars

'The Magical Magyars' the English press dubbed them, after they'd thrashed England 6-3 at Wembley in 1953. The Hungarians of the early 1950s were Europe's first great national side after the war. They lost only one match between 1952 and 1956, the year the team broke up. But it was the one they most wanted to win – the 1954 World Cup final. Even now, Hungarians still wonder how they lost 3-2 to West Germany.

Hungary made the world take note when they won the 1952 Olympic football tournament in Finland. By then, the stars were already in place. Ten of the team that beat Yugoslavia 2-0 in the Olympic final played against the Germans two years later. Legendary coach Gustav Sebes had made just one change, Jozsef Toth for Peter Palotas up front.

Sebes knew how to get the best out of the players. He was an innovative tactician too. He was the man who confused conventional defences by dropping centre-forward Nandor Hidegkuti deep to link up with right-half Jozsef Bozsik in midfield. In 1958, the Brazilians would refine the system into 4-2-4. While Hidegkuti created from deep, Ferenc Puskas and Sandor Kocsis drove forward; supported from the flanks by Zoltan Czibor and Palotas or Toth.

In the Olympic tournament, Czibor and Kocsis scored to beat Romania 2-1 in the first round. Palotas(2) and Kocsis saw off Italy 3-0. The Hungarians ran riot against Turkey (7-1) then Sweden (6-0) to reach the final in Helsinki. There, goals by Puskas and Czibor clinched the gold medal.

The Hungarian goalkeeper Grosics in action against England at Wembley in 1953

That triumph boosted the morale of the Hungarian people. For much of the war Hungary had been a Nazi puppet state. Afterwards, it became a Soviet satellite, ruled by one of the most repressive Stalinist regimes in eastern Europe. The Hungarian people would explode in rebellion in 1956, with tragic consequences. But in the early 1950s, the football team restored their national pride.

What a team. In goal was the great Gyula Grosics. Mihaly Lantos and Gyula Lorant were stern defenders. Bozsik, later a member of the Hungarian parliament, was a classical attacking wing-half. Hidegkuti was the fulcrum. Czibor and Kocsis supplied the pace and power; Puskas's deadly left foot was the cutting edge.

Like other eastern European countries who maintained conscription, the Hungarian government set up a prestige army club, Honved – where the best players could train and play, unhindered by military duties. Puskas was even given the rank of major. Inevitably he was nicknamed the 'galloping major', though no-one who knew him could imagine Puskas breaking into a trot, let alone a gallop.

In November 1953, Hungary came to Wembley. England had never lost at home to a non-British or Irish team. By the final whistle, the Hungarians had shattered that record. Hidegkuti's role confused England. Who should mark him? Billy Wright and Harry Johnston didn't want to be drawn deep. None of the

English midfield players picked him either. So Hidegkuti wreaked havoc, and swept forward often enough – usually unmarked – to hit a hat-trick. During the warm-up, the English fans derided the squat and chunky Puskas. He answered with two cracking finishes. Bozsik scored the other one. England's reputation lay in tatters.

A year later, England's last warm-up match before the 1954 World Cup finals was a trip to Budapest. More than 92,000 crammed into the Nepstadion. England left dejected. Hidegkuti ran the game again, and hit Hungary's seventh goal. Lantos opened the scoring. Puskas and Kocsis netted twice. Toth struck from the left. 7-1 to Hungary: England's biggest-ever defeat.

Hungary's movement and passing had pulled England apart. As centre-half Syd Owen said afterwards: 'It was like playing people from outer space.' England were not the only famous team to suffer. Before winning at Wembley, the Hungarians went to Rome and demolished Italy 3-0.

So to the World Cup finals in Switzerland. Hungary began by routing South Korea 9-0. In their second game, they met West Germany. The Germans, cynical pragmatists as ever, reckoned they could lose to Hungary and still qualify for the quarter-finals by beating Turkey in a play-off. That way they'd also avoid Hungary and Brazil in the quarter-finals. So Sepp Herberger fielded virtually a reserve side. The Hungarians won, 8-3, but at a price. The German centre-half Werner Liebrich kicked Puskas so hard that he didn't play again until the final. Even then he was nursing a suspect ankle.

The Germans duly hammered Turkey 7-2 in the play-off, beat Yugoslavia 2-0 in the quarter-finals – then demolished an Austrian

TEAMS IN THE 1954 WORLD CUP FINAL

Hungary:
Grosics, Buzansky, Lantos, Bozsik, Lorant, Zakarias, Czibor, Kocsis, Hidegkuti, Puskas, Toth

West Germany:
Turek, Posipal, Kohlmeyer, Eckel, Liebrich, Mai, Rahn, Morlock, O.Walter, F.Walter, Schafer

team with little stomach for a fight 6-1 to reach the final.

Meanwhile the Magyars had won two of the most memorable matches in World Cup history. The quarter-final against Brazil has gone down as the 'Battle of Bern' because of its finale. Hidegkuti and Kocsis put Hungary two up after seven minutes. Djalma Santos replied from the penalty spot. Lantos converted a penalty for Hungary on the hour. Winger Julinho pulled one back five minutes later.

There had been an undercurrent of tension from the first whistle. Now the game erupted. English referee Arthur Ellis sent off Bozsik and Nilton Santos for fighting. With four minutes left, he dismissed Humberto for kicking Lorant. Kocsis netted Hungary's fourth, two minutes from time. The Brazilians were furious. After the game they tried to invade the Hungarian dressing room. A brawl ensued. Punches were thrown and bottles broken. In those days, three dismissals and such after-match scenes were virtually unthinkable. But ·FIFA took no action.

Hungary progressed to the semi-finals, where they met the holders Uruguay in Lausanne. It was one of the finest contests ever seen in the World Cup finals. Czibor and Hidegkuti made it 2-0 to Hungary by the 46th minute. Juan-Eduardo Hohberg replied with two late goals to

force extra time. Kocsis made the difference in the second period. He struck twice to earn Hungary a 4-2 win. His second was his 11th goal in the competition, then a World Cup record.

So to the final, again in Bern. Hungary started huge favourites. Puskas insisted on playing despite his dodgy ankle. He shot Hungary ahead after six minutes. Czibor added a second two minutes later. But Max Morlock replied immediately for the Germans and Helmut Rahn levelled after 18 minutes.

Thereafter, it was Hungary against the Germans' heroic goalkeeper Toni Turek. He made flying saves from Kocsis, Czibor and Puskas. With nothing to show for their domination, Hungary were vulnerable to a breakaway. Six minutes from time the Germans got it. Rahn collected the ball 30 yards out, burst into the Hungarian box and beat Grosics with a snap shot. Puskas had a seemingly good goal disallowed as the desperate Hungarians piled forward. Turek pulled off another amazing save from Czibor. As they did 20 years later against Holland, the Germans had beaten the world's greatest team in a World Cup final.

The Hungarian people felt let down. Sebes and several senior players needed protection when they returned to Budapest. It took an unbeaten run of two years to win back the people's confidence. Then came the uprising. While Russian tanks massed to cross the border and crush the rebellion, Honved were in Bilbao for a European Cup tie against Athletic. Most of the Hungarian players never went home.

Ladislav Kubala had shown the way when he defected to the west in 1950. He became a star with Barcelona. So, in time, did Kocsis and Czibor. Puskas, with Real Madrid, made the biggest impact of all. But Hungary's footballing dreams died along with the revolution.

Real Madrid 1954-60

The Spanish champions of Europe

The late 1950s Real attack: (l to r): Del Sol, Di Stefano, Puskas and Gento

The story of the early years of the European Cup is the story of Real Madrid. They dominated the competition. Their great stars made European club football fashionable.

If their opening movement was a 4-3 win over Reims in the first final, then the crescendo came at Hampden Park in 1960, when Real thrashed Eintracht Frankfurt 7-3.

Real's heroes were two of the greatest footballing figures of the century – the president, Santiago Bernabeu; and the legendary Argentinian centre-forward Alfredo Di Stefano. Bernabeu, a successful lawyer and ex-amateur Real forward, had a dream. He would build a great stadium, fit for champions – and the players would follow. Bernabeu, supported by an ambitious bond scheme,

presided over the building of such a ground. Its 106,000-capacity bulk towers over the Madrid suburb of Chamartin even now.

It was Bernabeu who encouraged the signing of stars from all over the world; Bernabeu who first realised the importance of Real winning the new-born European Cup. Bernabeu's vision created the background. The majestic Di Stefano turned dreams into reality.

Bernabeu dispatched his young finance director, Raimundo Saporta, to South America, to sign Di Stefano in 1953. In his first game, his four goals for Real in a 5-0 win over Real's bitter rivals Barcelona announced the arrival of a superstar. Di Stefano had it all: pace, power and massive skill. He could play up front, drop deep, score goals with feet or head, create chances,

and set the strategy of the whole team. 'El Rey' (the king) the fans called him. New arrivals at Real – even as distinguished as Ferenc Puskas – were expected to walk in his shadow.

In 1955-56, the Spanish Champions eased past Servette of Geneva, then beat Partizan Belgrade and AC Milan to reach the first-ever European Cup final, in Paris. Di Stefano was the class act, but he had massive support. Centre-half Marcos Marquitos was a superb stopper. His partner, Juan Zarraga, was a constructive defender of quality. Miguel Munoz was a dynamic attacking right-half. The Argentinian inside-forward Hector Rial made the ideal foil for Di Stefano. And on the left flank, Real boasted the speediest winger of the age, Paco Gento.

Reims, inspired by their great centre-forward Raymond Kopa, pushed Real all the way in the final. Reims led 2-0 after 12 minutes, through Michel Leblond and Jean Templin. Di Stefano was stirred to action. He started and finished the move for Real's first. Rial headed them level. But Michel Hidalgo nodded in Kopa's free kick to give Reims a 3-2 lead. Marquitos, bursting forward, cracked a fortuitous equaliser, off Templin's knee. Eleven minutes from time, Gento broke on the right and crossed for Rial to hit Real's winner. Templin struck the bar with time running out, but Real survived. Gento thought it was the hardest victory of all Real's five successive wins.

Kopa joined Real the following season. But he was stuck on the right wing – a waste of a

European Cup winners: 56, 57, 58, 59, 60
Spanish champions: 53/4, 54/5, 56/7, 57/8

Di Stefano scores Real's first
goal in their 7-3 victory over
Eintracht Frankfurt in 1960

great talent. No-one was allowed to upstage Di Stefano.

After a play-off win against Rapid Vienna, Real ran into Manchester United, their biggest obstacle on the route to the 1957 final. A 3-1 win in Madrid and a 2-2 draw in Manchester saw them through. The final, against Fiorentina, was on Real's home ground. They took full advantage. Di Stefano opened the scoring from the spot, after Enrique Mateos was fouled. Kopa sent Gento through to make it 2-0.

Real signed a new centre-half for the 1957-58 campaign – the Uruguayan international, Jose Santamaria. Marquitos moved to right-back to accommodate him.

The Munich air crash had wrecked United. So Real met AC Milan in the final in Brussels. Another Uruguayan, Juan Schiaffino, put Milan ahead. Di Stefano levelled. The Argentinian Ernesto Grillo made it 2-1 for Milan. That lead lasted barely a minute before Rial equalised. In extra time, Milan's Antonello Cucchiaroni hit the bar. But Gento grabbed the winner, driving home the rebound after his first shot was blocked.

Now Real made another vital addition – Ferenc Puskas, the great Hungarian inside-left. Puskas was already 31. Critics claimed he was overweight. Puskas replied that he could sprint

when he needed to. He just didn't need to very often. What no-one doubted was the quality of Puskas' crashing left foot. By the 1959 semi-final, the Argentinian goalkeeper Rogelio Dominguez had taken over from Juan Alonso, a victim of lung trouble. He had a crucial role to play in Real's run to their fourth final.

The holders eased past Besiktas of Turkey and Austria's Wiener SK – to a clash with their bitter local rivals Atletico. Real offered Atletico the chance to make money by playing both games at Chamartin. Atletico refused. They decided to play their home leg at Vicente Calderon.

Atletico should have gone into that match with a 2-2 draw under their belts. In the opening game, Chuzo gave Atletico a surprise lead. Rial pulled Real level. Puskas whacked home a penalty. Then Atletico's Brazilian centre-forward Vava had the chance to equalise from the spot. Dominguez stretched full length and saved the kick. That stop was vital to Real's season... 2-1 to Real. Atletico winger Enrique Collar scored the only goal in the return.

These days, Atletico would have gone through on away goals. Then, such affairs were settled by a play-off on a neutral ground. The teams met again, in Zaragoza. Puskas, injured for the second leg, cracked a penalty winner after Collar had wiped out Di Stefano's opener for Real. Atletico cursed Dominguez's penalty save.

Puskas was injured for the final too, a low key 2-0 win over Kopa's old club Reims in Stuttgart. Mateos and Di Stefano scored Real's goals. Kopa took a kicking from his France team mate Jean Vincent. Mateos missed a penalty. But Real had made it four in a row.

There were more changes for Real's next defence. Enrique Pachin, from Osasuna, came in at left-back. On the right wing, the Brazilian, Canario, came in for the semi-finals, replacing Kopa, who'd returned to Reims. Luis Del Sol arrived from Betis of Seville to fill Rial's role as the linking inside-forward.

Ex-captain Munoz became coach, to the delight of the players. Real beat Luxemburg's Jeunesse d'Esch and the French Champions Nice to reach another all-Spanish semi-final. Or rather: Madrid against Barcelona, the symbol of Catalonia.

Helenio Herrera had made Barca a formidable side. But he went his own way. To the fury of the Barca fans, he left out the brilliant Hungarian attackers, Ladislao Kubala and Zoltan Czibor, following a dispute over bonuses. Angry fans attacked Herrera after Real's victory. Real won both games 3-1. Di Stefano dominated the match in Madrid, and scored twice. At the Nou Camp, Puskas – who'd played alongside Kubala and Czibor for Hungary – killed the tie with two more goals.

Now for Eintracht Frankfurt in the final. Di Stefano and Puskas ran riot. Real seemed omnipotent. But it would be their last hurrah in a European Cup final until 1966.

Brazil 1958

4-2-4 triumphs in Sweden

Vava lashes in Brazil's first goal in the final against Sweden

They are still fondly remembered, those Brazilians of 1958; World Cup winners in Sweden, the first of Brazil's world-beating teams. Yet – like so many World Cup-winning sides, their team didn't fall into place until the closing stages. It wasn't until the final group game against the Soviet Union that coach Vicente Feola – at the insistence of senior players – brought in Garrincha on the right wing. The 17-year-old prodigy Pele returned

after missing the opening matches against Austria and England through injury. Out went Joel and striker Jose Altafini. Feola settled on Vava at centre-forward. Now Brazil had a settled attack.

Feola's undistinguished playing career came to an end in his mid-20s. He made up for that as a coach, first with Sao Paulo, then as a member of the Brazilian federation's technical staff. In

1958, four months before the finals, he took over as national coach. Brazil had built a new side since the 1954 finals. Only Djalma Santos (restored by Feola for the Final), left back Nilton Santos, midfield general Didi and reserve goalkeeper Castilho remained from that squad. But the Brazilians had talent to burn – and Feola devised the ideal system to bring the best out of them. The great Hungarian team had been playing a variant of 4-2-4, with

The Brazilian team line up in the 1958 World Cup finals

forward Nandor Hidegkuti dropping back into midfield. Now Feola refined the formation for Brazil. Bellini and Orlando became the two centre-backs in front of goalkeeper Gilmar. Right half Zito filled the midfield fetcher and carrier role, while Didi dictated the tempo.

By the quarter-finals, Feola's forward four were in place too – Garrincha on the right, Vava in the centre, Pele breaking through the middle and the tireless Mario Zagalo on the left. If Brazil's midfield pair needed support, then Zagalo dropped back. He didn't have to drop back very often.

Brazil had qualified from a group containing only themselves and Peru. After a 1-1 draw in Lima, Didi's free-kick saw Brazil through at the Maracana. Didi and Garrincha were masters of such bending free kicks – 'banana shots', the British commentators christened them. They would marvel at more Brazilian skills before the finals were over.

Brazil came to Sweden oozing class. Feola had instilled another vital quality too: discipline. No longer did Brazil lose their tempers if circumstances ran against them – as they did in the notorious 'Battle of Bern' against Hungary in the previous finals. In 1958, such outbursts were never on the agenda, even when Just Fontaine equalised Vava's early goal in the semi-final. Didi shot Brazil in front. Pele hit a second-half hat-trick. Roger Piantoni's reply was only a consolation as Brazil eased through 5-2. Feola's team had peaked at the right time.

They had shown their intent in their opening group match, crushing Austria 3-0. Altafini opened the scoring after 38 minutes, Nilton Santos netted a second four minutes after half time and Altafini struck in the last minute. The only game Brazil didn't win was their next group match against England – the first 0-0 draw in World Cup finals history. England had

beaten Brazil 4-2 at Wembley two years earlier. But the Munich air crash had robbed England of some of its great young stars.

England manager Walter Winterbottom had done his homework, shrewdly advised by Bill Nicholson. Full-backs Don Howe and Tommy Banks tight-marked the Brazilian wingers. Bill Slater went man-for-man on Didi. Eddie Clamp and Bobby Robson congested midfield and Brazil couldn't find their usual rhythm.

Feola was delighted that he had a fit Pele to come back. He also knew he had to find another option, to stretch teams who played like England. The players made up his mind for him. A deputation approached the Brazilian coach and called for Garrincha's inclusion. Garrincha, the 'Little Bird' was an instinctive winger with pace, a dazzling swerve and stinging shot. He supplied that extra dimension. If he was exceptional in Sweden, then he reached his peak four years later, when Brazil retained the Cup in Chile.

Vava, already a target for Italian clubs, scored both goals as the new-look Brazil beat the Soviet Union 2-0 to top Group Four. That

brought them up against another stern British defence – the Welsh. Wales were without their injured star, the great Juventus centre-forward John Charles. Brazil attacked in waves. But Wales's Arsenal goalkeeper Jack Kelsey pulled off save after save. The Brazilians called him 'O Marvailhoso' (The Marvellous). Kelsey himself thought it was the best game he ever played for his country. But 17 minutes from time, Pele pounced from close range to break down the Welsh resistance. It was the first of six goals in three games for the teenage attacker.

Semi-final victory over France set up a showdown with hosts Sweden. The Brazilians' 5-2 success remains the most dominant performance ever seen in a World Cup Final. Four years later, in Chile, Pele was injured in the group game against Czechoslovakia. Another young forward, Amarildo, replaced him. Zele Moreira had taken over from Feola. But eight of Feola's team – Gilmar, Djalma Santos, Nilton Santos, Zito, Didi, Garrincha, Vava and Zagalo – played in the side that beat Czechoslovakia 3-1 in the Final. Even then though, they knew, they had played the best football of their lives in those closing matches in Sweden.

Manchester United

The Era of the Busby Babes

Matt Busby had already built one fine team for Manchester United, after the war. In the mid-1950s, he would build an even better one.

Busby took over at United in the spring of 1945. The Luftwaffe's bombs had left Old Trafford in ruins. They had to share with City at Maine Road. United's players – those that remained – were all over the world on war service. Yet within two years, Busby had built a side that finished second in the League, one point behind Liverpool. They finished runners-up for the next two seasons too. In 1948, they came from behind to beat Blackpool 4-2 in the FA Cup final. Centre-forward Jack Rowley scored twice that day. His success showed Busby's shrewdness in the transfer market. The ex-Bournemouth forward had been one of Busby's first signings. The United boss had pulled off another transfer coup when he brought Celtic outside-right Jimmy Delaney to Manchester.

The great Irish full back Johnny Carey was skipper. Centre-half Allenby Chilton, inside-left Stan Pearson and left-winger Charlie Mitten provided more experience. But Busby had already shown he was prepared to give youth a chance. Young hopefuls like left-back John Aston (father of the 1968 hero), left-half Henry Cockburn and inside-forward Johnny Morris all played at Wembley. League runners-up again in 1951, United finally collared the elusive title the following year.

But Busby knew he had to rebuild. Already he had a plan in mind. United would find the best schoolboy talent in the country, then turn them

into senior stars. Chelsea, under Ted Drake, had pioneered youth development in the south. They won the championship in 1955. They were dubbed 'Drake's Ducklings'. Almost inevitably United became known as 'The Busby Babes'. Other clubs, with less developed scouting networks, resented United's aggressive recruiting policy. United took Duncan Edwards from Dudley, on the doorstep of Wolves and West Bromwich. They lifted Bobby Charlton from under Newcastle's nose.

In Manchester and suburbs, United reigned supreme. Skipper and left-back Roger Byrne was Manchester-born His full-back partner Bill Foulkes came from St Helens. Right-half Eddie Colman was from Salford. Inside-forward Dennis Viollet was another Mancunian. Versatile forward David Pegg came from a little further afield – Doncaster; and United began to strengthen their Irish connection too. Centre-half Jackie Blanchflower – Danny's younger brother – arrived from Belfast. Forward Liam Whelan came from Dublin junior club Home Farm.

In Bert Whalley, United's youngsters found a knowledgeable and sympathetic coach. Busby and his assistant Jimmy Murphy had made sure of that. Busby had been shrewd in the market too. He signed a young goalkeeper called Ray Wood from Darlington and picked up right-winger Johnny Berry from Birmingham. He also broke the British transfer record for Barnsley centre-forward Tommy Taylor. The fee was £29,999 – because Taylor didn't want to be the first '£30,000 player'.

By the start of the 1955-56 campaign, the

Babes – fifth the previous season – were raring to go. They won the Championship with eleven points to spare over their closest pursuers, Blackpool. Wood, Byrne, Edwards and Taylor became England stars. Pegg joined them. Charlton would soon follow.

Byrne captained his country as well as his club. He personified calm and composure. Left-half Edwards was a massive amalgam of pace, power and touch, scoring thunderous goals against Scotland and West Germany. Taylor was quick, strong in the air and boasted a vicious left-foot shot, an all-round striker. Colman – 'Snakehips' – improved with every match. What might they have achieved for United – and for England in the World Cup finals – in 1958?

That Championship gave United entry into the European Cup, then approaching its second year. Or did it? The Football League had stopped Chelsea taking part in the inaugural tournament. United were not so simply deterred. Busby wanted to go in. Chairman Harold Hardman stood up to the League. United became England's first representatives in a European competition.

What a start they made. They beat the Belgian champions Anderlecht 2-0 in Brussels, then ran riot in Manchester. Viollet scored four and United ran out 10-0 winners. The rest of Europe sat up. Violett scored two more against Borussia Dortmund at Maine Road in the second round. United led 3-0 at half time, but the West German champions pulled back two goals by the end. On a freezing night in

1952-58

Manchester United, 1956 - 57: (l to r, back) Taylor, Jones, Wood, Foulkes, Edwards;
(l to r, front) Whelan, Colman, Berry, Viollet, Pegg, Bent

Germany, a goalless draw was enough to see United through.

The proud Basques of Athletic Bilbao, Spanish Champions while Real Madrid won the first-ever European Cup, followed. Whelan's goal – a 40-yard dribble on a snowy pitch – that cut Bilbao's home lead to 5-3 , proved crucial in the tie. United's aircraft had problems taking off from Bilbao, because of ice and snow. Busby's team had two goals disallowed in the return – but still won 3-0. Viollet scored again. Taylor was inspired, heading the second and creating the winner for Berry.

Then came the crunch – Real Madrid. In front of 120,000 at the Bernabeu, Hector Rial and the great Alfredo Di Stefano gave the holders a 2-0 lead. Taylor pulled one back, but Jose Mateos scored a third for Real. At Old Trafford Real

came to defend. Taylor was a particular target for rough attention and the holders wasted time at every opportunity. Raymond Kopa and Rial scored in breakaways. Taylor and Charlton replied for United. Busby's team were out, but their average age was little more than 21. Surely their best was yet to come?

That was borne out by the English table. United romped away with the title again, scoring 103 goals and finishing eight points ahead of runners-up Spurs. They reached the FA Cup final too, bidding for the first 'double' of the 20th century. They lost 2-1 to Aston Villa after Peter McParland's collision with Wood. Wood was so badly hurt that after treatment he had to play on the wing. Busby had to sign Northern Ireland international Harry Gregg from Doncaster, to replace him for the following season.

United were well in contention for a third successive title in 1958. Their 5-4 win at Arsenal, in the last game the Babes played in England, left them in a challenging position. But their sights were set on the European Cup. Di Stefano had forecast that United would eventually succeed Real. Busby and his players wanted to make it sooner rather than later. United had seen off Shamrock Rovers and the Czech champions Dukla. In the quarter-final first leg, Charlton and Colman scored as United beat Red Star Belgrade 2-1. In Yugoslavia, Violett struck first and Charlton netted twice to give United a 3-0 half-time lead. Red Star pulled back to 3-3, but the Babes were through.

They never played again together. The Munich air crash saw to that. Truly, in the title of the famous book about the disaster, it was 'The Day a Team Died.'

Tottenham Hotspur

Glory Glory Spurs land the 'double'

Before 1961, only two teams had ever done the 'double' – lifted the Championship and FA Cup in the same season: Preston and Aston Villa, both in the 19th century. Pundits of the late 1950s reckoned the feat was impossible, given the gruelling demands of the English season. However, in 1958 Spurs captain Danny Blanchflower forecast: 'The "double" will be done – and Spurs will be the team to do it.' At the time it seemed a rash prediction. Tottenham were nearer the bottom than the top of the First Division. They had some excellent individuals – most of all, Blanchflower himself – but the team needed rebuilding.

Enter a new manager. Bill Nicholson, stalwart right-half in Spurs' 1951 Championship side, took over from Jimmy Anderson in 1958. Nicholson would rebuild. Blanchflower would be the leader on the pitch – and off it. But their early relationship was far from harmonious.

Both were remarkable in their own ways. Blanchflower was a romantic, and a radical. In tandem with inspirational manager Peter Doherty, he had led unfancied Northern Ireland to the 1958 World Cup quarter-finals. The cause appealed to him. For Blanchflower, football was not about life or death, or even winning or losing. As he often said: 'It's about glory.' About realising dreams and weaving legends. Blanchflower did both.

He was a captain of rare authority, though never one to shake his fist. He was also one of the great wing-halves of his age: graceful, skilful, with a magical eye for a defence-splitting pass

He was never short of an opinion either. When he arrived at Barnsley from Belfast, the players trained without the ball for most of the week. Blanchflower demanded more ball work. 'If you don't see the ball during the week, you'll be

Bobby Smith (on ground) scores Spurs' first goal past Gordon Banks in the 1961 FA Cup Final

hungry for it on Saturday,' he was told. 'If I don't see the ball during the week, how will I know what it looks like on Saturday?' replied Blanchflower.

Those were the days of the maximum wage, when players were supposed to know their place. Blanchflower never played that game. It was no surprise that after he retired he wrote one of the punchiest football columns in the English press.

Spurs had been Nicholson's life since he was a boy. He was a clever tactician, a determined motivator, and a shrewd judge of a player. 'Double' heroes Peter Baker, Maurice Norman, Bobby Smith and Terry Medwin were already in place, along with Blanchflower, when Nicholson took charge. He wanted to add

1961-63

quality and Spurs were prepared to pay for it. Nicholson signed Swansea winger Cliff Jones for £35,000. The tough, dynamic Hearts wing-half Dave Mackay followed, for £30,000. Action man Mackay was the antithesis of the classical Blanchflower, but a perfect foil for him. No-one dared kick Tottenham players with Mackay around.

Nicholson raided Scotland again for Dundee's Bill Brown, the last great Scottish goalkeeper, and a frail Falkirk inside-forward called John White. What a partnership they formed, White 'The Ghost' and Blanchflower! Les Allen from Chelsea was another vital signing. He and Smith shared more than 50 goals in the 'double' season.

Nicholson promoted from within too. Shoreditch-born Ron Henry took over from Mel Hopkins at left-back. Terry Dyson, a £10 signing from (then) non-League Scarborough challenged Medwin and Jones for a place on the wing. Frank Saul made an all-purpose reserve forward.

In 1959-60, Spurs showed their potential. They led the table for much of the season, only to falter at the death. They won just three of their last seven games, and finished third, two points behind Champions Burnley.

The following season, they showed no such hesitancy. They won their first 11 matches, dropped only one point out of their first 32 (a home draw against Manchester City) and didn't lost until their 17th match, a 2-1 defeat by Sheffield Wednesday at Hillsborough. By the new year, they were ten points clear of their nearest pursuers. They clinched the title with three matches to spare, after a 2-1 win over Wednesday at White Hart Lane. As one newspaper headline had it: 'Spurs are streets ahead. They can score goals almost to order.' They did too, 115 in 42 League matches. If

Smith and Allen led the way, then the wingers grabbed their share, especially the flying Jones, who netted 15.

With the title already sewn up, they could concentrate on the FA Cup. Spurs beat Charlton, Crewe, Villa and Sunderland to reach the semi-final. At Villa Park, Jones opened the scoring and Smith struck twice, to demolish Burnley 3-0.

Tottenham met Leicester at Wembley. It was a great occasion but a low-key match. Leicester defender Len Chalmers was injured in an early collision with Allen and had to go off in the second half. There were no subs in those days. Spurs turned the screw. Smith struck with 21 minutes left, then Dyson tucked away the goal that clinched the 'double'. Blanchflower lifted the Cup, celebrated Tottenham's achievement, then spoke of his own role: 'I could change the rhythm and the pace, speed it up or slow it down. I had the ball much more than anyone else – so I should have done something with it, shouldn't I?'

The following season, Nicholson signed England's finest goalscorer, Jimmy Greaves, and Spurs set their sights on the European Cup. Three 'Glory Glory Hallelujah' nights followed at White Hart Lane as Tottenham saw off Gornik Zabrze, Feyenoord and Dukla Prague, before running into Cup holders Benfica. Slack defending – and a marginal offside decision against Greaves – meant they left Lisbon 3-1 down. Rui Aguas put Benfica ahead at Tottenham. Smith levelled and Blanchflower netted a 48th-minute penalty, but somehow the Portuguese Champions held out.

Ipswich – managed by Nicholson's old title-winning colleague Alf Ramsey – pipped Spurs for the Championship. But Spurs retained the Cup, beating old rivals Burnley 3-1 at Wembley. A year later, Tottenham became the first

Danny Blanchflower and Bobby Smith hold the FA Cup as Spurs complete the 'double' in 1961

English club to lift a European trophy, beating Atletico Madrid 4-1 in the European Cup Winners Cup final in Rotterdam.

It was the crowning – and final – glory of a great team. Brown, Baker, Henry, Norman, Blanchflower and Smith had grown old together. White was to die in a tragic accident, struck by lightning on a golf course. Nicholson had to rebuild again. He did. But Spurs could never match the glory of that fabulous 'double' side. They became the standard by which every Tottenham team is judged.

Champions: 60/1
FA Cup winners: 61, 62
European Cup Winners Cup winners: 63

DID YOU KNOW?

When Spurs won the title in 1961, they equalled Arsenal's record points total of 66 set in 1931. Spurs also set a record of 31 wins in a First Division season. But their goal tally of 115 was 12 behind Arsenal's 127 in 1931.

Benfica 1960-68

The Flying Eagles of Portugal

Benfica before their 3-1 victory over Tottenham in March 1962: (l to r, back) Angelo, Mario Joao, Cavem, Cruz, Germano, Costa Pereira; (l to r, front) Jose Augusto, Eusebio, Aguas, Coluna, Simoes

After Real Madrid came Benfica. There was a world of difference between Real's polyglot squad and Benfica, who employed only Portuguese players – or players from Portugal's colonies. For nearly three years – until a cynical foul robbed them of the 1963 European Cup – the Portuguese champions dominated Europe all the same.

What a contribution they made, those stars from Mozambique and Angola: the brilliant left-footed Mozambican Mario Coluna, midfield general and inspirational captain, the skilful Angolan inside-right Joaquim Santana; and his countryman Jose Aguas, an all-round

target man before the role became fashionable. Then came the most exciting of them all, the explosive Mozambican, Eusebio, who took over from Santana and became one of the world's greats.

The Brazilian, Otto Gloria, had signed Coluna, Santana and Aguas in the 1950s. Bela Guttmann, the Hungarian who replaced Gloria in 1959, used them to brilliant effect. He was the man who signed Eusebio too. The ex-Brazilian international Carlos Bauer alerted Guttmann to Eusebio's potential. Guttmann moved fast and snapped up Eusebio from Lourenco Marques – for a mere £7,500!

Benfica boasted plenty of Portuguese stars too. Goalkeeper Antonio Costa Pereira was one of the best in Europe. Half-backs Neto and Cruz provided physical presence. The versatile Domiciano Cavem gave Benfica stalwart service in almost every position.

Guttmann added important signings. The unyielding centre-half Figueiredo Germano, of the bald head and massive moustache, arrived from minor Lisbon club Atletico for just £2,000. The flying right-winger Jose Augusto came from Barreirense.

In 1959, as Porto's coach, Guttmann had snatched the Championship from Benfica. Under Guttmann's control, Lisbon's 'Eagles' made certain the following year. Then they launched their European assault. They began by beating Scottish champions Hearts 2-1 in Edinburgh and 3-0 at the Estadio da Luz. They followed up by thrashing the Hungarians Ujpest Dosza 6-2 – making a 2-1 defeat in Budapest a minor trifle. Two wins and a 7-3 aggregate took Benfica past Aarhus of Denmark to the semi-finals. There they ran into Rapid from Vienna. Benfica cruised through the first leg 3-0. The return at the Prater ended 1-1. But – after the English referee Reg Leafe refused them a late penalty – Rapid players attacked their opponents. Fans ran on to join in. The Vienna police had to break up the fighting, then escort Benfica – and Leafe – to the safety of the dressing rooms.

In the final, in Berne, Benfica 'only' had to worry about Barcelona, who started firm favourites. They had knocked out the five-times winners

Real. Their attack included the famous Hungarians, Sandor Kocsis, Zoltan Czibor and Ladislao Kubala, as well as the Brazilian, Evaristo. The great Spanish inside-forward Luis Suarez pulled the strings from midfield.

Guttmann admitted he was worried. After 19 minutes, Kocsis finished Suarez's centre with a diving header. 'Keep competing,' Guttmann had told his team. They gave him the perfect answer with two goals in a minute. Coluna split the Barcelona defence, Cavem crossed and Aguas netted the equaliser.

Then Neto's lob glanced off Barcelona defender Gensana. The renowned keeper Antonio Ramallets could only push the ball against a post, and it dropped into the net. After 55 minutes, Coluna's stinging volley from Cavem's cross made it 3-1. Benfica rode their luck. Kocsis and Kubala hit the woodwork. Czibor pulled back a 75th-minute goal. But Benfica were Real's successors as Champions of Europe.

The following season, Guttmann flung in Eusebio. He mixed explosive pace with a lethal right-foot shot. He seemed like a force of nature. He inspired Benfica, and Portugal, for a decade. Guttmann introduced another Portuguese great too, the nippy, 17-year-old left-winger Antonio Simoes. How many goals did his crosses make for Aguas, and his towering successor, Jose Torres?

Benfica comfortably saw off FK Austria , then recovered from a 3-1 deficit to hammer West German Champions Nurnberg 6-0, before meeting Spurs in the semi-finals. In the Estadio da Luz, Bill Nicholson used Tony Marchi as sweeper in a five-man defence. It wasn't Spurs' game. Benfica pulled them apart early on. Simoes and Jose Augusto gave the holders a 2-0 lead. Bobby Smith pulled one back. Jose Augusto scored again.

At White Hart Lane, Jimmy Greaves had an early 'goal' controversially disallowed for offside. Aguas netted in a counter attack. Smith equalised. Blanchflower, from the penalty spot – three minutes into the second half – gave Spurs hope. Germano and Costa Pereira were outstanding in the second half...and the woodwork saved Benfica again. Spurs struck it three times in those last 42 minutes.

The final, in Amsterdam, was the last of the great attacking European Cup extravaganzas. Benfica against Real, the new masters against the old. Ferenc Puskas scored a first-half hat-trick for Real. Aguas and Cavem replied for Benfica, but Real led 3-2 at the break. At half time, Guttmann set Cavem to tight-mark Real's inspiration, the great but aging Alfredo Di Stefano. That halted Real's supply lines. Coluna lashed a memorable 30-yarder to level. Eusebio, brought down, got up to crash in the penalty. Then Eusebio cracked a free-kick that deflected off a Real defender. Benfica were undoubted masters now.

Guttmann quit while he was ahead, and left that summer. The Chilean, Fernando Riera, took over. In their second defence of the Cup, Benfica eased past Norrkoping from Sweden, before surviving a difficult quarter-final against the Czech champions Dukla Prague. Benfica only won 2-1 in Lisbon. They needed a rare defensive performance to go through after a goalless draw at Juliska. In the semi-final they beat Feyenoord 3-1 in Lisbon, after another goalless draw in Rotterdam.

The final, against AC Milan, was at Wembley on a Wednesday afternoon. By now the giant Torres had replaced Aguas. But Benfica had injuries at half-back which forced them to re-organise their defence. They were also missing a vital component, injured centre-half Germano. And Gino Pivatelli's cynical foul on Coluna ruined Benfica's afternoon.

European Cup winners: 61, 62
European Cup runners-up: 63, 65, 68
Portuguese Champions: 59/60, 60/1, 62/3, 63/4, 64/5, 66/7, 67/8, 68/9
Portuguese Cup winners: 62, 64, 69

Benfica started so brightly. Torres fed Eusebio, who raced on to score with a shot off an upright. But Benfica couldn't press home their advantage. Milan's young midfield star, Gianni Rivera, crossed for the Brazilian Jose Altafini to equalise, 13 minutes into the second half . A minute later, Pivatelli tripped Coluna. Down he went. There were no substitutes in those days. Benfica effectively played the last half-hour with ten men. Rivera split Benfica's defence again and Altafini grabbed the winner, a rebound after Costa Pereira saved his first shot.

It was a harsh result, but it signalled the end of Benfica's dominance. They were still keen contenders – Eusebio's prowess saw to that. They lost the 1965 final 1-0 to Inter in the cauldron of San Siro, where only the bravest referees gave important decisions against the home club.

In 1966, Benfica provided all six midfielders and attackers (now strengthened by Jaime Graca) to the Portuguese team that took third place in the World Cup. Two years later, Benfica lost the European Cup final in extra time at Wembley to Manchester United – after Alex Stepney had pulled off an incredible save from Eusebio near the end with the score at 1-1.

They had contributed so much to the joy and excitement of the European Cup. But their reservoir of talented youngsters was drying up. They would never threaten Europe so seriously again. The early 1960s were Benfica's halcyon days.

Liverpool 1962-73

The team that Shankly built

Ian St John heads for the winner in the 1965 FA Cup final against Leeds United

Bill Shankly created the modern Liverpool. The great Bob Paisley, then Joe Fagan and Kenny Dalglish, were the heirs to Shankly's legacy.

A tough Scottish international wing-half, who made his name with Preston before the war, Shankly became the embodiment of the Anfield club. His tongue-in-cheek quote, that 'Football isn't life or death. It's far more important than that,' has passed into legend – in a way that Shankly never meant. But when he said: 'There are two great teams in Liverpool – Liverpool and Liverpool reserves,' he meant it all right. That typified his commitment to Liverpool's cause.

He managed Carlisle, Grimsby and Workington, then Huddersfield, before the Liverpool board asked him to take over in December 1959. Liverpool were a big club, fallen on hard times.

Champions in 1946-47, FA Cup runners-up three years later, they had dropped into the Second Division.

Liverpool's directors were wise enough to give Shankly a free hand – and Shankly's bubbling energy gave Liverpool purpose. He set about building a side to compete with Europe's finest. First though, Liverpool had to gain promotion. They accomplished that in 1962, winning the Second Division title by eight points.

The following season, they consolidated. Liverpool finished eighth while bitter rivals Everton took the Championship. But Shankly was building shrewdly. Right-back Chris Lawler and Scottish goalkeeper Tommy Lawrence had risen through the Anfield youth ranks. So had left-back Gerry Byrne and right-winger Ian Callaghan. Top scorer Roger Hunt had joined

the Anfield club in 1959 after military service. Another Scot, centre-half Ron Yeats, was Shankly's colossus. 'Six feet two, fourteen stone and not an ounce of fat on him,' Shankly proudly told the waiting media when Yeats arrived from Dundee United. Alongside him, Liverpool unveiled another local product, the young hard man Tommy Smith. When Liverpool first won the European Cup, in 1977, he would score a vital goal.

Skilful right-half Gordon Milne arrived from Shankly's old club, Preston. On the left of midfield was Willie Stevenson, the ex-Rangers star who'd come home after a spell in Australia. If Liverpool needed back-up, they had Jimmy Melia; another Liverpudlian, and an England inside-forward.

Shankly had signed Hunt's partner, Ian St John, from Motherwell. St John had the ability to play up front, or drop deep and draw defenders out. 'What will you do when the Lord comes?' demanded religious posters in Liverpool at the time. 'Move St John to inside left,' scribbled blasphemous Anfield fans in reply.

On the left wing, Shankly had recruited another ex-Preston man, Peter Thompson, a jinking, twisting trickster, in a tradition the Liverpool boss well understood. Shankly's idol was his Preston colleague Tom Finney, a great winger who doubled as a brilliant centre-forward. Thompson was neither as direct, nor as versatile as Finney. But his maverick dribbling turned many a match, set up countless chances – and won several vital penalties.

John Toshack (left) and Peter Cormack keep their eyes on the ball

League Champions: 63/4, 65/6, 72/73
FA Cup winners: 65, 74
UEFA Cup winners: 73

In 1964, Liverpool arrived. They won the Championship by four points from Manchester United. Everton finished a further point behind. St John(2), Thompson(2) and Alf Arrowsmith scored as Liverpool demolished Arsenal 5-0 to clinch the title.

That took Shankly's team into the European Cup. They thrashed the Icelandic champions KR Reykjavik, then beat Anderlecht home and away. In the quarter-finals, they needed the toss of a coin to get past Bundesliga Champions Cologne – after two goalless games, and a 2-2 draw in the play-off in Rotterdam.

Then Liverpool's problems began. By then, they'd reached the FA Cup final, but conceded their title to Manchester United. Their season depended on the cups. Geoff Strong, the former Arsenal forward, was outstanding as deputy for the injured Milne as Liverpool beat Leeds 2-1 in extra time to take the FA Cup at Wembley. Hunt and St John scored the goals. But Shankly's team were shattered.

Somehow they found the energy to beat European Cup holders Inter 3-1 the following Tuesday. Hunt drove home Callaghan's centre to put Liverpool in front. Sandrino Mazzola levelled after an uncharacteristic mistake by Yeats. Callaghan cracked home a well-worked free kick to make it 2-1. St John netted the third, after Giuliano Sarti had saved Hunt's shot.

At San Siro, Liverpool went down 3-0. These were what Brian Glanville called: 'The Years of the Golden Fix' – years when certain Italian clubs bribed referees. It's still a matter of conjecture how the Spanish referee, Ortiz de Mendibil, reached some of his decisions that evening. Mario Corso was allowed to score direct, from an indirect free-kick. Giacinto Facchetti ran 70 yards to net Inter's third. His finish put to shame what had gone before.

In 1966, Liverpool finished six points ahead of Leeds at the top of the table. Hunt played for England's World Cup winners. But Liverpool lost the European Cup Winners Cup final 2-1 to Borussia Dortmund in Glasgow, despite Hunt's equalising Siggi Held's opening goal. The European Cup the following season was a disaster. Shankly's team crashed 1-5 to Ajax – and a young man called Johan Cruyff – in Amsterdam and went out on a 7-3 aggregate.

Liverpool's squad was breaking up. They remained a force in England - but not in Europe. Shankly patiently built a new team. In came goalkeeper Ray Clemence from Scunthorpe, defender Emlyn Hughes from Blackpool, left-back Alec Lindsay from Bury and Alun Evans from Aston Villa. The muscular Bristolian Larry Lloyd replaced Yeats. Shankly signed the Cardiff striker John Toshack as a target man. Another brilliant left-wing dribbler, Steve Heighway, arrived from the amateur club Skelmersdale.

In 1971, Shankly's 'new boys' finished fifth in the League and lost to 'double' winners Arsenal in the 1971 FA Cup final. The following season they finished third, a point behind Champions Derby.

Fresh talent emerged – another ex-Scunthorpe star, the all-action Kevin Keegan, and the Liverpudlian centre-half, Phil Thompson. Shankly signed Forest's Peter Cormack.to pull the midfield strings along with Callaghan.

In 1973, Liverpool beat off Arsenal's challenge to win the Championship. They lifted the UEFA Cup too. In the final, two goals by Keegan and a Lloyd header built a 3-0 lead over Borussia Moenchengladbach. Gladbach could only win 2-0 in Germany. Yet Shankly and his 'Boot Room' trust of Paisley and Fagan already knew: for Liverpool to win the European Cup, they'd have to change their style and play with patience. Defeat by Red Star Belgrade the following season gave them the impetus.

Liverpool finished League runners-up, and reached the FA Cup final. Two goals by Keegan and another from Heighway demoralised Newcastle 3-0. It was Shankly's last game in charge. His final act was to sign Ray Kennedy from Arsenal that summer. Then he stepped down. Paisley was the heir to Shankly's kingdom. He made it his own.

England 1966-72

Ramsey's Wingless Wonders

When he took over as England manager in 1962, Alf Ramsey was asked if England could win the 1966 World Cup. 'Yes,' he replied – a bold statement from a usually cautious man.

Four years later, Ramsey built a team that won the World Cup. England were hosts, so they didn't have to qualify. They had the advantage of playing all their games at Wembley. But Ramsey's team were the most efficient unit England have ever fielded. What they lacked in aesthetic appeal, they made up in hard graft.

Ramsey, the former Spurs and England right-back, had worked miracles as a club manager with Ipswich, leading a team without stars from the Second Division to the Championship.

England offered more promising material. In the 1962 World Cup finals, Bobby Moore had already proved himself a defender of the highest class. He became Ramsey's captain and leader on the field. Bobby Charlton was in his prime, a menace at outside-left or in midfield, where he finally settled. Jimmy Greaves was a supreme goalscorer, a penalty area poacher, though Ramsey always seemed suspicious of his maverick quality. Gordon Banks was developing into a magnificent goalkeeper. Ray Wilson was already a fine left-back.

Ramsey insisted on full control of team selection. He broke decisively with the days of his predecessor Walter Winterbottom, when committees picked the England side.

But fitting the pieces together was a problem. England's first match under Ramsey was a disaster. They lost 5-2 to France, which killed any hopes of qualifying for the 1964 European Championship finals.

Gradually though, Ramsey introduced key personnel. Banks became England's regular keeper. In 1964, George Cohen – one of the first overlapping full-backs – captured the right-back slot from Jimmy Armfield. A year later, the giant Jack Charlton, Bobby's big brother, was called in at centre-half. A solid defence took shape.

Finding the right formula in attack proved harder. Ramsey experimented with George Eastham as playmaker in a 4-2-4 formation – then sidelined Eastham and his creative partner Gordon Milne. Ramsey wanted a different balance – penetration, combined with strength. He switched Bobby Charlton, of the raking passes and stinging long-range shots, to be England's midfield general. Alongside him Ramsey chose a controversial figure, Nobby Stiles. Stiles was a defender for Manchester United. His special talent was man-to-man marking. Ramsey made him England's midfield destroyer.

Stiles was a hard man. In the group games of the 1966 World Cup finals, he clattered the Frenchman Jacky Simon, at Wembley. The FA secretary Denis Follows told Ramsey to drop Stiles for the next match. Ramsey replied that, if Stiles went, he would leave too. Stiles stayed.

Finding gifted wingers was another problem. Ramsey tried, then discarded, another maverick, Liverpool's mazy dribbler Peter Thompson. Terry Paine, John Connelly and Ian Callaghan were other options. None quite fitted the bill either. Ramsey's teams have gone down in history as 'wingless wonders'. But it wasn't until the 1966 quarter-final against Argentina that England dropped conventional wingers.

The rise of two young midfield players gave Ramsey crucial options. Alan Ball had energy to burn. The stealthy Martin Peters was always likely to nick a goal. So England used Ball to work the right flank and Peters to drift in from the left. Ramsey had effectively invented 4-4-2.

Greaves and Liverpool's unsung hero Roger Hunt were the front men. At least they were until Greaves was injured against France. Geoff Hurst replaced him – and stayed in for the Final, even though Greaves was fit. There were no substitutes in those days, so Greaves didn't even have the chance to step off the bench. His career was never the same afterwards.

England began their 1966 run-up to the World Cup finals with a 1-1 home draw against Poland. They followed up with impressive wins over West Germany (1-0), Scotland (4-3), Yugoslavia (2-0), Finland (3-0), Norway (6-1), Denmark (2-0) and Poland (1-0). But Ramsey was still searching for his most effective combination. A 0-0 draw against Uruguay in the opening game of the 1966 World Cup dampened England's mood of optimism. Then Charlton and Hunt scored in a 2-0 win over Mexico and Hunt hit both goals as England beat France 2-0 to reach the quarter-finals.

Ramsey's England celebrate their 4-2 victory over West Germany in the 1966 World Cup Final

That game against Argentina was nasty. Hurst netted England's winner after West German referee Rudolf Kreitlein sent off the Argentinian captain Antonio Rattin. Later, the angry Argentinian players tried to break down the door of the England dressing room. Ramsey called them 'animals' – a remark that reverberated in South America for years.

In the semi-final, England met Portugal. The great Eusebio was Portugal's inspiration. The gritty Stiles stuck to him. Eusebio scored with a penalty, but by then Charlton had lashed in two of his specials to put England in command.

Hurst scored a hat-trick in the final – though the legitimacy of England's crucial third goal remains a matter of debate. But England were World Champions. They never scaled such heights again.

In 1968, Dragan Dzajic's late goal earned Yugoslavia a 1-0 win over England in the European Championship semi-finals in

Florence – after Alan Mullery was sent off. Ramsey's team beat the USSR 2-0 in the third place play-off.

Two years later, great things were expected of the holders at the 1970 World Cup finals in Mexico. England boasted an even stronger squad than four years before. Leeds brilliant left-back Terry Cooper had taken over from Wilson. Brian Labone had displaced Jack Charlton. Mullery was a more attack-minded midfielder than Stiles. The emergence of Colin Bell, Francis Lee and Peter Osgood had given Ramsey extra options going forward.

The day it all turned sour was 14 June 1970. With 20 minutes left, England led West Germany 2-0 in the quarter-final in Leon. Goals by Mullery and Peters emphasised England's dominance. Franz Beckenbauer pulled one back. Banks was out with food poisoning. His deputy, Peter Bonetti, failed to gather Franz Beckenbauer's low shot. Two minutes later, Ramsey substituted Bobby Charlton.

Beckenbauer, who'd been marking him, immediately pushed forward – and the Germans seized the initiative.

Helmut Schoen had already sent on Jurgen Grabowski to run at England's tiring full-backs. Uwe Seeler forced extra time and Gerd Muller grabbed the Germans' winner.

Two years later, in the European Championship quarter-finals, the Germans were England's downfall again. By now Bobby Charlton had retired from international football. England had found no successor. The hopefuls of Mexico 1970 had not fulfilled their potential. Banks had retired too. Hurst, Ball and Peters had seen better days. Cooper was injured. So was centre-half Roy McFarland. Gunter Netzer dominated midfield that night at Wembley. West Germany won 3-1. They went on to lift the trophy.

They ended an era in English football too. Not until 1990 were England able to compete again with the world's best.

Celtic 1965-75

Jock Stein's Lions of Lisbon

Celtic 1967: (l to r, back) O'Neill, McNeill, Craig, Gemmell, Simpson, Hughes, Murdoch, Clark;
(l to r, front) Johnstone, Lennox, Wallace, Chalmers, Gallagher, McBride, Auld

European Cup winners: 67
European Cup runners-up: 70
Scottish Champions: 65/6, 66/7, 67/8, 68/9, 69/70, 70/1, 71/2, 72/3, 73/4
Scottish Cup winners: 65, 67, 69, 71, 72, 74, 75
Scottish League Cup winners: 66, 67, 68, 69, 70, 75

Celtic's great team was Jock Stein's creation. Once a modest centre-half with Albion Rovers, Llanelli and Celtic, the 'Big Man' began his coaching career with the Parkhead reserves in the late 1950s. He led Dunfermline to a Scottish victory, then managed Hibernian, before returning to Celtic Park in 1965.

Rangers, including such luminaries as Eric Caldow, Ronnie McKinnon, John Greig, Willie Henderson and the great Jim Baxter were Glasgow's leading team. Not for long. Stein

rebuilt Celtic into Champions of Europe. He restored the veteran goalkeeper Ronnie Simpson to the first team, made one of his ex-reserves, Billy McNeill, the Celtic captain – and encouraged a tiny winger called Jimmy Johnstone.

In 1965, Celtic beat Dunfermline 3-2 to win the Scottish Cup final. The following season, they won the Scottish Championship and reached the European Cup Winners Cup semi-final, losing to Liverpool. Stein knew how he wanted

Celtic to play – attacking at a ferocious pace, from all angles and positions.

By now his team had taken shape. Jim Craig was at right-back, with the great attacker Tommy Gemmell on the left. Centre-half McNeill was the lynchpin, supported by John Clark. Stein had shrewdly converted ex-Birmingham left-winger Bertie Auld to Celtic's midfield provider. Auld and partner Bobby Murdoch were two of the most accurate – and positive – passers in the game. Johnstone

'Jinky' Johnstone,
Celtic's dazzling winger

tormented opponents on the right. From the left, Bobby Lennox cut inside to become a prolific scorer. Steve Chalmers was at centre-forward, backed up by Joe McBride – or Willie Wallace. Stein signed Wallace from Hearts after McBride suffered a long-term injury. Celtic had magnificent forward cover in the versatile John 'Yogi Bear' Hughes, who could play anywhere along the line.

They won all three Scottish trophies in 1967. Then they achieved an even more remarkable feat: they became the first British team to lift the European Cup. Celtic knocked out Zurich of Switzerland, the French Champions Nantes, then met the Yugoslav title holders, Vojvodina Novi Sad. Celtic lost the first leg 1-0. At Parkhead, Chalmers levelled and McNeill scored an 89th minute winner to take Celtic through to the semi-finals.

Stein's side beat the Czech army team Dukla 3-1 in Glasgow, when Wallace netted twice – then defended for a goalless draw in Prague. Their final win over Inter, in Lisbon, has passed into legend. Those players will forever be known as the 'Lisbon Lions.'

Between 1966 and 1975, Celtic's domination of the Scottish game was so complete that only their rare defeats made news. Their 'nine in a row' Championships between 1966 and 1975 was a record. Rangers' 'Old Firm' derby wins in that time were few and far between.

Celtic's real proving ground was the European Cup. They never quite scaled the heights of 1967 again. But they reached another final, lost two more semi-finals, and gave Scotland a presence at the peak of European football that no other small country could match.

Celtic, the holders, went out in the first round in 1967-68. Dynamo Kiev, inspired by Anatoly Byshevetz, sneaked a 2-1 win at Parkhead.

Murdoch was sent off in Ukraine. Lennox put Celtic ahead on the night. Byshevetz levelled in the last minute. 3-2 to Dynamo on aggregate. Maybe Stein's team had been affected by three despicable matches against the Argentinian title holders Racing Club, for the 1967 World Club Championship. McNeill's header won the first game at Hampden Park 1-0. Before the return in Buenos Aires, Simpson was laid out by a missile from the crowd. Reserve goalie John Fallon took over. Celtic were kicked to a 2-1 defeat.

The play-off was across the Uruguayan border in Montevideo. Racing kicked hell out of Celtic again. Six players were sent off, two from Racing, four from Celtic, including Hughes and Gemmell for retaliation. Celtic lost 1-0. Atletico Madrid, managed by the Argentinian, Juan Carlos Lorenzo, would remind Celtic of those tactics seven years later.

The following season, Celtic knocked out St Etienne and Red Star Belgrade, then drew 0-0 against AC Milan at San Siro. In Glasgow, a rare McNeill error allowed Pierino Prati to score the only goal. In 1969-70, Celtic beat Basle, Benfica and Fiorentina, then Leeds in the semi-final. New stars had emerged: the all-action David Hay at right-back, Jim Brogan as McNeill's partner, George Connelly in midfield. Hughes

had taken over from Chalmers. In the final, Stein changed Celtic's tactics from the 4-3-3 that had dominated Leeds to 4-2-4. Feyenoord's playmaker Wim van Hanegem ran the game. Celtic lost 2-1 in extra time, despite taking the lead.

Cruyff's Ajax beat Celtic 3-1 on aggregate in the 1971 quarter-finals The following year, Stein's team – now including Danny McGrain, Kenny Dalglish and Lou Macari – saw off BK Copenhagen, Sliema Wanderers and Ujpest Dosza. In the semi-finals, they met Inter. The Italian champions were lucky to be there. They'd survived despite losing 7-1 to Borussia Monchengladbach – a result UEFA declared void after Inter's appeal, in somewhat dubious circumstances. The first leg at San Siro finished goalless, 0-0. Celtic couldn't finish the job at home. Inter won 5-4 on penalties, and duly lost to Ajax in the final.

Ujpest took their revenge for the previous year, knocking Celtic out in 1972-73. The next season marked Celtic's last great campaign in Europe – halted by more cynical brutality. Stein's team beat TPS Turku, Vejle from Denmark, and Basle, to reach the semi-finals,. There they ran into Atletico Madrid. In Glasgow, Lorenzo's team pursued a policy of systematic intimidation. The Turkish referee Dogan Barbacan did his best to rein them in, sending off three Atletico players. But Johnstone was kicked from pillar to post and it was impossible for Celtic to build up any rhythm amidst all the fouling. Stein was incensed when UEFA decided the second leg should go ahead in Madrid. In an atmosphere of rabid hostility, Celtic went down 2-0 to two late goals. With hindsight, that was the end of Celtic as a major force in Europe.

But Celtic had shown the way. They'd won the European Cup while English clubs still dreamed about it.

Manchester United

Busby rebuilds after Munich

Bobby Charlton holds up the European Cup watched by Alex Stepney and Bill Foulkes

Matt Busby had built a great team before the Munich air crash. In the 1960s, he built another one.

Busby's assistant, Jimmy Murphy, had kept United's flame alive – while the manager decided if he wanted to return to football, after the injuries he'd suffered at Munich.

Busby eventually took the plunge again. United finished League runners-up in 1959, though six points behind Champions Wolves. They spent the next three years plunging down the table, to 15th in 1962. Busby had cash to spend. That summer, he made some vital signings. The best of all was Denis Law, the Scottish inside-forward who Busby

rescued from Torino. The Turin fans loved the ex-Huddersfield and Manchester City attacker. But Law hated the regimentation of Italian football. Torino's loss was United's gain. Law had pace, power, a prodigous leap and a poacher's eye for a goal. He also had the vision to drop deep and create chances, with subtle passes. No-one more deserved to play for United's 1968 European Cup final winners. But knee trouble kept him out.

Pat Crerand, a creative wing-half with a hard streak, arrived from Celtic. Crerand wanted to play with style. The cynicism that crept into the game in the latter 1960s dismayed him. Arsenal's leading scorer, David Herd – son of a former Manchester City star – came too.

Busby already had experience at his disposal. Northern Ireland goalkeeper Harry Gregg, defender Bill Foulkes, and Bobby Charlton, had survived the Munich disaster. Noel Cantwell and Maurice Setters had made their names with West Ham and West Bromwich. Inside-forward Albert Quixall had come for a record fee from Sheffield Wednesday. Full-backs Shay Brennan and Tony Dunne, both from Dublin, had risen through United's youth system.

However, the 1962-63 League season was tough for United. It took a while for the new players to settle in. United finished only three points clear of relegation. In the FA Cup though, it was a different matter. Inspired by Law and Charlton, they powered to Wembley and a meeting with Leicester. Fourth-placed Leicester were one of the most consistent teams of the early 1960s. They wanted to make

1962-68

up for losing the 1961 final to Spurs 'double' team. United beat them out of sight, 3-1. Law was magnificent. Herd scored twice. Law's goal was the icing on the cake.

Busby had more young stars coming through: a tough wing-half, Nobby Stiles, and a former England amateur international, David Sadler, signed from Maidstone. In 1964, United unveiled another precocious talent – George Best.

He was a revelation as United beat Sporting Lisbon 4-1 at Old Trafford in the European Cup Winners Cup quarter-final. Alas for United, Sporting won 5-0 in Lisbon. But two years later, Best would make his mark in the Portuguese capital – on Sporting's eternal rivals, Benfica.

In 1964, Busby strengthened the attack by signing the Burnley winger John Connelly. By now, Charlton had moved from the left wing to midfield, for United and England.

United scored 89 goals and pipped Leeds to the 1964-65 Championship on goal average. Best started on the left now. He had it all: devastating ability, good looks and charm. He became the first player to make the crossover from football star to media celebrity. It was a tortuous path, and Best's undoing. But in 1965, he was a teenage starlet helping United win the Championship.

Liverpool lifted the title the following season, while United concentrated on the European Cup. 'It's the one we want. We all know that,' said Charlton. United saw off Vowarts from East Germany and HJK Helsinki, before meeting Benfica in the quarter-finals. United won 3-2 at Old Trafford, then travelled to Lisbon with some trepidation. They needn't have worried. Best ripped Benfica to shreds with two early goals. Connelly, Crerand and Charlton made it 5-1 on the night.

How then, did United lose to Partizan Belgrade in the semi-finals? Maybe it was because Best played in Belgrade when he wasn't fit – and he missed the return. Partizan won 2-0 at home, lost 1-0 at Old Trafford, then went down 2-1 to Real Madrid in the final.

United hit a domestic peak the following season. A 6-1 rampage at West Ham – who included England World Cup heroes Bobby Moore, Martin Peters and Geoff Hurst – clinched the title with a week to spare. But many of United's stars were aging. Busby knew they had to make the most of their chance in the European Cup in 1967-68.

United had accquired a key figure, goalkeeper Alex Stepney, from Millwall via Chelsea, to replace Gregg. Busby rated the south Londoner the best keeper he'd seen at Old Trafford. Stepney's save from Eusebio in the 1968 European Cup final virtually repaid the £65,000 fee alone. United also had a new young hero to accompany Best: Brian Kidd from the Manchester suburb of Collyhurst. He celebrated his 19th birthday in style at Wembley.

The Championship race turned into a Mancunian derby. Joe Mercer and Malcolm Allison had revived City. United made the running for so long, but they dropped too many points at home – a warning of problems ahead. City scored a vital 3-1 win at Old Trafford. On the last day of the season, United lost 2-1 at home to Sunderland, while City clinched the title by winning 4-3 at Newcastle. United had to win the European Cup to top that.

They'd made tough progress to the semi-finals. Dispatching Hibernians of Malta in the first round was a simple task. The Yugoslav champions Sarajevo were tougher opponents. The United trainer Jack Crompton came on so often in the goalless draw in Sarajevo that

Crerand muttered: 'I bet half the crowd thought he was playing.' John Aston and Best scored the decisive goals at Old Trafford.

That took United through to meet the Polish champions Gornik Zabrze. Gornik had knocked out Dynamo Kiev, first-round conquerors of holders Celtic. Gornik stars Szgfryzd Szoltysik and Wlodek Lubanski were at the heart of Polish football's revival in the late 1960s and early 1970s – and Gornik outplayed United at Old Trafford. They created chances but couldn't score. Then Best conjured an opening out of nothing, though it went down as an own goal by Stefan Florenki. In the last minute, Kidd drove a low shot past Gornik goalkeeper Hubert Kostka. On a frozen surface in Chorzow, roared on by a 78,000 crowd, Gornik could only score once, through Lubanski.

In the semi-final against Real Madrid, at Old Trafford, Best drove United ahead, after Crerand had hit a post. The second leg has passed into United folklore. Pirri and Gento gave Real a two-goal lead before Zoco sliced Dunne's centre into his own net. Amancio buried another shot past Stepney. At 3-1 down at half time, United had to pile forward. With 18 minutes left, Sadler headed on Best's flick to make it 3-2. Five minutes later, Foulkes finished off Best's cross for United's winner. Foulkes had played against Real in the 1957 semi-finals. There seemed a symmetry and a justice to the move.

In the final, at Wembley, United overcame Benfica 4-1 in extra time. It was the pinnacle of Busby's career. He'd coveted the European Cup since 1956. Now Old Trafford's great manager had it in his grasp.

European Cup winners: 68
League Champions: 64/5, 66/7
FA Cup winners: 63

Leeds United 1965-75

The formidable Revie machine

Billy Bremner with the 1974 League Championship trophy

Leeds were England's most consistent team over a decade But they never turned that consistency into the pile of trophies they could have won. Two Championships, an FA Cup, a League Cup and two UEFA Cup wins sound a reasonable return: until you consider the times that Leeds were pipped at the post.

There were reasons, of course. In 1970, a gruelling fixture list caught up with Don Revie's team. In the space of 18 days, Leeds' tired squad lost both the FA Cup final and the European Cup semi-final. The following year, Arsenal's 'double' team pulled out a

superhuman effort, snatching the title from Leeds after winning their final game, at Tottenham. Never had a team amassed 64 points, yet finished runners-up. In 1972, Leeds needed only to draw their last game, at Wolves, to deprive Derby of the Championship on goal average. Wolves beat them 2-1.

In the 1973 FA Cup final, second division Sunderland somehow shocked them 1-0, when Jim Montgomery pulled one of the finest saves ever seen at Wembley. In the 1973 European Cup Winners Cup final – and the European Cup final two years later – Leeds were victims of incompetent refereeing. But few outside west Yorkshire wept for Leeds. They had made many enemies on their way to the top.

When Don Revie took over at Elland Road in 1961, Leeds were battling against relegation to the Third Division. The club had never recovered from selling the great John Charles to Juventus in 1957. In 1960, they were relegated. Two years later, Revie dragged them clear of the drop – they finished 19th – then set about re-building.

Leeds' biggest asset was their crop of home-grown youngsters – Welsh goalkeeper Gary Sprake, full-backs Paul Reaney and Terry Cooper, tough centre-back Norman Hunter and a fiery Scottish midfielder, Billy Bremner. As the 1962-63 season progressed, Revie flung them in alongside seasoned pros like Jack Charlton and left-back Willie Bell. Leeds finished fifth. The revival was under way. Revie made two important signings – Manchester United right-winger John Giles and Everton inside-forward

Bobby Collins. Combative veteran Collins was Leeds' inspiration as they eased to promotion, two points ahead of Sunderland, in 1964.

Revie's team astonished the First Division in their first season back. They finished level on points with Champions Manchester United, losing the title on goal average. Only United conceded fewer goals than Leeds. Bremner and Collins were inspirational in midfield. Giles and the South African, Albert Johanneson provided a stream of crosses for Alan Peacock. Leeds reached the FA Cup final too, for the first time. Bremner equalised Roger Hunt's goal, but Ian St John hit Liverpool's winner in extra time. It had been the greatest season in Leeds' history. At a price. The word went round: Leeds pushed gamesmanship to its outer limits. They explored every avenue to gain an advantage.

Meanwhile, the Leeds manager was rebuilding his forward line. Runners-up again in 1966, fourth in 1967, Revie knew Leeds needed more firepower. A young Scot with an explosive shot, Peter Lorimer, had risen through Leeds' youth ranks. Centre-forward Mick Jones arrived from Sheffield United.

After Collins' departure, Revie shrewdly converted Giles from a winger to an old-fashioned inside-forward. That was a master-stroke. On the left, another young Scot, Eddie Gray, brimmed with promise. Paul Madeley, the most versatile Englishman of his generation, gave Revie even more options.

But controversy stalked Leeds. In 1967, Revie devised a new tactic for corners. Charlton

Mick Jones and Spurs' Mike England compete for the ball, with Allan Clarke in attendance

stood in front of the opposing goalkeeper and blocked him as he tried to reach the ball. Leeds won their first honour in 1968, beating Arsenal 1-0 in the League Cup final – and Arsenal insisted that Charlton fouled goalkeeper Jim Furnell before Cooper's winner.

Leeds' players regularly tried to influence the referee. Take another game against the Gunners, at Highbury in 1969. Sprake had laid out the Arsenal striker Bobby Gould. As skipper Bremner later admitted, the Leeds' players surrounded referee Ken Burns to make sure he didn't send off Sprake. Hunter was known as 'Bites Yer Legs.' Charlton said he kept a 'little black book' of players he'd like to kick over the touchline before he retired. Bremner and Giles were abrasiveness personified.

Yet Leeds had so much quality, they didn't need to fight or stretch the rules. In 1968, Mick Jones's goal was enough to beat the crack Hungarians, Ferencvaros, over two legs of the UEFA Cup final. The following season, Leeds won their first Championship, with six points to spare over Liverpool. That summer, Revie added the final piece to his attacking jigsaw. Allan Clarke came from relegated Leicester for £165,000. 'Sniffer' Clarke scored 17 League goals, but Leeds won nothing.

Everton, inspired by the Kendall-Ball-Harvey midfield trio, took Leeds' title. Revie's team finished runners-up, nine points behind. But they'd set their sights on the European Cup. They demolished Lyn Oslo 16-0 on aggregate, beat the declining Ferencvaros 3-0 home and away, then squeezed through against Standard Liege. That brought them up against Celtic. George Connelly of Celtic scored the only goal at Elland Road. In the second leg, Celtic shrugged off Bremner's goal to win 2-1; 3-1 on aggregate.

In between the matches with Celtic, Leeds had

League Champions: 68/9, 73/4
FA Cup winners: 72
League Cup winners: 68
UEFA Cup winners: 68, 71

drawn the FA Cup final against Chelsea 2-2. Gray was majestic at Wembley, skipping past defenders at will. But Ian Hutchinson netted a late equaliser: and in the replay at Old Trafford on 29 April – two weeks after Leeds' defeat in Glasgow – David Webb's header won the Cup for Chelsea.

In 1971, with Arsenal in hot pursuit, Leeds were undone by controversial refereeing, in a home match against West Bromwich. Ray Tinkler allowed Tony Brown to burst forward – although Colin Suggett was clearly offside – and square the ball for Jeff Astle to score Albion's winner. Leeds protested long and loud. So did the fans, who invaded the pitch. Leeds were made to play their first three home games of 1971-72 away from Elland Road. Arguably that decision cost them another title.

They had the consolation of winning the FA Cup for the first time, when Clarke's header beat Arsenal at Wembley.

After the disappointments of losing to Sunderland the following season – and to AC Milan, and some highly dubious refereeing in Salonika – Leeds set about the League with a vengeance. New stars had emerged: David Harvey in goal, Eddie Gray's younger brother Frank at left-back and tough midfielder Terry Yorath. Centre-half Gordon McQueen from St Mirren had replaced Charlton. Another no-nonsense Scot, centre-forward Joe Jordan, had arrived from Morton.

Leeds were unbeaten in their first 29 games. They won the title with five points to spare over Liverpool.

It was probably Revie's greatest managerial triumph – and his last. Revie left at the end of the season, to follow caretaker Joe Mercer as England manager, successor to Alf Ramsey. The ex-England full-back Jimmy Armfield restored peace at Elland Road, after Brian Clough's traumatic 44 days in charge. Clough had threatened revolution. Armfield left well alone. Leeds' target was the European Cup. In the semi-finals, they knocked out a Barcelona side including Johan Cruyff and Johan Neeskens.

In the final, they faced cup-holders Bayern in Paris. The French referee, Michel Kitadjian, refused two plausible penalty appeals against Franz Beckenbauer, then disallowed a Lorimer 'goal' with the score at 0-0. Leeds fans went wild. Franz Roth and Gerd Muller netted to win the game for Bayern.

Leeds were banned from Europe for three years. The Leeds team broke up. Giles went off to West Bromwich. Bremner moved to Hull. The glory days were over.

Brazil 1970

Wonderful World Cup winners

They have passed into legend now, those Brazilians of 1970. They defied the spirit of an age, in which football became dour and cynical. It wasn't just that they won the World Cup. It was how they won it.

Joao Saldanha, the ex-academic who put the side together, never listened to those voices who insisted on being sound at the back and keeping clean sheets. Maybe they weren't as solid all round as their great World Cup-winning predecessors of 1958. But going forward – has there been another team to match them? Saldanha knew that Brazil had six sublimely gifted attacking players who could shatter the meanest of defences.

Remember the names? Clodoaldo, the loping young midfielder who never seemed to tire. Oliveira Nunes Gerson, the general, a smoker with a stoop. Who could consider him an athlete – until he had a football at his feet? The chunky Rivelino, of the bristling moustache and the devastating left foot, a wizard at dead-ball kicks. Up front, Jairzinho, all pace and power, played on the right. A central striker with his club Botafogo, he made the switch so Brazil could use Tostao in the middle. He scored in every round of the finals. Tostao's career had been saved by an eye operation in America. His darting runs and on-field vision made him a nightmare for defenders. Then there was Pele. Injured when Brazil won in 1962 and kicked out of the 1966 finals, he reasserted himself triumphantly in 1970.

Saldanha, an active socialist, first established his coaching credentials when he led

BRAZIL'S ROUTE TO THE FINAL

v Czechoslovakia (Guadalajara) 4-1
Half time: 1-1
Brazil scorers: Rivelino (24 minutes), Pele (59 minutes), Jairzinho 2 (61 and 81 minutes)

v England (Guadalajara) 1-0
Half time: 0-0
Brazil scorer: Jairzinho (59 minutes)

v Romania (Guadalajara) 3-2
Half time: 2-1
Brazil scorers: Pele 2 (19 and 67 minutes), Jairzinho (22 minutes)

Quarter-final:

Peru (Guadalajara) 4-2
Half time: 2-1
Brazil scorers: Rivelino (11 minutes), Tostao 2 (15 and 52 minutes), Jairzinho (75 minutes)

Semi-final:

Uruguay (Guadalajara) 3-1
Half time: 1-1
Brazil scorers: Clodoaldo (44 minutes), Jairzinho (76 minutes), Rivelino (89 minutes)

Botafogo – including Didi, Garrincha and Nilton Santos – to the 1957 Rio Championship. But his iconoclastic style made him no friends in high places. When he – with tongue somewhat in cheek –

threatened to drop Pele, Brazil went wild. Saldanha's emotions were often his worst enemy. He lost the Brazil job three months before the 1970 World Cup finals. He'd burst into Flamengo's training ground to remonstrate with coach Durnival Knippe, who'd criticised him in the media. The altercation ended with Saldanha waving a gun. The CBF, the Brazilian federation, replaced him with Mario Zagalo, forthwith. As he showed in 1974, Zagalo's spirit was rather more conservative. At Mexico 1970 though, he wisely let Brazil follow their attacking dream.

Their detractors claimed they had a dodgy back four, and a goalkeeper, Felix, who wasn't up to international standard. Yet Carlos Alberto was the classiest right-back of his time and centre-half Wilson Piazza later proved himself with St Etienne – he was a crucial force in their team that reached the 1976 European Cup final.

Brazil's critics missed the point though. Brazil didn't go in to stop other teams. Their approach was simple: if you score three, we'll score four. They had massive belief too. When Ladislav Petras put Czechoslovakia ahead 11 minutes into their opening group game in Guadalajara, the Brazilians never panicked. They just moved up a gear. Rivelino levelled. Pele made it 2-1. Powerhouse Jairzinho added two more.

They kept their nerve after Tostao made the incision and Jairzinho scored the only goal against holders England. In the semi-final

Brazil before the group match against England: (l to r, back) Carlos Alberto, Brito, Wilson Piazza, Felix, Clodoaldo, Everaldo. (l to r, front) Jairzinho, Rivelino, Tostao, Pele, Paulo Cesar

against Uruguay, they fell behind again. Half time was a barely a minute away when Clodoaldo equalised. After that though, there was only one winner. Rivelino blasted a second and Jairzinho added a third in the 89th minute.

They knew when they could ease down – in the closing minutes against the Czechs, in a 3-2 group win over Romania when qualification was already assured; and in the 4-2 quarter-final demolition of Peru. Tostao scored twice that day, proving he could tuck away chances as well as make them.

They provoked memorable images too; Pele's header against England which forced that

incredible save from Gordon Banks; Tostao's shimmy, in the same game, to fool some of the world's best defenders and set up Jairzinho's goal; Pele almost scoring from the halfway line against the Czechs; Rivelino's free kick routines; wondering how Gerson would ever last 90 minutes in Mexico's heat and altitude.

If there's one incident that sums up the sheer exuberance of that side though, it was the last goal in the final. Brazil had beaten down Italy, the world's most effective defensive unit, to lead 3-1. Pele was playing keep ball, as if he were on the beach at Copacabana. Suddenly he picked out Carlos Alberto who thundered a right-foot shot into the Italian net.

Four years later, in West Germany, the Brazilian side was unrecognisable. In Zagalo's preferred starting line-up, only Rivelino and Jairzinho remained from the greats of 1970. Both carried massive burdens of expectation, trying to lift less experienced players. Retirement and injuries had taken their toll. Zagalo practised pragmatism, at times negativity. In the decisive second-phase match against Holland, Brazil lost 2-0 and Luis Perreira was sent off for a high tackle on Johan Neeskens. Thus did the champions lose their world crown. But that squad had a murderously hard act to follow...the greatest Brazilian attacking team in the history of football.

West Germany

Netzer and Beckenbauer take over

World Cup winners: 74
European Champions: 72

West Germany's 1972
European Champions: Maier,
Hottges, Schwarzenbeck,
Beckenbauer, Breitner, Wimmer,
Netzer, Hoeness, Heynckes,
Muller, E.Kremers

The creative force behind the 1972 West German team, Gunter Netzer, considers his options

West Germany took third place in the 1970 World Cup finals. But Helmut Schoen knew he had to rebuild. Within two years, he had created the most exciting German side ever.

The Germans' 1-0 win over Uruguay, in the third place play-off in Mexico City, marked the last big game appearance of a national icon, the Hamburg centre-forward Uwe Seeler.

Seeler was strong, powerful, tenacious and an inspiring leader. He had come to symbolise German football in the 60s.

The man who became German football's symbol in the 1970s was altogether more elegant and laid-back: Franz Beckenbauer. As Brian Glanville wrote in 1972: 'The Germans' ego-ideal has changed, from Seeler to Beckenbauer.' Beckenbauer's move from midfield to defence after the 1970 finals was a key component of the Germans' success. There, he created from the back – and 'invented' the role of attacking sweeper. In the 1972 side, he teamed up with another creative genius, midfield general Gunter Netzer. Netzer, suave and fashionable, was one of a new generation of German stars, a world removed from the disciplined and regimented stereotype. So, even more abruptly, was the outspoken and politically active young full-back Paul Breitner.

Besides Seeler, Karl-Heinz Schnellinger, Willi Schulz, Klaus Fichtel, Bernd Patzke, Hannes Lohr and Reinhard Libuda also stepped down from the national team in the year following the 1970 finals. Schoen still had solid foundations to build on. Beckenbauer, of course. Goalkeeper Sepp Maier and prodigious striker Gerd Muller had proved themselves in Mexico. So had defender Berti Vogts. Winger Jurgen Grabowski, a tactical substitute in 1970, became a regular.

Of the old guard from the 1966 World Cup, only four remained, apart from Beckenbauer: defenders Horst Hottges and Wolfgang Weber, forward Siggi Held and midfielder Wolfgang Overath. Now Schoen used them as cover – though Overath returned to enjoy his greatest moments in the 1974 World Cup final.

By the time of the qualifiers for the 1972 European Championship, George Schwarzenbeck, the Bayern stopper, had broken through alongside club colleague Beckenbauer. The tireless Herbert Wimmer had become the midfield ball-winner. Young forward Uli Hoeness scored on his debut, against Hungary. Jupp Heynckes, strong and unselfish, joined Muller in attack. Erwin Kremers supplied blistering pace on the left. By now, Schoen had switched systems, from the 4-2-4 of 1970, to 4-3-3; with Muller flanked by two wide men. Whatever the formation though, there was almost a club ethos about the German team. Maier, Beckenbauer, Breitner, Schwarzenbeck, Hoeness and Muller came from Bayern. Vogts, Wimmer, Netzer and Heynckes played for their leading rivals, Borussia Moenchengladbach.

The Germans had already shown their competitiveness. They qualified from a group including Poland, Turkey and Albania, after a 3-1 win over Poles in Warsaw. Poland went on to win the 1972 Olympic football tournament.

1970-76

Many of the Germans – like Breitner, Schwarzenbeck and Hoeness – were virtually unknown in Britain. That changed inside two hours one Saturday night. The date was April 29, 1972 – the occasion, the quarter-final first leg against England at Wembley. Alf Ramsey had forecast that England would beat the Germans and go on to win the European Championship.

Vogts was injured. So were Grabowski and Heynckes. Hottges and Held stepped in. Hoeness won only his second cap. But Beckenbauer was impeccable, and Netzer ran the match. Ramsey picked a midfield without a marker or tackler. Netzer took full advantage. His vision, passing and dead ball delivery tore England apart. Hoeness fired the Germans ahead. Netzer scored the second from the penalty spot. Muller's goal sealed the Germans' 3-1 victory.

Ramsey picked a defensive team for the second leg, a 0-0 draw in West Berlin. Netzer complained that nearly all the England team had 'autographed' his legs.

No matter. The finals tournament was held in Belgium. It was Netzer's long pass that set up the opening goal for Muller in the semi-final, as Germany beat the hosts Belgium 2-1 in Antwerp. Muller netted again 18 minutes from time, and Odilon Polleunis's reply came too late to bother the Germans.

Netzer dominated the final too, against the Soviet Union. Muller hit two more, Wimmer added a rare goal, and the Germans won 3-0 in a canter.

Naturally, West Germany were installed as favourites for the 1974 World Cup finals, on their home soil. The Germans didn't have to qualify, so Schoen spent the next two years experimenting with his line-up. By the time

Gerd Muller scores West Germany's first goal in the 1972 final

the Germans opened the 1974 finals – with a 1-0 win over Chile – Netzer was out of favour with Schoen, despite his popularity with the German public. Netzer was a genius, but a maverick. After his performances in 1972, he was a marked man too, sometimes to his own fury. Schoen had turned instead to the less gifted but more consistent Overath.

The West Germans scored another laboured win, 3-0 against Australia. Their final group game was against East Germany. Jurgen Sparwasser scored the only goal, for the East, 13 minutes from time. Netzer had come on as a 70th minute substitute for Overath. He couldn't turn the game, against super-fit opponents. He never played again in the competition.

Schoen's team qualified for the second phase anyway. In their first match, against Yugoslavia, Schoen added a vital cog, the all-action Gladbach midfielder, Rainer Bonhof. The Germans won, 2-0. By now, the Frankfurt winger Bernd Holzenbein was a fixture on the left. But it wasn't until the closing stages of the 4-2 win over Sweden – when Grabowski came on as a sub for Dieter Herzog – that Schoen found his winning team.

Grabowski played from the start in the 1-0 win over Poland. Muller, almost inevitably, twisted to snatch the only goal, after the kick-off had been delayed because of a near-flooded pitch.

In the final, another Muller twist and turn conjured up the winner against Holland. Schoen beamed as Beckenbauer lifted the World Cup. They'd both been waiting a long time. Immediately Muller retired from international football. So did Grabowski. So did Breitner, whose attacking runs had been crucial to his side's success. West Germany may have won the World Cup, but the cavalier Breitner thought they were unimpressive. Netzer didn't want to play for Schoen either.

The bulk of the team though – led by Beckenbauer – remained and grew old together. West Germany topped their group, then beat Spain 3-1 on aggregate, to qualify for the 1976 European Championship finals in Yugoslavia. Along came another Muller, Dieter, from Cologne. He hit a second-half hat-trick as the Germans beat the host country 4-2 in the semi-finals.

Muller scored again, against Czechoslovakia in the final. By then though, Jan Svehlik and Karel Dobias had given the Czechs a two-goal cushion. Schoen's team were as competitive as ever. Holzenbein's goal forced extra time. But the Czechs, inspired by the heroism of goalkeeper Ivo Viktor, kept the Germans out. So to penalties. Four Czechs scored. Then Uli Hoeness missed his kick and Panenka drove home the Czechs' spot kick winner. That goal signalled the end of an era in German football.

Ajax 1966-73

Cruyff inspires three European Cup victories

Ajax: in Britain in the mid-1960s it was the name of a floor cleaner. Then, in the second round of the 1966-67 European Cup, Holland's champions wiped the floor with Liverpool 5-1. Bill Shankly, ever one for a good line, said he didn't know how the Reds had been thrashed by a defensive team.

Some 'defensive team'! Ajax drew the return at Anfield 2-2. A slight, fast, technically brilliant young forward called Johan Cruyff dominated both matches. The Dutch club lost 3-2 on aggregate to the Czech army side Dukla Prague in the quarter-finals, but Ajax had already sewn the seeds of their great teams of the early 1970s. And Cruyff was the pick of the crop.

Ajax had spotted his precocious talent early. By giving his widowed mother a job as a cleaner, they helped the family survive – and ensured young Johan's loyalty. Cruyff gave the best years of his playing life to Ajax. When he left for Barcelona after the 1973 European Cup final, Ajax's glory began to fade

Cruyff had pace, vision and a blistering finish. His movement pulled defenders all over the pitch. His passing and eye for a chance bore the hallmarks of a great midfielder – and he could score with feet or head. For all his regular contractual disputes with the club, Cruyff was the heart of Ajax.

In 1969, Ajax reached the European Cup final for the first time. Typical Ajax. They lost their home quarter-final first leg 3-1 to Benfica. In Lisbon, it was all or nothing. Ajax attacked from the start. Cruyff inspired a 3-1 win. The

Johan Cruyff out-jumps Juventus's Morini in the 1973 European Cup final

Dutchmen won the play-off in Paris 3-0. They pipped another Czech team, Spartak Trnava, 3-2, to reach the final. They crashed 4-1 to AC Milan. But the side was taking shape. Right-back Wim Suurbier and centre-half Barrie Hulshoff were already fixtures in defence. Sjaak Swart was a veteran on the right wing. Cruyff and left-winger Piet Keizer were key attackers.

The following season, coach Rinus Michels added Nico Rijnders in midfield and another vital figure, the left-footed midfielder Gerrit Muhren from FC Twente. Ajax lost to Arsenal in the Fairs Cup semi-final.

Yet their strength was growing. Johan Neeskens, a midfield army of one, had joined

HONOURS

European Cup winners: 71, 72, 73
European Cup runners-up: 69
Intercontinental Cup winners: 72
Dutch Champions: 65/6, 66/7, 67/8, 69/70, 71/2, 72/3
Dutch Cup winners: 67, 70, 71, 72,

Johnny Rep playing against Feyenoord in 1973

from Haarlem. Dick van Dijk had arrived to support Cruyff. Youngsters called Arie Haan and Ruud Krol were rising through the ranks.

In 1971, Ajax won the European Cup – the first of three successive triumphs. They disposed of Nendori Tirana, Basle, Celtic and Atletico Madrid to reach the final at Wembley. Ajax's finest display came in the semi-final second leg against Atletico. They attacked in breathless waves. Keizer wiped out Atletico's 1-0 lead from the first leg. Fourteen minutes from time, Suurbier broke forward to make it 2-1 on aggregate. Then Neeskens surged from the back to lash a third.

Ajax started huge favourites against Panathinaikos at Wembley – and eased home 2-0. Van Dijk's early goal from Keizer's cross killed the contest. Substitute Haan scored the second and Yugoslav defender Velibor Vasovic lifted Ajax's first European trophy.

The following season, Michels refined the side even further. He confirmed the multi-talented Krol at left-back, and deployed the German, Horst Blankenburg – another Wembley sub – as attacking sweeper to replace departed stopper Vasovic. He switched Ajax's formation from 4-2-4 to 4-3-3 too. Neeskens and Haan joined Muhren in a three-man midfield, with van Dijk an occasional tactical substitute.

Neeskens became a vital foil for Cruyff. He offered strength, boundless energy, a great touch and a stinging right-foot shot. Neeskens was Ajax's enforcer too. Only real hard men argued with him. One who did was

Anderlecht's Jan Verheyen. Their clashes in Holland-Belgium matches would make so-called modern hard men wince. Michels had another youngster bubbling under too – Johnny Rep, who would replace Swart.

Arsenal proved Ajax's biggest obstacle in 1971-72. Ajax comfortably disposed of Dynamo Dresden and Marseille before meeting the Gunners in the quarter-finals. The Cup holders won 2-1 in Amsterdam, after trailing to Ray Kennedy's 15th-minute score. A 27th-minute goal by Gerrit Muhren deflected in by Peter Simpson, and a dodgy 74th-minute penalty, also converted by Muhren, saw Ajax home. At Highbury – uncharacteristically – Ajax shut up shop. Peter Marinello missed an early chance, then George Graham's own goal gave Ajax a platform. They defended it with vigour.

Swart's header in Amsterdam was all that separated Ajax and Benfica in the semi-finals. So Ajax met Inter in the final in Rotterdam, home of their bitter rivals Feyenoord. Inter were hugely fortunate even to be in the competition after their 1-7 defeat by Borussia Monchengladbach – wiped out following an Inter protest that was

contentious to say the least. Ajax were magnificent, passing with magical fluency. The goals were just a matter of time. Krol hit a post. Cruyff shot Ajax ahead after Inter failed to clear Suurbier's cross. The man the Ajax fans called 'De Koning van Europa' headed his second from Keizer's free kick. Only Ivano Bordon's agility saved Inter from humiliation.

The following season, Hungarian-Romanian Stefan Kovacs took over from Michels, who'd joined the Dutch national team. Rep scored Ajax's winner in a disappointing European Cup final against Juventus in Belgrade – a disappointment too for Kovacs, who encouraged his team to attack even more than Michels did. But Ajax turned on one of their greatest-ever displays in the quarter-final first leg, thrashing their leading rivals, Bayern Munich, 4-0 in Amsterdam. Haan netted twice. Muhren and Cruyff scored the others, making the second leg a formality. Two wins over Real Madrid took them to another final.

Ajax's glory could not continue. Too many clubs with loads of money wanted their best players. Cruyff was on his way to Barcelona. Neeskens soon followed. No team could replace such legends. Those losses ripped the soul out of Ajax, especially when stars like Suurbier and Muhren were waning too.

It would be 20 years before young Dutchmen like Marc Overmars and the de Boer twins formed the nucleus of another side to beat Europe's finest. They followed in a noble tradition of fluent attacking – pioneered by Johan Cruyff.

Bayern Munich 1966-76

The German champions of Europe

Franz Beckenbauer – 'Der Kaiser' – was the man who led Bayern Munich to become the greatest club side of the mid-1970s.

Bayern's president, the mason-turned-millionaire Wilhelm Neudecker, had a dream. He pumped millions of marks into the club so they could beat the best in the Bundesliga, then the best in Europe. Inspired by Beckenbauer, Bayern made the dream come true.

the Cup Winners Cup, just up the autobahn in the northern Bavarian city of Nuremburg. Franz Roth scored the winner, just as he did in the European Cup final against St Etienne in Glasgow nine years later.

Roth joined Bayern from an amateur club in 1966. He was one of the originals of Bayern's great team. Roth won 44 caps, though he never became an international star like

that big. Maybe his low centre of gravity helped. He had massive thighs, strong shoulders and held off the toughest opponents. And he could turn on a pfennig.

Muller was deadly with either foot, or his head. He manufactured goals out of nothing – like West Germany's winner in the 1974 World Cup final. He set records for Bayern and his country – more than a goal a game – that will never

Uli Hoeness scores the second goal in the 1974 European Cup final replay against Atletico Madrid

No matter who was coaching the team, Beckenbauer was the heart of Bayern. He made his debut on the left wing as an 18-year-old in 1964. Two years later, he had established himself as an attacking right-half of the highest quality. Bayern beat MSV Duisburg 4-2 in the West German Cup final that year – and Beckenbauer was a sensation for the German team that reached the World Cup final against England.

The following season, Bayern won their first European trophy. They pipped Rangers 1-0 in

Wolfgang Overath, Gunter Netzer, Helmut Haller or Rainer Bonhof. But his touch and stealthy breaks from midfield were vital to Bayern for a decade.

Sepp Maier and Gerd Muller played in that Bayern side too. The hollow-cheeked Maier was probably Germany's greatest-ever keeper. A brilliant shot-stopper and a master at dealing with crosses, his giant gloves became his hallmark across the world. Muller – Der Bomber' was the most lethal striker of his time. He was a genius in the penalty area. He wasn't

be beaten. His two goals in the 1974 European Cup final replay against Atletico Madrid made sure Bayern won the trophy for the first time.

Bayern took a while to realise their potential. They lifted the German Cup again in 1967, and secured the German 'double' two years later. They were Bundesliga champions again in 1972, only to lose 4-0 to Ajax in the European Cup quarter-final the following season.

European Cup winners: 74, 75, 76
European Cup Winners Cup winners: 67
Intercontinental Cup winners: 76
West German Champions: 68/9, 71/2, 72/3, 73/4
West German Cup winners: 66, 67, 69, 71

Sepp Maier grabs the ball from
Leeds United's Allan Clarke in the
1975 European Cup final

The departure from Ajax of Johan Cruyff, to join his old mentor Rinus Michels in Barcelona, gave Bayern their chance.

By then, Beckenbauer had dropped back. The great wing-half had found a new role. Did Beckenbauer invent the attacking sweeper by accident or design? Was his move a reaction to the foul that effectively knocked him out of the 1970 World Cup semi-final against Italy? Or had he realised that, in those days of congested midfields, back players had more space to create?

Whatever the reasons, the switch was hugely successful for West Germany – who won the European Championship in 1972 and the World Cup two years later – and for Bayern. Beckenbauer probed and prompted from the back – and Bayern boasted a quality cast to support him as they pursued the 1973-74 European Cup.

Their old guard had been reinforced by new talent. Centre-back Georg Schwarzenbeck, a tough stopper with a knack of hitting vital goals, ideally complemented Beckenbauer. Winger Uli Hoeness pulled defences out of position. The Swede, Connie Torstensson – signed from Atvidaberg, the Swedes who gave Bayern such a hard time in the first round – made an unselfish foil for Muller. Then there was Paul Breitner, an attacking full-back of genius.

Breitner was a radical. On the field and off it: he adopted a Vietnamese orphan and was always keen to espouse third world causes. On the field, Breitner burst forward with panache, bursting down the left, then cutting inside to shoot. He scored crucial goals for club and country, notably in the 1974 World Cup finals.

Bayern overcame Dynamo Dresden, CSKA Sofia and Ujpest Dosza to reach the 1974 European Cup final. Their opponents in Brussels were Juan Carlos Lorenzo's Atletico Madrid. Atletico had intimidated their way to the big occasion. In the semi-final against Celtic, for instance, Turkish referee Dogan Barbacan sent off three Atletico players after they'd kicked Celtic all over Parkhead.

The final was goalless after 90 minutes. Luis Aragones gave Atletico an unexpected extra time lead. The minutes ticked away. Bayern needed Schwarzenbeck, rumbling forward, to drive a last gasp equaliser and force a replay. This time they made no mistake. Muller and Hoeness scored two each as Bayern dispatched Atletico 4-0.

The following season, they disposed of Magdeburg, Ararat Erevan and St Etienne, before meeting Leeds in the final, in Paris. Maier was inspired that night. He made flying saves from Billy Bremner, John Giles, Paul Madeley and Peter Lorimer. Leeds' supporters thought the French referee Michel Kitadjian contributed at least as much to Bayern's victory. First he refused a penalty when Beckenbauer fouled Allan Clarke. Then he controversially disallowed Lorimer's 'goal' for offside.

Bayern took advantage. Roth – who made a habit of scoring at vital times – rifled home their first. The inevitable Muller netted the second from Jupp Kapellmann's centre. In their next defence of the European Cup, Bayern saw off Jeunesse d'Esch and Swedish champions Malmo, before meeting Benfica. Bayern drew 0-0 in Lisbon, then annihilated Benfica 5-0 at the Olympic Stadium. Muller and Bernd Durnberger scored twice. It was probably their finest-ever display in Europe.

Muller scored twice to settle the semi-final second leg against Real Madrid. So Bayern met St Etienne in the final at Hampden Park. St Etienne had knocked out Bayern in the 1969/70 first round. Bayern had taken revenge in the previous season's semi-final.

Bayern fielded a new forward star, the young Karl-Heinz Rummenigge. But they had to ride their luck again. The French team dominated. Dominique Bathenay and Jacques Santini hit the woodwork. But Roth, the old stager, won it for Bayern with a lethal 57th-minute finish. St Etienne gambled on the barely-fit Dominique Rocheteau for the closing minutes. He tormented the Bayern defence, and almost scored himself, as well as setting up a chance for Herve Revelli. But Bayern survived.

Three in a row for Bayern. But their reign was almost over. Dynamo Kiev beat them in the 1977 quarter-finals. Beckenbauer and Muller retired. Breitner had already joined Real Madrid where he became a midfield player. Torstensson had gone too. Suddenly Bayern were in transition. Their glory days were behind them.

Liverpool 1974-83

The Bob Paisley Years

Jimmy Case and Terry McDermott, two key members of Paisley's team, celebrate another Liverpool victory

Bill Shankly had built Liverpool's first great side in the mid-1960s, a team that lost the 1965 European Cup semi-final to Inter in highly dubious circumstances. When that side began to break up, Shankly created another one. By 1973, Liverpool were English Champions again and they beat Borussia Monchengladbach 3-2 on aggregate to win the UEFA Cup final. The following year, Liverpool won the FA Cup, outplaying Newcastle 3-0 at Wembley. Two more important things happened. In the European Cup, Red Star Belgrade passed Liverpool off the pitch at Anfield and knocked them out of the competition. Then, at the end of the season, Shankly – citing tiredness – suddenly retired.

Paisley succeeded him. Shankly, a bundle of energy, had a telling gift for the memorable phrase. Paisley was quiet and introverted by comparison. But he had accumulated huge knowledge through years as a member of Liverpool's famous 'Boot Room'. He put that knowledge to emphatic use. He inherited a powerful team, of course. Ray Clemence was one of Europe's finest goalkeepers. Skipper Emlyn Hughes and centre-half Phil Thompson were strong, constructive defenders. Terry

McDermott popped up with vital goals from midfield. In attack, Liverpool boasted the all-action Kevin Keegan and the mazy dribbler Steve Heighway.

Paisley quickly made his mark with a remarkable switch. Ray Kennedy, the former Arsenal striker and 'double' hero had been Shankly's last signing. Paisley saw his potential as a midfield player, a natural left-footer who could give Liverpool balance as well as power.

Paisley put another vital change into practice. That defeat by Red Star convinced the 'Boot Room' team – Shankly, Paisley, Joe Fagan and Ronnie Moran – that Liverpool needed more subtlety and control to compete with Europe's very best. Paisley stressed the value of accurate passing. He instilled a less frantic approach.

In 1975, Liverpool finished the season with just a UEFA Cup place to show. In 1976, they saw the first fruits of Paisley's work. Liverpool beat off Manchester United and Derby for the Championship, and defeated FC Bruges in the UEFA Cup final. Liverpool won 3-2 at Anfield, then defended with great composure to clinch a 1-1 draw in Bruges. It was a sign of things to come.

Another Championship followed. Old rivals Manchester United stopped Liverpool completing the 'double', beating them 2-1 at Wembley. But Paisley's team gained more than adequate compensation. They won the European Cup for the first time, showing style and flair to beat Borussia Moenchengladbach (again) 3-1 in the final in Rome.

The elegant Alan Hansen in action against Manchester United

League Champions: 75/6, 76/7, 78/9, 79/80, 81/2, 82/3, 83/4
FA Cup winners: 74
League Cup winners: 81, 82, 83
European Cup winners: 77, 78, 81
UEFA Cup winners: 76

Liverpool eased past Crusaders from Belfast and Turkey's Trabzonspor. In the quarter-finals, they met St Etienne, unlucky runners-up the previous year. Liverpool played the first leg, in France, without the injured Keegan. Dominique Bathenay scored the only goal. At Anfield, Liverpool were missing Thompson, out for the rest of the season with a cartilage injury. The old war horse Tommy Smith replaced him. Liverpool threw up a new hero, 'supersub' David Fairclough. Keegan gave Liverpool a third-minute lead. Bathenay equalised. Ray Kennedy made it 2-1. Liverpool were still behind on away goals. Enter Fairclough. He chested down Kennedy's pass, beat two defenders and lashed in Liverpool's winner. They demolished FC Zurich 6-1 on aggregate in the semi-final. On to Rome...

That summer, Keegan left for Hamburg. Paisley signed the great Celtic forward Kenny Dalglish to replace him, then captured a young Scot of huge potential, centre-half Alan Hansen.

Brian Clough's Nottingham Forest pipped Liverpool to the title and the League Cup. But Liverpool reigned supreme in Europe. By the quarter-finals – against Benfica – Paisley had bought another vital Scottish presence, the rugged midfield general Graeme Souness from Middlesbrough. Liverpool won 2-1 in Lisbon and 4-1 at Anfield. In the semi-final, a 3-0 home win- against Monchengladbach again – wiped out a 2-1 defeat in Dusseldorf. Bruges, conquerors of Juventus, were Liverpool's final opponents at Wembley. Their coach, Ernst Happel, admitted they'd come to defend, and try to force penalties. Heighway started the

move for Liverpool's winner. Souness split the Bruges defence and Dalglish finished calmly.

Clough's Forest did for Liverpool in the European Cup the following season, after a massive rearguard action at Anfield. Dynamo Tbilisi played the two games of their lives to beat Liverpool in 1979-80.

On the domestic scene though, only Forest could come near the Anfield club, who won the Championship again in 1979 and 1980. Manchester United never quite made the breakthrough. Arsenal had gifted individuals but were reluctant to spend to boost their strength in depth.

Under Paisley few home-grown players came through. Fairclough and the small, energetic midfielder Sammy Lee were exceptions. Paisley reasoned that Liverpool were playing so many tough matches, they needed ready-made players to pull them through. Only under the management of Dalglish, then Souness, did Liverpool's youth system revive.

In 1981, Liverpool 'only' finished fifth. Long-term injuries to Hansen and Thompson were the reason for that. But they won the League

Cup for the first time – and the European Cup again. Liverpool knocked out OPS Oulu from Finland, Alex Ferguson's Aberdeen, then CSKA Sofia, who'd beaten holders Forest. In the semi-final, the discipline Paisley had instilled showed itself once more. After a goalless draw at Anfield, Ray Kennedy's late strike in Munich disposed of Bayern on away goals.

The final against Real Madrid was deadly dull. Neither side wanted to take a chance. Hansen and Thompson were magnificent. But Liverpool needed a defender, new left-back Alan Kennedy, to score the winner, in a rare moment of adventure. Liverpool were Champions of Europe for the third time. But CSKA took their revenge in 1982, beating Liverpool in the quarter-finals. The following year, the Poles Widzew Lodz, inspired by the great Zbigniew Boniek, knocked them out at the same stage.

At home though, Liverpool remained imperious. They won the Championship in 1982 and 1983, the League Cup again in 1982 (beating Tottenham) and 1983 (a 2-1 win over Manchester United).

Paisley had brought in new faces before he stepped down at the end of the 1982-83 season – goalkeeper Bruce Grobbelaar, Ronnie Whelan, Craig Johnston, Steve Nicol, and a young centre-forward called Ian Rush. They were all regulars as Liverpool made it three Championships in a row, won the League Cup again – and the European Cup against Roma – under the shrewd Fagan a year later. But, as he acknowledged, Paisley had left him a wonderful legacy.

Nottingham Forest

Clough leads Forest to European glory

Trevor Francis heads the only goal and winner against Malmo in the 1979 European Cup final

Nottingham Forest...Champions of Europe. It was an unlikely scenario when Brian Clough took over a second division club with better days behind it, in 1975. But Clough – and his assistant Peter Taylor – had worked miracles at Forest's bitter rivals Derby. They did the same for Forest.

It was a complementary arrangement. Clough was the motivator, the dictator, a man with a vision. Taylor found the players; soothed them and built their confidence. After leaving Derby in 1973, Clough and Taylor moved to Brighton.

Then Clough took over from the legendary Don Revie at Leeds United. In just 44 days, the senior players – unreceptive to Clough's methods – chased him out. Taylor meanwhile, stayed at Brighton and became manager, while Clough took charge at Forest. It was 18 months before Clough asked Taylor to join him again.

Now the partnership was reborn. Taylor spotted the potential of an overweight Scottish left-winger called John Robertson. Between them, Clough and Taylor turned him into the most effective winger in Britain. Robertson could dance past defenders at will and deliver wicked crosses. He was crucial to Forest's success. So was a young left-sided forward from the mining village of Eastwood, Tony Woodcock. So too was another ex-youth team star, right-back Viv Anderson, the first black player to play for England.

Martin O'Neill, the Northern Ireland midfielder, blossomed under Clough and Taylor. Frank Clark, the former Newcastle left-back found a new lease of life. Centre-half Larry Lloyd was rejuvenated too. Likewise midfielder Ian Bowyer, who'd seen glory days with Manchester City. Taylor spotted burly centre-forward Peter Withe playing for Birmingham. Clough brought him to Nottingham and he

prospered. Clough also imported two old faithfuls – midfielder John McGovern, who'd been with him as a 16-year-old at Hartlepool, and forward John O'Hare from Derby.

These were the stalwarts of the Forest side that won promotion in 1977. Clough made three vital signings as Forest returned to the top division. England goalkeeper Peter Shilton arrived from Stoke. Archie Gemmill, the left-footed maestro of Clough's old Derby midfield, joined Forest that September.

Then there was Kenny Burns. Clough wanted a dominating centre-back, who could pass the ball, to play alongside the towering Lloyd. Taylor hit on Burns: quick, skilful and fiery. It was one of their best-ever deals. Clough and Taylor showed confidence in Burns. He repaid them by becoming a pillar of the team. Forest began with a 3-1 win at Everton. A 3-0 loss at Arsenal was the only defeat they suffered in their first 12 games. They had a wobbly spell in early November, losing to Chelsea and Leeds. Then they went 26 League matches unbeaten. They didn't lose a home League game all season. They won the title by seven points from defending Champions Liverpool. Ironically, their last game of that title-winning season was a goalless draw, in front of 50,000 at Anfield. Forest had also beaten Liverpool 1-0 in a League Cup final replay.

Forest fans wondered when they'd wake up. But in 1979, their team reached the peak. They won the European Cup. In the first round, they met the holders, Liverpool. Clough and Taylor had decided the way to play in Europe was to

1977-80

Larry Lloyd in the 1980
European Cup final
against Hamburg

counter-attack. Forest had sold Withe and replaced him with a youngster from Long Eaton called Garry Birtles. Taylor had convinced Clough to sign him. Birtles would be the fulcrum of Forest's attack for years to come. Forest won 2-0 in Nottingham. Birtles and reserve defender Colin Barrett scored the goals. At Anfield, Forest defended in depth. Anderson made two goal-line clearances. Shilton pulled off two majestic saves from Kenny Dalglish. And Forest went through.

Forest saw off AEK Athens and Grasshoppers of Zurich, then met the German Champions Cologne in the semi-final. Japanese substitute Yasuhiko Okudera scored a late equaliser at Nottingham to earn Cologne a 3-3 draw and elicit the memorable headline 'Forest sunk by Japanese sub.'

Forest were given little chance in the return leg in Cologne. English bookmakers were offering 4 to 1 against them. How little they knew of Forest's resolve. Bowyer knocked in Lloyd's flick for the only goal, after Cologne's playmaker Dieter Muller had been sent off.

By now Forest had signed England's first £1 million player, Trevor Francis from Birmingham. He made his first European appearance in the final against Malmo and scored the only goal. On the stroke of half time, Robertson nipped past the Malmo cover and crossed. There was Francis, rising to head the winner. It was the pinnacle of Clough's career. And Taylor's.

Forest hadn't done too badly at home either.

They'd won the League Cup again, coming from behind to beat Southampton 3-2 at Wembley, with two goals by Birtles and one from Woodcock. They'd finished League runners-up to Liverpool.

The following season, Forest slipped to fifth in the League and lost yet another League Cup final 3-2 to Wolves. Clough had mysteriously sold Gemmill to Birmingham and signed the Manchester City midfield player Asa Hartford. The eccentric Clough then sold him to Everton after only three League appearances.

Later in the season, Forest gambled on Stan Bowles. Bowles had been a majestic attacker for Queens Park Rangers. He walked out on Forest when a European Cup medal was in his sights. Was it possible that Clough and Taylor were losing their touch?

They made a much shrewder signing when they brought in attacking left-back Frank Gray from Leeds, to replace the aging Clark. But doubts had surfaced. Forest comfortably saw off Osters Vaxjo from Sweden and the Romanian champions Argesul Pitesti in the opening rounds of their European Cup defence. The quarter-final was much tougher,

Dynamo Berlin's star, Hans-Jurgen Riediger, had scored the only goal of the first leg in Nottingham. In Berlin, Taylor noted that the Dynamo players didn't know how to approach the game. Should they attack or defend? Francis made such arguments redundant with two early goals. Robertson netted a third from the penalty spot and Forest went through.

Francis and Robertson – again from the spot – scored as Forest beat Ajax 2-0 in the semi-final first leg. Shilton was magnificent in Amsterdam. So were Lloyd and Burns. Ajax won 1-0, but Forest reached the final.

This was Forest's last hurrah. Perhaps the signs were already showing. Gary Mills was the only young player coming through. Francis had ripped an achilles tendon. Forest had never replaced Gemmill. Robertson was passing his peak. So was O'Neill, who'd contributed so much unsung heroism. Lloyd and Burns were coming to the end of a forceful partnership. Forest's slide the following season would confirm such anxieties.

In Madrid – against Kevin Keegan's Hamburg – they staged a massive rearguard action to retain the European Cup. Robertson scored the only goal. Mills was outstanding in midfield. Despite the efforts of Keegan, Manny Kaltz and Horst Hrubesch, Hamburg couldn't conjure up an equaliser. It was a desperately dull game. But Forest remained Champions of Europe.

Clough, without Taylor, built another successful side in the late 1980s. But Forest would never reach such heights again.

France 1982-84

Platini inspires 'Les Bleus'

In 1982, France were cheated out of a place in the World Cup final. Two years later, by way of compensation, they won the European Championship at the Parc des Princes.

France's story revolves around a group of remarkable players – and a coach who gave them the freedom to play. Michel Hidalgo, the former Reims wing-half, was that coach. Hidalgo led France for eight years, three months, and 75 matches. His teams won 41 and lost just 18.

In Spain in 1982 England caught them cold in the opening game. Bryan Robson scored after 27 seconds and England won 3-1. But a 4-1 win over Kuwait and a 1-1 draw against Czechoslovakia took the French through to the second phase. There, they beat Austria 1-0 and hammered Northern Ireland 4-1 to reach the semi-finals.

Hidalgo's squad had grown hugely in stature since England beat them in Bilbao. Marius Tresor was an imposing, constructive centre-back. The full-backs, Manuel Amoros and Maxime Bossis, loved to go forward. Winger Rocheteau proved his class year after year with St Etienne in Europe. But the crowning glory of the French team was its midfield – the darting little Giresse from Bordeaux buzzed like a bee. His tall, elegant club-mate Jean Tigana found time and space in the tightest areas. Michel Platini – originally from Nancy, later a hero at Juventus – was the golden vision, the supreme strategist. He could slow the play or speed it up. He conjured openings where none existed and picked out colleagues with passes like

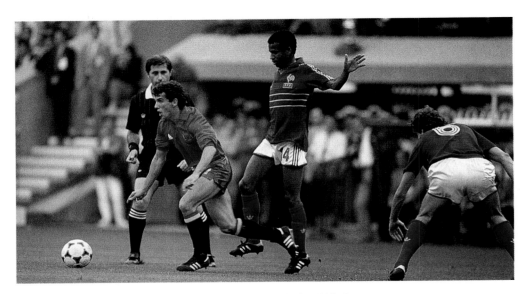

Jean Tigana (centre), the stylish French midfield star, in action against Spain in the 1984 final

homing missiles. His powerful shooting made him a constant threat too.

What France lacked was a penalty box poacher. That has been a theme in French football for more than 40 years – ever since Just Fontaine wrote his name into the record books as leading scorer in the 1958 World Cup finals.

In the 1982 semi-finals, France met West Germany in Seville. After the halcyon days of Beckenbauer and Netzer, the Germans had slipped back into their traditional role as Europe's least-loved team. That night German cynicism triumphed – with a little help from the Dutch referee, Charles Corver. Pierre Littbarski gave the Germans an early lead.

Platini levelled from the penalty spot. The match settled into a pattern: French flair against German defence. Extra time was needed. After two minutes, Tresor nodded France ahead. Six minutes later, Giresse made it 3-1. Surely France were through? No. They didn't know how to shut a game up – and they were wrecked by an appalling decision.

German goalkeeper 'Toni' Schumacher's appalling foul on French sub Patrick Battiston – as he burst into the box, threatening to put the match beyond the Germans – was one of the most cynical ever seen in the World Cup finals. Corver didn't even caution Schumacher, let alone send him off. By then, Karl-Heinz Rummenigge had pulled one back. But

European Championship final
27 June 1984 at Parc des Princes, Paris
FRANCE 2 SPAIN 0

FRANCE: Bats, Battiston (Amoros, 72 minutes), Le Roux, Bossis, Domergue, Fernandez, Tigana, Giresse, Platini, Lacombe (Genghini, 80 minutes), Bellone
SPAIN: Arconada, Urquiaga, Salva (Roberto, 85 minutes), Gallego, Julio Alberto (Sarabia, 77 minutes), Senor, Victor, Camacho, Francisco, Santillana, Carrasco

Giresse shields the ball in the 1984 final

Germany, down to ten men, including a sub goalie, would have been there for the taking. Instead that brutal incident disrupted France's rhythm. Klaus Fischer added a third to force penalties and the Germans' apologists trotted out the old cliches about their staying power.

Psychologically the Germans held the upper hand. The French hung on in the penalty shoot-out until it reached 4-4. Then it was sudden death. Schumacher saved Bossis' spot kick. Horst Hrubesch netted. The Germans were through. Justice had not been done. In the final, Italy beat them 3-1. That was no consolation to France.

Hidalgo, the idealist, had learned. He didn't become a cynic; merely a realist. He tweaked the team between Spain and the 1984 European Championship finals, when France were the hosts. Tresor was gone, but Bossis had switched to fill his place, alongside the spiky Monaco centre-back Yvon Le Roux. In midfield, Hidalgo added a fighter, Luis Fernandez from Paris St Germain, to protect his creative trio. He forgot about two wingers and opted for the solidity of 4-4-2, sometimes with Didier Six as a deep-lying winger.

Problems up front remained. Hidalgo permed two from Bernard Lacombe, Bruno Bellone and Bernard Genghini. None came close to filling Fontaine's shoes. Fortunately for France, they didn't need to.

In the opening phase, the French took charge. They beat Denmark 1-0, annihilated Belgium 5-0, then pipped Yugoslavia 3-2. Spain edged the other group from Portugal – on goals scored – after beating the Germans 1-0. In the semi-finals, France met Portugal in Marseille. It was a night to remember. Jean-Francois Domergue, the Toulouse left-back, gave the home team a 25th-minute lead. Benfica's Jordao levelled with 16 minutes left. Disaster threatened in extra time when Jordao grabbed a second. Five minutes remained, when Domergue bundled in the French equaliser. Penalties again? Platini was having none of that. The clock was running into the final minute as he swept home Tigana's cross. *Allez les bleus*! France were in the final.

There they faced Spain, penalty winners over Denmark, after a 1-1 draw. Miguel Munoz sent his team out to defend. The French battered away for nearly an hour. Then the Spanish goalkeeper, Luis Arconada, gifted them the breakthrough. Platini hit a curling free kick. Arconada, so impressive earlier, let the ball slip through his fingers.

France being France, they had to make life hard for themselves. Ten minutes from time, referee Vojtech Christov sent off Le Roux for a second bookable offence. At last Spain piled forward. In the 89th minute, all their outfield players were camped in the French half, when Tigana intercepted a pass and launched a long ball towards Bellone. The Monaco striker ran on, waited for Arconada to commit himself, then chipped him to kill the game. France were Champions of Europe. Platini lifted the trophy and Hidalgo, only 51, retired from international coaching a winner and a happy man.

Henri Michel took over and preserved Hidalgo's line-up. France reached the 1986 World Cup semi-finals. The Germans were laying in wait again. France didn't deserve to lose 2-0, but they did. The Germans had destroyed French hopes in 1982. Four years later, that German victory signalled the break-up of France's great team.

Fittingly, Platini was one of FIFA's head honchos when his countrymen won the World Cup at Stade de France in 1998. Jacquet's French side will go down as the most successful his country has ever seen.

Zinedine Zidane was an imperious playmaker with a knack of scoring vital goals. But France were pragmatic like everyone else. Where was the magic in their game...the spark that Platini, Tigana and Giresse supplied?

Holland 1988

Van Basten and Gullit dominate Europe

At last: Holland won a trophy. And victory was sweet. Because the Dutch didn't just win the European Championship. They won on the soil of their bitterest rivals, West Germany – after beating the Germans in the semi-finals. Holland's 2-1 victory over West Germany in Hamburg was historic; their first win over the West Germans for 32 years. It opened the way to the final, against the Soviet Union.

The Soviets, heavily dependent on Ukraine's finest from Dynamo Kiev, had beaten Holland in the group matches. That was no pointer to the showdown in Munich. Fourteen years earlier, another great Dutch side had gone down to defeat – to the Germans – in the Olympic stadium. This time Holland made no mistake.

The connecting link was the coach, Rinus Michels. The brains behind Ajax's rise to glory, he had led the Dutch that Sunday afternoon in 1974. Holland had never won when it mattered. Not just in 1974. In the 1976 European Championship, they lost to Czechoslovakia in the semi-finals. Two years later, they went down to Argentina in Buenos Aires, in extra time of the World Cup final.

After that, Dutch football contemplated its own navel, threatening to implode with internal arguments. By November, 1984, the KNVB (the Dutch FA) were desperate to find a respected figure to restore stability. When Kees Rijvers resigned, they turned to Michels, then a successful Bundesliga coach with Cologne. Michels' nicknames were 'The General' and 'The Bull'. He was not a man to stand any nonsense. His commitment cost

him nearly a year out of the game for heart surgery. But he earned the respect of the players – and he came back to guide them to triumph in Munich.

The Dutch qualified from a group containing Greece, Poland, Hungary and Cyprus. They crossed the border into Germany with quiet confidence. They had good reason. For once the egos in the squad weren't at each others' throats nor were they criticising the coach. That had become a Dutch custom. Michels stamped it out.

Ronald Koeman holds off the attentions of Soviet attackers in the 1988 final

Frank Rijkaard, one of Holland's key players, remembered: 'Michels was charismatic. He helped give us the spirit you need to succeed. There was no envy. We had a combination of players who wanted to work together. There was no problem over who was the most clever or important.'

A new generation of Dutch stars had grown up. Hans van Breukelen was one of Europe's finest goalkeepers. Centre-back Ronald Koeman was one of the best long passers in the game – and a deadly dead ball merchant. Rijkaard, his partner, was really an elegant midfielder, creating from the back. Shades of Arie Haan in 1974. In 1988 though, the

Ruud Gullit delivers a warning in the 1988 European Championships

TEAMS IN THE FINAL

HOLLAND: Van Breukelen, Van Aerle, Rijkaard, R.Koeman, Van Tiggelen, Vanenburg, Wouters, Muhren, E.Koeman, Gullit, Van Basten
SOVIET UNION: Dasaev, Demianenko, Aleinikov, Khidiatulin, Rats, Litovoyenko, Zavarov, Mikhailichenko, Gotsmanov (Baltacha, 67 minutes), Belanov, Protasov (Pasulko, 71 minutes)

Germans didn't have a Gerd Muller to torment the Dutch defenders..

The dreadlocked Ruud Gullit, a massive amalgam of skill and energy, led Holland's creative thrust. Arnold Muhren, of the cultured left foot, offered perceptive passing in support. Jan Wouters was a steely anchor man. In attack, the Dutch boasted the most lethal striker of the age, Gullit's Milan colleague, Marco van Basten. 'He had such football intellect,' said Rijkaard. 'He was a beautiful player. But he played for the team, not for himself.'

Yet their team's start set Dutch nerves jangling. They lost 1-0 to the Soviets in Cologne, after Vasily Rats swept in Igor Belanov's cross. Only two teams from the two groups of four qualified for the semi-finals. So Holland had to beat England in Dusseldorf. Van Basten responded with a murderous hat-trick.

Two minutes before half time, he controlled Gullit's far post cross and drove past Peter Shilton. Bryan Robson levelled, eight minutes into the second half, following a one-two with Gary Lineker. Van Basten lashed in another Gullit pass after 71 minutes, to restore Holland's lead. Four minutes later, he tucked away sub Wim Kieft's knock down from Erwin Koeman's corner. It was finishing of the highest class.

Ireland provided tough opposition in the final group game. Johan Cruyff had warned before the competition, no-one would enjoy playing Jack Charlton's team. England and the Soviets had discovered that already. Holland needed a fortuitous 81st minute goal from Kieft to win. Ronald Koeman's hurried shot bounced in front of Pat Bonner. Kieft's head guided home the rebound. The Irish claimed van Basten was offside, but the goal stood.

The semi-final win over the Germans has passed into Dutch folklore. The team in orange triumphed 2-1 after they'd fallen behind to Lothar Matthaus's penalty. Ronald Koeman's equaliser from the spot revived Dutch hopes. Van Basten's late winner seemed to settle a catalogue of ancient scores. It was if justice had been done at last. Millions came out on to the streets of Holland to celebrate the country's success.

The Dutch still had to beat the Soviets in the final. The great Kiev coach Valeri Lobanovski had drilled his team in the pressing game. They'd squeezed the life out of Italy to win the other semi-final 2-0. But Holland took charge from the start. The determination in the Dutch team reeked of Michels' influence. After 32 minutes, van Basten headed on Erwin Koeman's corner, and Gullit powered through to head Holland in front.

Van Basten hit the decisive goal, eight minutes into the second half. Adri van Tiggelen picked up a loose ball and found Muhren on the left. He arrowed a pass towards van Basten on the edge of the box. Van Basten moved on, took it in stride and hammered a ferocious volley that left Renat Dasaev rooted to the spot.

It was a popular victory.

AC **Milan** 1988-96

Berlusconi funds the Italian masters

AC Milan before the 1989 European Cup final: (l to r, back) Maldini, Van Basten, Gullit, Ancellotti, Rijkaard, Galli;
(l to r, front) Baresi, Donadoni, Costacurta, Colombo, Tassotti

Milan's domination of European football was the culmination of one man's driving ambition. Media mogul Silvio Berlusconi was determined to leave his mark on Italian society. He used his multi-media empire to launch himself into politics. For a few months, he even became prime minister of an Italian coalition government.

He left his mark on football too – as the Milan president who restored the club's glory days after a decade of failure. Berlusconi bought his way to success – putting up the money, for instance, to sign the famous Dutch trio of Ruud Gullit, Marco van Basten and Frank Rijkaard. Yet other clubs, notably Inter and Juventus, spent

as least much for far less reward. Berlusconi also made an inspired choice when he brought in a little-known coach from Second Division Parma: Arrigo Sacchi. Sacchi had no experience as a player. He had been a successful youth coach with Fiorentina. That's how he landed the Parma job. But Sacchi's team gave Milan such a fright in an Italian Cup tie that, in 1987, Berlusconi offered him the reins at San Siro.

Sacchi was a rarity in Italian football. He wanted to attack. He favoured a back four, told the team to 'press' all over the pitch and wanted to win the ball back as close to his opponents' goal as possible.

In the summer of 1987, Milan signed Gullit, midfield strategist of PSV and Holland, for £6 million. The great striker Van Basten, out of contract at Ajax, arrived for £1.5 million. After spells with Sporting Lisbon and Real Zaragoza, Rijkaard joined his old Ajax colleague at San Siro the next summer.

It was easy to describe that Milan team as 'Holland on tour,' but Italian players made a huge contribution too. Franco Baresi was one of the world's most perceptive centre-backs. Mauro Tassotti was a determined full-back. Two more vital links in the defensive chain rose through Milan's ranks – Paolo Maldini and Alessandro Costacurta. Roberto Donadoni was a gifted right-side midfielder. All played in Milan's 1989 European Cup final triumph over Steaua Bucharest.

In 1988, Sacchi's team pipped Napoli for the Italian title. The crucial game was Milan's 3-2 late season win in Naples, when Van Basten scored their third goal. Milan had not won the European Cup since 1969. In 1989, they ended the wait. Their bitter rivals Inter had snatched the Italian title. But Sacchi's squad lifted the biggest prize. Milan needed penalties to put out Red Star Belgrade in the second round, then squeezed past Werder Bremen 1-0. In the semi-final first leg, Van Basten scored to earn Milan a 1-1 draw at Real Madrid. In the second leg, Milan were dazzling. Carlo Ancelotti opened the scoring. Rijkaard, Gullit, Van Basten and Donadoni made it 5-0. Steaua rolled over in the final. Gullit and Van Basten scored two each and Milan won 4-0 at a canter.

European Cup winners: 89, 90, 94
Italian Champions: 87/8, 91/2, 92/3, 93/4, 95/6

Frank Rijkaard, shortly after his arrival at the San Siro in 1988

The following season, they did the double – European Cup and Italian League – despite losing Gullit to repeated knee surgery for much of the season. Milan knocked out HJK Helsinki, Real Madrid (again), KV Mechelen and Bayern, on away goals, to reach the final, where Rijkaard scored the only goal against Benfica in Vienna.

That series of operations had taken a toll on Gullit. Ankle injuries were catching up with Van Basten. So were the kickings he suffered. In the second round at Bruges, he had elbowed his marker in retaliation and been sent off.

The Italian federation wanted Sacchi as national coach. Berlusconi agreed. He thought Sacchi had reached the end of his achievements at San Siro.

Sacchi's successor Fabio Capello, had been a great Milan midfielder. But he kept the team playing in the same style. His impact was immediate. With no European distractions, Milan ran away with the Championship. They were unbeaten in 34 League matches, winning 22. Baresi, Costacurta, Tassotti, Maldini and Donadoni remained the nucleus of the side.

By now Gullit was with Sampdoria. Giovanni Galli had joined Napoli and Sebastiano Rossi was in goal. The muscular Demetrio Albertini had reinforced midfield. Daniele Massaro and Marco Simone added variety in attack.

For their assault on the European Cup, Capello signed French striker Jean-Pierre Papin from Marseille, the Croat midfielder, Zvonimir Boban, the Serb, Dejan Savicevic and Gianluigi Lentini

from Torino. Milan ran away with Serie A again, losing just twice. In the final stages of the European Cup, they beat IFK Gothenburg, PSV Eindhoven and Porto; home and away. No wonder they started favourites for the final, against Marseille in Munich.

Milan dominated but couldn't score. Marseille defender Basile Boli hit the only goal, a minute before half time. Milan had won every battle but the last. Rijkaard left. Van Basten retired the following year. Once more Berlusconi opened his wallet. In came Marcel Desailly, Brian Laudrup and Florin Raducioiu. Christian Panucci, another Milan product, broke through to provide versatile cover in defence.

Milan won a third successive championship – and the European Cup. They qualified for the semi-final, one leg only that season, without losing a game. They played that at home too. Desailly, Albertini and Massaro scored to beat Arsene Wenger's Monaco 3-0.

Milan saved their best for the final when they crushed Barcelona 4-0 in Athens. Massaro struck twice in the first half. Savicevic made it 3-0, and Desailly added a fourth. Milan seemed invincible. But 1994-95 was a big disappointment. Milan finished only fourth in the League. But Boban's last minute winner in the semi-final first leg at Paris St Germain – and Savicevic's two goals at San Siro – carried Milan to another Champions League final. This time, Ajax's young team beat them 1-0 in Vienna. Patrick Kluivert's 85th-minute goal was a warning: Milan's supremacy was fading.

Berlusconi spent again. Capello signed Roberto Baggio from Juventus, George Weah from Monaco and the winger Paulo Futre from Porto. With no European Cup to play for, Milan concentrated on Serie A. They won their fourth title in Capello's five years as coach, but only reached the UEFA Cup quarter-finals.

That summer Capello left for Real Madrid. His successor, Oscar Washington Tabarez had to handle a squad stronger on paper than on the pitch. Baresi finally hung up his boots. Michael Reiziger and Edgar Davids, new recruits from Ajax, failed to settle. Monaco's Christophe Dugarry wasn't an instant hit either. Milan slid to tenth in the League – and failed to qualify from the European Cup group. The Norwegians, Rosenborg Trondheim, ended their hopes with a 2-1 win at San Siro.

It was the death knell of Milan's decade of domination. But maybe their Italian Championship win of 1999 will herald the dawn of a new era?

Barcelona 1989-99

Homage to Catalonia

Michael Laudrup on the attack during the 1992 European Cup final

Barcelona are more than a football club. They are the symbol of Catalonia. The Catalan people of Spain's north-east have always stood out against central control from Madrid. Barcelona have mirrored that determination on the football pitch. Barca's bitter rivalry with Real Madrid is one of the great causes of Spanish football.

Real could claim the biggest honours, most of all in the European Cup. By the time Johan Cruyff became Barcelona's coach, in the summer of 1988, Real had won Europe's premier trophy six times; Barca never. They had reached two finals. Helenio Herrera led them to the 1961 showdown with Benfica in Bern. Barca lost, 3-2. In 1986, Terry Venables

took Barcelona to their second final – when they lost on penalties to the Romanian army club Steaua Bucharest in Seville.

Both times Barca had started favourites. Both times their army of fans was disappointed. Cruyff, a Barca player in the mid-1970s, knew all about the expectations of the Catalan public. He also knew about winning the European Cup. The great Dutch forward inspired Ajax to victory in 1971, 1972 and 1973. In 1992, he coached Barcelona to their first-ever European Cup triumph. Cruyff took over from Venables, who'd fallen foul of the club hierarchy and had returned to London. Meanwhile, Gary Lineker stayed at the Nou Camp. He didn't rejoin Venables – then Tottenham's manager – until the summer of 1989.

In 1988-89, Barca finished runners-up in the League to Real. But they lifted the European Cup Winners Cup. Julio Salinas and sub Lopez Rekorte scored as Barcelona beat Sampdoria 2-0 in Bern, in a rehearsal for the European Cup final three years later. The following season was a disappointment. Cruyff's team finished third in the Primera Division and lost to Anderlecht in the Cup Winners Cup second round. But redemption was at hand. Barca beat Real 2-0 in the Spanish Cup final. Cruyff had plenty of talent at his disposal. Andoni Zubizarreta had proved himself one of Europe's top goalkeepers. Salinas and Artor Beguiristain provided the cutting edge. Amor was a powerful midfielder. So was the young hopeful Jose Bakero. Eusebio did a fine job as the holding midfield player. Roberto added valuable goals.

Cruyff had made two important signings – the great attacking defender Ronald Koeman from PSV Eindhoven, and the Danish attacker Michael Laudrup. Koeman blasted 14 goals from dead-ball kicks that season. Laudrup set up many more for Salinas and Beguiristain.

Barca lost the Cup Winners Cup final 2-1 to Manchester United. But they won the Spanish title. That was Cruyff's priority. He had been building his squad for an assault on the European Cup. New stars had been bedded in: full backs Nando and Albert Ferrer (later to play for Chelsea), Guardiola at centre-back, along with Nadal – giving Koeman freedom to roam; midfield hard man Goicoechea, and the explosive Christo Stoichkov. The Bulgarian striker hit 14 League goals in his first season and went on to score more than 100 in his Barca career.

In 1992, Barcelona won the Spanish title again – and faced Sampdoria once more in the European Cup final at Wembley. Nearly 40,000 came from Catalonia to support Barca that night. It was 0-0 at full time: Koeman's blast in the 22nd minute of extra time decided the contest. Barca were Champions of Europe. They had waited a long while, since Herrera's side had lost to Benfica.

Two more Spanish championships followed. Real were eclipsed. But Barcelona's real tests came in Europe. CSKA Moscow knocked them out, 4-3 on aggregate, in the 1992-93 third round. Cruyff responded by bringing in Sergi to reinforce the back line – and by signing Romario from PSV.

Barca celebrate with Cruyff after the 1992 European Cup final victory over Sampdoria at Wembley

Like Koeman, Romario proved another sensational buy from Eindhoven. The Brazilian striker hit 30 goals in 33 League appearances in his first season, as Barca clinched another Spanish title – though only on goal difference. The highlight was a 5-0 home win over Real in January, when Romario hit a hat-trick. The decisive result though, was a 3-0 win over closest pursuers Deportivo La Coruna at Nou Camp, when Stoichkov, Laudrup and Romario all scored. That was vital, as Barca won the title on goal difference.

In 1994, Barcelona reached the final again – then collapsed. AC Milan thrashed them 4-0 in Athens. It was hard to believe that so many class players could surrender so easily.

The following season, cracks started to appear. Barca crashed 5-0 at the Bernabeu that January, and went down by the same score at unfashionable Santander five weeks later. They finished only fourth in the League and lost to Paris St Germain in the European Cup quarter-finals.

Third place next season, and no European glory, moved the Barcelona board to act. On 19 May 1996, they sacked Cruyff. Carlos Rexach became caretaker coach. Ex-England manager Bobby Robson took over from Rexach. Robson brought in players he knew from his time in Portugal – goalkeeper Vitor Baia, Fernando Couto and Figo.

Another promising young striker arrived from Brazil – Ronaldo. Barca finished runners-up again, and beat Paris St Germain 1-0 in the Cup Winners Cup final in Rotterdam. Ronaldo struck the only goal, from the penalty spot. Barca won the Spanish Cup as well, beating Real Betis. Then Robson moved 'upstairs'.

Barca brought in Louis van Gaal, coach of Ajax's 1995 European Cup winners. Shades, maybe, of Cruyff. Van Gaal brought in Dutch goalkeeper Ruud Hesp and defenders Winston Bogarde and Michael Reiziger. He added more Brazilians, Giovanni, Rivaldo and Sonny Anderson. But Ronaldo moved to Inter. In 1998, Barcelona won the League title and pipped Real Mallorca on penalties in the Spanish Cup final.

But next season they crashed out of the European Cup at the group stage. Van Gaal has some work to do before he can compete with the record of his illustrious Dutch predecessor. Maybe Barca's 1999 Spanish Championship will be the launching pad?

European Cup winners: 92
European Cup Winners Cup winners: 89, 97
Spanish Champions: 90/1, 91/2, 92/3, 93/4, 97/8
Spanish Cup winners: 90, 97, 98

Juventus 1994-98

The team of the modern age

Twenty-year-old Alessandro del Piero in action against Steaua Bucharest in 1995

At the end of the 20th century, Juventus had been one of Europe's great clubs for years. Their 1985 team – inspired by Michel Platini and Zbigniew Boniek – beat holders Liverpool 1-0 in the European Cup final; though hardly anyone now remembers the result. The pre-match tragedy that night at Heysel made the game almost irrelevant. Juve had reached two other European Cup finals. In 1973, they lost to Johan Cruyff's great Ajax side. Ten years later, they went down to Hamburg.

Backed by the Agnelli family, the owners of FIAT cars, Juve had the resources to sign the world's finest players. *LaVecchia Signora* (the

Old Lady, as the club is known in Italy) had eclipsed local rivals Torino. Club president Gianni Agnelli was equally keen to ensure they stayed ahead of Inter and AC, their bitter rivals from Milan.

AC Milan dominated the late 1980s and early 1990s, in Serie A and the European Cup. But Juve were on the brink of the greatest period in their long history.

The catalyst was a change of coach. In the summer of 1994, Giovanni Trappatoni joined Bayern. His replacement was Marcello Lippi, a 46-year-old from Viareggio, who'd made his

name with Cesena and Napoli. One of his first moves was to sign centre-half Ciro Ferrara from Napoli and make him the cornerstone of Juve's defence. That Juventus side included Gianluca Vialli and Fabrizio Ravanelli – who struck 31 League goals betwen them – goalkeeper Angelo Peruzzi, Roberto Baggio, Moreno Toricelli, Antonio Conte, Angelo Di Livio, Paulo Sousa from Portugal, the French midfielder Didier Deschamps; and a young attacker called Alessandro Del Piero.

They clinched the Serie A title with a 2-0 triumph over Milan at San Siro on 1 May. Three days later, they won 2-1 at Borussia Dortmund (4-3 on aggregate) to reach the UEFA Cup final. Dino Baggio scored the only goal, for Parma, in the first leg. Parma held on for a 1-1 draw in Turin: 2-1 on aggregate.

Lippi's team returned even stronger the following season. Milan pinched their Championship. But Juve had their sights set higher – on the European Cup. Attilio Lombardo, Vladimir Jugovic and veteran defender Pietro Vierchowod arrived from Sampdoria. Michele Padovano came from Reggiana. Lippi snapped up defender Gianluca Pessotto from Torino.

Juventus had to be at their best in the quarter-final. They trailed 1-0 to Real Madrid after the first leg in Madrid. At the Stadio delle Alpi, Del Piero gave them a 16th-minute lead. Padovano grabbed the winner, eight minutes after half time. In the semi-finals, Juve beat Nantes 4-3 on aggregate, to meet holders Ajax in Rome.

Gianluca Vialli rounds the Ajax goalkeeper in the 1996 European Cup final, which Juventus won on penalties

**Italian Champions: 94/5, 96/7, 97/8
European Cup winners: 96, runners-up 97, 98**

signed striker Filippo Inzaghi from Atalanta to replace Vieri, who'd joined Atletico Madrid, then added Holland star Edgar Davids from Milan during Italy's December 'transfer window.'

In the quarter-finals, Juve met Dynamo Kiev. They were lucky to escape with a 1-1 draw in Turin, after English referee Paul Durkin waved away what seemed a blatant trip on Sergei Rebrov. In the second leg though, Juve were inspired. Inzaghi scored a hat-trick. Juve won 4-1, then eased past Monaco into the final, against Real Madrid in Amsterdam.

Del Piero had enjoyed a majestic season, scoring 21 goals in Serie A. But Real centre-back Fernando Hierro dominated in defence, and Predrag Mijatovic scored the only goal, after 66 minutes.

In the last complete season of the 20th century, Juve struggled in the League early on. That was the cue for the Juventus praesidium to sack Lippi – however much he'd done for them. Carlo Ancelotti took his place.

The European Cup was Juve's target again. In the semi-final second leg, Dwight Yorke, Roy Keane and Andy Cole scored for Manchester United in Turin, to end the dream. 4-3 to United on aggregate. Where do Juventus go from here?

Ravanelli fired Juventus into a 12th-minute lead. Ajax's Finnish forward Jari Litmanen levelled. Extra time couldn't separate the teams. In the penalty shoot-out, Peruzzi outdived Edwin van der Saar. Juve won 4-2 and became Champions of Europe.

Lippi signed Alen Boksic and Christian Vieri that summer. Vialli and Ravanelli both moved to England. Paolo Montero arrived from Atalanta. So did another Portuguese international, Dimas from Benfica, Nicola Amoruso from Padova, and Salernitana's Mark Juliano.

Then Lippi won the race for the most prized signature of all – Bordeaux and France's playmaker, Zinedine Zidane.

It was if the Juve coach had built a new team during the close season. The 'Zebras' carried on regardless. A 6-1 win over Milan at San Siro was the high point of their progress towards

their 24th Italian title. Jugovic and Vieri scored twice, Zidane and Amoruso once.

In Europe, Juve pulled out two remarkable semi-final performances, to demolish Ajax. Vieri and Amuroso scored in a 2-1 win at the Ajax Arena. In Turin, Juve ran out 4-1 victors. 'They're playing football from a different planet,' said Ajax's captain Frank de Boer.

Juve started favourites to beat Borussia Dortmund in Munich. But Otmar Hitzfeld's team had huge organisation – and Karlheinz Riedle – on their side. Riedle netted twice in the first half. Del Piero, amazingly, only a sub, replied after 64 minutes. Then Hitzfeld sent on Lars Ricken. It was a decisive substitution. Ricken hit Dortmund's third. Juve were out of the argument.

Europe was Juve's target again in 1998. They won the Italian Championship as well as reaching the European Cup final. Lippi had

Manchester United 1999

The Reds grab the elusive 'treble'

United celebrate the 'treble' in Barcelona

The date was 26 May 1999. The venue, the Nou Camp in Barcelona. Forty seconds into injury time; Manchester United trailed 1-0 to Bundesliga Champions Bayern Munich. David Beckham's corner was only half-cleared. Ryan Giggs swung a boot, sub Teddy Sheringham helped the ball on, past Bayern keeper Oliver Kahn. United were level.

Extra time seemed inevitable. Sheringham flicked on another Beckham corner. Another sub, Ole Gunnar Solskjaer, poked out a foot to deflect the ball wide of Kahn. Italian referee Pierluigi Collina blew the final whistle seconds later. Bayern were devastated. United were Champions of Europe.

They had made English football history. Never before had any team won the Championship,

FA Cup and European Cup in the same season. Liverpool had come so close in 1977 – but United beat them 2-1 in the FA Cup final.

United had been building up to that triumph in Barcelona for years. Ever since 1993 – when Alex Ferguson's team lifted the club's first championship for 26 years. The following season, United won the 'double'. During the 1994-95 season, Ferguson added the Blackburn defender David May and Newcastle top scorer Andy Cole to his squad. That season, they lost the title on the last day of the season, drawing at West Ham when victory would have carried them past Champions Blackburn.

Then Ferguson dropped his bombshell. That summer, he allowed Paul Ince (to Internazionale), Andrei Kanchelskis (Everton)

and Mark Hughes (Chelsea) all to move on. Ferguson knew his nucleus was sound. Peter Schmeichel was a great goalkeeper, Denis Irwin a full-back of metronomic consistency. Roy Keane was the engine of the team. Ryan Giggs added quality on the left.

Now Ferguson wanted to blood his rising generation of young stars – David Beckham, Paul Scholes, the Neville brothers, Gary and Phil, and Nicky Butt. 'You'll win nothing with kids,' said BBC TV pundit Alan Hansen – the ex-Liverpool defender – after United crashed 3-1 at Aston Villa in August 1995. Fergie's team proved him wrong with a vengeance. They won the Championship yet again – and beat Liverpool 2-0 in the FA Cup final. Suddenly, the 'double' didn't seem so difficult.. By then, Ferguson had added Sheringham, the Norwegians Solskjaer and Ronny Johnsen – and three vital signings for the new campaign – Jaap Stam, Jesper Blomqvist and Dwight Yorke.

Arsenal fought United all the way through the Premiership campaign. They even thrashed United 3-0 at Highbury. Over a season though, United were too strong. In hindsight, Cole's equaliser against the Gunners, at Old Trafford in February, assumed huge significance. On the last day of the Premiership season, United had to beat Tottenham at Old Trafford to be sure of the title. Les Ferdinand gave Spurs an early lead. Beckham equalised. Cole – an ex-Gunner – hit the winner. That was typical of United's usual response to adversity. If the comeback against Bayern was the most famous example, then United had already demonstrated their strength of will – against

Juventus in Turin, and Liverpool and Arsenal in the FA Cup. In the fourth round against Liverpool, United trailed 1-0 until the 89th minute – then Yorke and Solskjaer scored. A foretaste maybe to Barcelona?

United's progress against Arsenal in the semi-final was equally heart-stopping. After a goalless draw Beckham gave United an early lead. Dennis Bergkamp equalised. Keane was sent off for a second bookable offence. In stoppage time, Phil Neville hauled down Ray Parlour. Bergkamp took the penalty. Schmeichel guessed right, flung himself across and saved. In extra time, Giggs pounced on Patrick Vieira's misplaced pass, hared off towards the Arsenal goal, beat off three tackles, then unleashed a thunderous shot past David Seaman. United had ridden their luck . But as Ferguson said: 'We never give up.'

It was if United had debts to settle with Arsene Wenger's team too. Giggs was one of several United stars who revealed how much Arsenal's 1998 'double' success had hurt them. 'We were very disappointed,' said Ferguson, 'but sometimes in life you have to be.'

That disappointment galvanised the Old Trafford club. United plc realised Ferguson had to bring in major signings. The towering Dutch defender Stam arrived to solve the centre-back problems that had plagued United throughout the previous season. Swedish winger Jesper Blomqvist gave Ferguson even more options in attack. Then, as the season opened, Ferguson staged his greatest coup. He wanted a striker to partner Cole. He hit upon Aston Villa's Dwight Yorke. The fee was £12.6 million, a United record. Yorke delivered from day one: eight goals at the highest level in Europe, 29 in all, 53 in partnership with Cole. Meanwhile, United's youth system continued to turn out impressive products. Defender Wes Brown was the latest.

United are the richest, best-supported club in England. They had built by far the strongest squad. That was a key factor in their success. Arsenal, for instance, could never match United's formidable back-up. Neither, in

Barcelona, could Bayern. As Sir Bobby Charlton put it: 'Perhaps in the past we've not appreciated how much has been asked of a relatively small group of players. This season the squad has been used fully. It takes a brave man to make that system work. So Alex deserves great credit for his vision.'

United's squad did the business again at Wembley in the FA Cup final. Keane limped off after eight minutes against Newcastle, following Gary Speed's early tackle. On came Sheringham, to score 96 seconds later, then create the second for Scholes: 2-0 to United; a third 'double' – one more than Arsenal.

Four days later, United stuffed taunts of 'What have you done in Europe?' down their critics' throats. Squad success again. Keane and Scholes were suspended for the final. Goal heroes Sheringham and Solskjaer climbed off the bench to deliver glory.

Ferguson's team had reached the European Cup semi-finals in 1997, but lost to eventual winners Borussia Dortmund. The following year, David Trezeguet's quarter-final goal for Monaco at Old Trafford ended their hopes on

away goals. In 1999, United were a different proposition. Ferguson's recruiting had given them so many more options.

As English League runners-up, they had to beat the Polish champions LKS Lodz to qualify for the Champions League. In the group games, United drew each of four titanic clashes against Bayern and Barcelona. But their wins over Brondby from Denmark took them into the quarter-finals. Yorke scored both goals in the first leg against Inter in Manchester. In Milan, Scholes netted to earn United a 1-1 draw. That set United for a semi-final clash with Juventus,. Antonio Conte put Juve ahead at Old Trafford. Giggs gave United hope with a late equaliser. In Turin, Juve made a flying start. Filippo Inzaghi struck twice in the first 11 minutes. United refused to buckle. Keane headed home a corner. Yorke, twisting and turning, buried a second; United ahead on away goals. Juve were demoralised. Cole made it 3-2.

Bobby Charlton summed up what United's achievement meant, throughout the world: 'English football has been in the wilderness for a long time. Now we're back on the world stage. It's been a sensational season!'

Ole Gunnar Solskjaer scores the last-second winner for United against Bayern

Great Games

A great game of football normally lasts for only 90 minutes but can live in the memory for a lifetime. For instance, who can forget the marvellous 1960 Eintracht Frankfurt v Real Madrid European Cup final or the 1970 Brazil v Italy World Cup Final, thrilling matches which represented the ultimate in footballing skill and artistry?

In this section we look back at the top 20 games of the century, ranging from the 'Wembley Wizards' rout of England in 1928 to the 1996 Liverpool v Newcastle 4-3 thriller, and bring these great contests dramatically back to life.

England v Scotland 1928

The Wembley Wizards rout England

Alan Morton, the 'wee blue devil' of Rangers and Scotland

31 March 1928, Wembley (international match)
ENGLAND 1 SCOTLAND 5

Scots will lionise the 'Wembley Wizards' for ever more. England included such stars as Roy Goodall, Willis Edwards, Joe Hulme, Dixie Dean and Bob Kelly – and Scotland thrashed them.

The Scots fielded one of the smallest forward lines ever seen at Wembley – none of them was over 5ft 7in – yet they shredded the England defence. Huddersfield winger Alec Jackson scored a hat-trick. Alex James, later to become an Arsenal legend, added two more. England were humiliated.

As Ivan Sharpe, the leading football journalist of the time, wrote: 'It was the finest football ever seen in Britain and the most memorable afternoon in the history of the Scottish FA Remember the names of the famous five: Jackson, Jimmy 'Ginger' Dunn, the great Hughie Gallacher, James, and the 'wee blue devil' Alan Morton.

Sharpe wrote of England's centre-half – Jackson's Huddersfield colleague Tom Wilson: 'His head is a great force when the ball is in the air. He must have wondered whether there was any air at Wembley. The ball was never there when Scotland played it.'

James and Morton were at the heart of Scotland's triumph. James proved himself a complete inside-forward. Morton gave a wonderful display of accurate crossing. 'I tried to place my centres to the far side of their goal because I thought that would help us,' said Morton.

After five minutes, James sent Morton away on the left. He crossed low, and Jackson, coming in from the right, stooped to nod Scotland in front. Thirteen minutes later, James intercepted Billy Smith's back pass – then took off on a dribble past Harry Healless, Wilson and Herbert Jones, before planting a low shot past Ted Hufton.

Twenty minutes into the second half, Jackson made it 3-0 from another Morton centre. Within 60 seconds, James had netted Scotland's fourth. Gallacher was tackled close to goal. The ball ran loose. James reacted first. His shot was going in anyway, but a deflection off Herbert Jones made certain.

The Scots could do no wrong. Typical was

centre-half Tom 'Tiny' Bradshaw, of Liverpool, winning his only cap. A Liverpool director, Harvey Webb, said: 'He's a wonderful player, but he gives us a heart attack every match by dribbling in his own penalty area.' Bradshaw gave no such hostages to fortune at Wembley.

Five minutes from time, Morton sped down the left again. In nipped Jackson, ahead of Jones and Hufton, to score his hat-trick. Kelly's last minute free-kick for England was not even a consolation. The Scots were rampant.

THE GOALS

5 minutes	Alec Jackson heads Scotland in front
18 minutes	Alex James hits Scotland's second
65 minutes	Jackson makes it 3-0
66 minutes	James scores Scotland's fourth, via a deflection
85 minutes	Jackson completes his hat trick
90 minutes	Bob Kelly pulls one back for England

THE TEAMS

ENGLAND: Hufton, Goodall, Jones, Edwards, Wilson, Healless, Hulme, Kelly, Dean, Bradford, Smith
SCOTLAND: Harkness, Nelson, Law, Gibson, Bradshaw, McMullan, Jackson, Dunn, Gallacher, James, Morton

England v Italy 1934

The Battle of Highbury

The Italian goalkeeper Ceresoli saves at Highbury

**14 November 1934, Highbury (international match)
ENGLAND 3 ITALY 2**

The English didn't enter the World Cup until 1950. So, in 1934, Italy – under the leadership of Vittorio Pozzo – became the first European team to win the trophy. In the final, on home ground in Rome, they beat Czechoslovakia 2-1 after extra time. But England had drawn with Italy 1-1 in Rome eleven months before that World Cup victory. Now the world champions wanted to prove they were more than a match for football's 'old masters'.

It was the time of 'Il Duce', Mussolini, who saw sporting success as a way of restoring Italy's glory. Politics and football became intertwined. The football writer Ivan Sharpe, remembered: 'Every game became a victory for fascism. Bonuses to win therefore became too big. For those reasons, the match between England and Italy at Arsenal developed into a match of blood and bruises – the roughest I've ever seen. The "state" was too much at stake.'

England had never lost at home to European opponents. Pozzo's team were confident they could break that record. England were almost like a club team that day. Seven of the team – Frank Moss, George Male, skipper Eddie Hapgood, Wilf Copping, Ray Bowden, Ted Drake and Cliff Bastin – from Champions Arsenal were playing on home territory. England piled forward from the start. After just 30 seconds, Drake challenged goalkeeper

THE GOALS
10 minutes	Eric Brook scores England's first
12 minutes	Brook scores his second
15 minutes	Ted Drake nets England's third
67 minutes	Giuseppe Meazza pulls one back
69 minutes	Meazza makes it 3-2

THE TEAMS
ENGLAND: Moss, Male, Hapgood, Britton, Barker, Copping, Matthews, Bowden, Drake, Bastin, Brook
ITALY: Ceresoli, Monzeglio, Allemandi, Ferraris, Monti, Bertolini, Gualiti, Serantoni, Meazza, Ferrari, Orsi

Carlo Ceresoli for a long ball. Full-back Eraldo Monzeglio joined in with such force that the Swedish referee, Olssen, awarded England a penalty. Ceresoli, the finest goalkeeper of the age, somehow palmed out Eric Brook's kick.

Brook soon took revenge. Ten minutes later, Stanley Matthews broke away on the right and delivered a perfect far-post cross. In ran Brook to score with a powerful header that gave

Ceresoli no chance. Two minutes later, the Manchester City forward crashed England's second, a free-kick from edge of the area. By the 15th minute, England were three up. Drake burst clear of the Italian defence and fired home from 15 yards.

Italy had lost their inspiration, the Argentinian – now a naturalised Italian – Luisito Monti, injured. Pozzo's men did not enjoy the tough English tackling. They knew what this game meant too, and not just in terms of football. They started kicking. England hard man Copping retaliated. Olssen was barely able to keep control.

Amidst the brutality, Italy's magical forward Giuseppe Meazza pulled out two pieces of top quality finishing inside two minutes, giving Moss no chance from inside the box. At 3-2 with 20 minutes left, Italy had a fighting chance. Fighting was the word. Male and Hapgood tried to steady England. Moss saved whatever Italy flung at him in a desperate finale. Somehow the battered English held out.

At the post-match banquet, Hapgood appeared with a broken bone in the nose. Brook's arm had been x-rayed. Drake's eyes were discoloured after the pounding he'd taken. Bowden limped in with a damaged ankle.

As for Pozzo's team it would be 1938 before they wiped out the memory of that defeat. Only by winning the World Cup for a second time could they redeem themselves in the eyes of their government.

Bolton v Blackpool 1953

The Stanley Matthews final

THE GOALS

75 seconds	Nat Lofthouse strikes for Bolton
35 minutes	Stan Mortensen equalises
39 minutes	Willie Moir restores Bolton's lead
55 minutes	Eric Bell nets Bolton's third
67 minutes	Mortensen makes it 3-2
89 minutes	Mortensen equalises
90 minutes	Bill Perry hits Blackpool's winner

THE TEAMS

BLACKPOOL: Farm, Shimwell, Garrett, Fenton, Johnston, Robinson, Matthews, Taylor, Mortensen, Mudie, Perry

BOLTON: Hanson, Ball, Banks, Wheeler, Barrass, Bell, Holden, Moir, Lofthouse, Hassall, Langton

Blackpool celebrate their last-minute Cup final victory

**2 May 1953, Wembley (FA Cup final)
BOLTON WANDERERS 3 BLACKPOOL 4**

Stanley Matthews was already 38. He had been on the losing side for Blackpool against Manchester United in 1948 and Newcastle three years later. This was his last chance of collecting an FA Cup winner's medal.

The papers had headlined Matthews' last chance for weeks. But Blackpool were more than a one-man team. Their forward line was one of the most lethal in the League: Matthews on the right, the South African Bill Perry on the left, inside-forwards Ernie Taylor and Jackie Mudie, fronted by another England hero, Stan Mortensen. Mortensen would play a crucial role too.

Bolton's defence against Blackpool's attack was the expected contest: though Wanderers boasted a lethal striker of their own, the great England centre-forward Nat Lofthouse.

Lofthouse made an impact within 75 seconds. His cross shot from the right screwed through George Farm's grasp, hit the Blackpool goalkeeper on the shoulder and bounced over the line.

It took Blackpool 34 minutes to level. Mortensen strode through the middle, shot, and the ball deflected off Bolton's Harold Hassall, past wrongfooted 'keeper Stan Hanson. Five minutes later though, Willie Moir lunged ahead of Farm to Bobby Langton's through ball and restored Bolton's lead.

The scoreline grew even worse for Blackpool, ten minutes after half time. Bolton's limping wing-half Eric Bell (there were no substitutes in those days) had been pushed up front. He met Doug Holden's centre with a firm header for Wanderers' third.

Enter Matthews – and Mortensen again. Matthews crossed to the far post. Hanson let the ball drift behind him. In slid Mortensen, foot colliding with a post, to touch it home, and bring Blackpool back with a chance.

Yet, with a minute left, Blackpool still trailed. Then Mudie was sandwiched five yards outside the box. Bolton's wall gave Mortensen no sight of goal as he placed the free-kick. Suddenly Mortensen spotted full-back Ernie Shimwell racing forward – and a Bolton defender peeling from the wall to track him. Mortensen saw his chance. He blasted his shot through the gap. A hat-trick for Mortensen: Blackpool level.

By now, Matthews was tormenting Bolton left-back Ralph Banks. As extra time loomed, the great man skipped past Banks again. Before Malcolm Barrass could cover, Matthews crossed. In ran Perry, to drive a low shot and seal one of the most dramatic Cup final victories ever. For Matthews it was the realisation of a dream.

Arsenal v Man United 1958

The Babes' last League game

1 February 1958, Highbury (League match)
ARSENAL 4 MANCHESTER UNITED 5

This was a historic game. Not just for the result. It was the last match the 'Busby Babes' played in England, before that brilliant side was cut to shreds by the Munich air disaster.

Of United's team that day, the great Duncan Edwards, skipper Roger Byrne and centre-forward Tommy Taylor died at Munich. So did centre-half Mark Jones and attacking wing-half Eddie Colman; along with Liam Whelan, David Pegg and Geoff Bent, who missed the Highbury thriller.

United had built a 2-1 lead over Red Star Belgrade in the European Cup quarter-final first leg. They drew 3-3 in Belgrade to reach the semi-final. They flew back in triumph. Then tragedy struck after their plane refuelled at Munich airport.

More than 63,000 Highbury fans saw the last of the Babes in England, playing at their finest. And Arsenal – re-building after their glory years – were crucial performers in a majestic drama. United had already won two consecutive titles. They fancied a hat-trick. They were gunning for European Cup holders Real Madrid too. Thoughts of impending doom seemed miles away, as a packed crowd lapped up a nine-goal feast.

By half-time, United led 3-0. Dennis Viollet and Albert Scanlon set up the first, lashed home by the imperious Edwards. Scanlon outpaced the Arsenal defence and chipped back for Bobby

Edwards clears at Highbury, watched by United 'keeper Harry Gregg

Charlton to drive United's second. A minute before the interval, Taylor cracked their third. Arsenal wouldn't lay down. Skipper Dave Bowen drove his team forward. They levelled inside three crazy minutes. David Herd – later a United star – launched the revival when he smashed home Bowen's pass on the volley. Vic Groves nodded down Gordon Nutt's centre to Jimmy Bloomfield, who blasted the second. Nutt drove over another cross, hard and low. Inside-forward Bloomfield flung himself full length. His header flew past Harry Gregg.

But Arsenal over-reached themselves, bursting for the lead. Charlton and Scanlon split the Gunners defence on the break and Viollet plundered United's fourth. Taylor cracked the fifth past Jack Kelsey from an incredible angle.

Arsenal refused to give in. Derek Tapscott slammed the Gunners' fourth goal. They pressed and pressed for the last 13 minutes. Somehow United held out. They showed they were worthy champions.

THE GOALS

10 minutes	Duncan Edwards scores
33 minutes	Bobby Charlton makes it 2-0
44 minutes	Tommy Taylor nets United's third
58 minutes	David Herd pulls one back
60 minutes	Jimmy Bloomfield nets Arsenal's second
61 minutes	Bloomfield heads the equaliser
65 minutes	Dennis Viollet restores United's lead
72 minutes	Taylor makes it 5-3
77 minutes	Derek Tapscott's goal ensures a thrilling finish

THE TEAMS

ARSENAL: Kelsey, S.Charlton, Evans, Ward, Fotheringham, Bowen, Groves, Tapscott, Herd, Bloomfield, Nutt
MANCHESTER UNITED: Gregg, Foulkes, Byrne, Colman, Jones, Edwards, Morgans, B.Charlton, Taylor, Viollet, Scanlon

Sweden v Brazil 1958

Pele arrives on the world scene

Pele scores Brazil's third goal against goalkeeper Svensson

29 June 1958, Solna (World Cup final)
SWEDEN 2 BRAZIL 5

The image shot round the world. The triumphant Brazilians parading the World Cup underneath a Swedish flag as a mark of respect for their defeated hosts.

The Swedish team had done their country proud. Coached by an Englishman, George Rayner, they reached the final without losing a game. They beat Russia 2-0 in the quarter-finals, then knocked out holders West Germany 3-1. Rayner had gambled on experience, putting faith in the attacking quality of 35-year-old Nils Liedholm and 37-year-old Gunnar Gren. How they had repaid him.

Brazil had been even more impressive. Only England took a point off them in the qualifying group. In the quarter-finals, Wales goalkeeper Jack Kelsey defied them magnificently until Vava scored the only goal. Brazil's 5-2 semi-final win over France was a classic, when a new prodigy, 17-year-old Pele, presented himself to the world.

In right-back Orvar Bergmark, centre-forward

Agne Simonsson and left-winger Lennart 'Nacka' Skoglund, Sweden also had quality players .

But Brazil had quality in every position. Djalmar and Nilton Santos were the world's finest full-backs. Didi was an inspirational provider in coach Vicente Feola's revolutionary 4-2-4 system. Garrincha was a thrusting winger of genius, while Mario Zagalo preferred to play deeper. Then there was Vava – and Pele.

The Swedes risked all on a fast start. It worked for them after four minutes. Liedholm picked his way inside the box and shot past Gilmar. That lead lasted five minutes. Garrincha left Sven Axbom and Sigvard Parling for dead and crossed for Vava to level. Garrincha was causing the Swedes all sorts of problems. After 33 minutes, he burst clear again, centred, and there was Vava to score his second.

Then there was Pele. Brazil's third will forever feature among the 'Golden Goals'. Pele controlled a cross on his chest, juggled the ball to his feet, rounded a defender and volleyed past Karl Svensson. Zagalo grabbed the fourth after 68 minutes. following up his

own half-cleared corner to ram home a 15-yard shot. Simonsson finished off a clever passing move, set up by Gren, to give Sweden brief hope with ten minutes left.

But Pele had the last word. His cunning back-heel fed Zagalo, who crossed for the teenage striker to score with a looping header. It was Brazil's first World Cup final victory. But not their last.

THE GOALS

4 minutes	Nils Liedholm gives Sweden the lead
9 minutes	Vava levels
33 minutes	Vava makes it 2-1 to Brazil
55 minutes	Pele nets his first
68 minutes	Mario Zagalo hits Brazil's fourth
80 minutes	Agne Simonsson scores for Sweden
90 minutes	Pele wraps up Brazil's victory

THE TEAMS

SWEDEN: Svensson, Bergmark, Axbom, Borjesson, Gustavsson, Parling, Hamrin, Gren, Simonsson, Liedholm, Skoglund
BRAZIL: Gilmar, D.Santos, N.Santos, Zito, Bellini, Orlando, Garrincha, Didi, Vava, Pele, Zagalo

Real v Eintracht 1960

The game of the century

THE GOALS

19 minutes	Richard Kress puts Eintracht in front
26 minutes	Alfredo Di Stefano equalises
29 minutes	Di Stefano makes it 2-1
45 minutes	Ferenc Puskas scores from an amazing angle
54 minutes	Puskas scores a penalty
60 minutes	Puskas nets a rare header
72 minutes	Puskas blasts Real's sixth
74 minutes	Erwin Stein replies for Eintracht
74 minutes	Di Stefano hits Real's seventh
76 minutes	Stein grabs a late consolation

THE TEAMS

REAL MADRID: Dominguez, Marquitos, Pachin, Vidal, Santamaria, Zarraga, Canario, Del Sol, Di Stefano, Puskas, Gento
EINTRACHT FRANKFURT: Loy, Lutz, Hofer, Weilbacher, Eigenbrodt, Stinka, Kress, Lindner, Stein, Pfaff, Meier

18 May 1960, Hampden Park (European Cup final)
REAL MADRID 7 EINTRACHT FRANKFURT 3

Many who watched it maintain it was the finest exhibition of football ever seen. Real, the masters of Europe, winners of all four European Cups, against the energetic pretenders from West Germany.

Real boasted greats like Alfredo Di Stefano, Ferenc Puskas, Jose Santamaria, Luis Del Sol and Paco Gento. But the Scottish fans who packed Hampden Park knew about Eintracht's quality too. They had destroyed the Scottish Champions Rangers – including Jim Baxter – 6-1 and 6-3 in the semi-finals.

Ferenc Puskas scores Real's fourth goal from the penalty spot

Midfield general Alfred Pfaff, winger Richard Kress and centre-forward Erwin Stein were Eintracht's stars.

Kress it was who opened the scoring, beating Rogelio Dominguez from close range. Real were roused. Del Sol dominated midfield. Gento's pace stretched Eintracht's defence. And Di Stefano and Puskas took advantage. Skipper Jose Maria Zarraga sent Canario away and Di Stefano converted his centre for the equaliser. The great Argentinian blasted the second when Eintracht goalkeeper Egon Loy couldn't hold Canario's shot. Puskas's famous left foot made it 3-1 as half-time approached. That was truly a goal from nothing. Puskas had won the ball barely a yard from the goal-line on the edge of the box, and drilled his shot from there.

In the second half, Puskas was rampant. He rammed home a penalty; and even scored a goal with his head. His fourth goal was another gem. Few players would even have reached Canario's centre. But the Hungarian maestro blasted a shot just under the bar and just inside a post.

Stein replied for Eintracht. They were determined to keep fighting, but Di Stefano, the match's creative force, who had given a bravura performance, killed any hopes of a rally. Puskas played the defence-splitting pass. Di Stefano ran on and beat Loy for Real's seventh. Stein pounced on a careless back pass to salvage pride and another goal for the German Champions. They had given everything. But they knew they had been outclassed.

Little did they know it, but it was the last hurrah for a long while – for both teams. It would be six years before Real won the European Cup once more. As for Eintracht, they have never appeared again in Europe's premier club competition.

127

England v W Germany 1966

"They think it's all over..."

30 July 1966, Wembley (World Cup final)
ENGLAND 4 W GERMANY 2
(after extra time)

Stiles, Moore, Hurst and Peters parade the World Cup trophy

THE GOALS

12 minutes	The Germans take the lead through Helmut Haller
18 minutes	Geoff Hurst equalises
78 minutes	Martin Peters puts England ahead
90 minutes	Wolfgang Weber nets the rebound from a free kick, to force extra time
101 minutes	Hurst restores England's lead with one of the most controversial goals in World Cup history
120 minutes	Hurst breaks away to complete his hat-trick and make the final score 4-2

THE TEAMS

ENGLAND: Banks, Cohen, J.Charlton, Moore, Wilson, Ball, Stiles, R.Charlton, Peters, Hunt, Hurst
WEST GERMANY: Tilkowski, Hottges, Schulz, Weber, Schnellinger, Haller, Beckenbauer, Overath, Held, Seeler, Emmerich

There's a difference of opinion about the 1966 World Cup final. England fans regard it as their country's finest hour – or two hours – in football. Germans still believe their team was robbed, claiming England's match-turning third goal didn't cross the line.

TV pictures and photo evidence never proved conclusive. It was 11 minutes into extra time. England midfield dynamo Alan Ball had swept past Karlheinz Schnellinger. He crossed to the near post. Geoff Hurst swivelled and shot past keeper Hans Tilkowski. The ball cannoned off the underside of the bar and bounced down.

Roger Hunt, the nearest England player, immediately celebrated a goal. Swiss referee Gottfried Dienst wasn't so sure. Nor were the Germans. Dienst consulted Soviet linesman Tofik Bakhramov. 'Goal', said Bakhramov. Dienst pointed to the centre circle. England were in command.

The Germans piled forward. But England's last-minute answer became part of the nation's folklore. Skipper Bobby Moore broke up a German attack and freed Hurst with a long pass. His West Ham colleague ran on and hammered the ball past Tilkowski. 4-2 to England; a hat trick for Hurst. As Kenneth

Wolstenholme said in his immortal TV commentary...'Some people are on the pitch. They think it's all over. It is now!'

The result was a triumph for Hurst – who hadn't played in England's opening game – and for manager Alf Ramsey. Hurst had come in for the injured Jimmy Greaves, and scored England's winner in a bad-tempered quarter-final against Argentina. Hurst stayed in for the final, even though Greaves was fit.

That was typical of the England boss. He did things his way. Like getting rid of wingers and switching to 4-4-2 long before it was fashionable. Ball and Martin Peters became the wide midfielders. Bobby Charlton was England's midfield supremo. Alongside him was Manchester United colleague Nobby Stiles, a defender for Matt Busby, but a midfield enforcer for Ramsey. Behind them was a back four superbly marshalled by Moore; and Gordon Banks, the world's finest goalkeeper.

For the Germans, 20-year-old Franz Beckenbauer had been a sensation in midfield. Centre-forward Uwe Seeler was a national celebrity. Schnellinger and midfielder Helmut

Haller had just made their names in Italy. Dortmund's Lothar Emmerich was the Bundesliga's leading scorer.

The Germans went ahead when Haller pounced on Wilson's weak clearance. Their lead lasted six minutes, until Hurst headed England level from Moore's free-kick. With 12 minutes left, Peters made it 2-1 when he forced home the rebound after Hurst's shot was blocked after a corner.

Injury time beckoned when Dienst awarded a free kick against Jack Charlton. Emmerich blasted it. The ball rebounded off Schnellinger to Sigi Held. His attempt came back off Cohen – and Wolfgang Weber poked in the goal that forced extra time.

Ramsey was sanguine. 'You've beaten them once – now go and do it again,' he told his tired team. They did. With the help of a linesman's vision.

Celtic v Inter Milan 1967

Celtic's greatest day

THE GOALS
6 minutes   Sandro Mazzola scores a penalty
62 minutes   Tommy Gemmell equalises
83 minutes   Steve Chalmers touches in Celtic's winner

THE TEAMS
CELTIC: Simpson, Craig, Gemmell, Murdoch, McNeill, Clark, Johnstone, Wallace, Chalmers, Auld, Lennox
INTER: Sarti, Burgnich, Facchetti, Bedin, Guarneri, Picchi, Domenghini, Mazzola, Cappellini, Bicicli, Corso

Steve Chalmers celebrates his winning goal against Inter

25 May 1967, Lisbon (European Cup final)
CELTIC 2 INTERNAZIONALE 1

They have gone down in history as 'the Lisbon Lions' – the first Scottish team, the first British team, to win the European Cup.

Jock Stein had built the team painstakingly. It was almost a Glasgow District XI. None of the players were born more than 20 miles from the city centre. Yet that May late afternoon in Lisbon, they overwhelmed the side that was Europe's dominant force of the mid-1960s.

The contrasts were obvious. Celtic were young, vibrant and committed to attack. They played at a ferocious pace. Inter, winners in 1964 and 1965, were vastly experienced and committed to defence. Coach Helenio Herrera, the high priest of negative tactics, had creative talents at his disposal – Sandro Mazzola, midfield general Luis Suarez (who missed the final through injury), Angelo Domenghini and Mario Corso. He just wouldn't unleash them. How much more

might Italian football have achieved down the years, given a spirit of adventure?

Narrow 1-0 defeats in Serie A by the likes of Lanerossi and Atalanta Bergamo meant Inter finished a point behind Champions Juventus, and suggested they weren't as strong as they had been. Yet they were still capable of beating Real Madrid home and away in the quarter-finals. 'We'll annihilate them 1-0', was the joke among Celtic's 10,000 travelling fans, well aware of Inter's defensive strength.

After six minutes, Celtic knew they had to score twice. Jim Craig, the dentist at right-back, tussled with Renato Cappellini. The Inter striker went down. Referee Kurt Tschentscher said penalty. Mazzola's finish was deadly.

Typically Inter settled back to defend their lead. Stein knew Celtic had the superior stamina - and the individuals to prise open Herrera's defence. Jimmy 'Jinky' Johnstone drifted inside to torment Tarcisio Burgnich. Bobby Lennox

tied up Inter's famous left-back Giacinto Facchetti. Bobby Murdoch dominated midfield. Full-backs Craig and Tommy Gemmell piled into the space left by the wingers.

After 17 minutes of the second half, Celtic equalised. Giuliano Sarti had no chance when Gemmell met Craig's pass with a lethal 25-yarder. Inter claimed two Celtic players were offside. Tschentscher waved away their appeals.

In training, Stein demanded that Celtic attack from all over the pitch. The variety of those attacks had Inter reeling. The closing minutes became a procession towards the Inter goal. Sarti rescued them again with a desperate one-handed save from Murdoch's header.

But Celtic would not be denied. Seven minutes from time, Gemmell burst forward again. He cut a centre back for Murdoch, who shot. Centre forward Steve Chalmers stuck out a foot that deflected the ball past Sarti. The European Cup was on its way to Glasgow's East End.

Man United v Benfica 1968

Ten years on … United triumph

THE GOALS

53 minutes	Bobby Charlton scores
81 minutes	Jaime Graca equalises
92 minutes	George Best restores United's lead
95 minutes	Brian Kidd makes it 3-1
98 minutes	Charlton wraps up United's victory

THE TEAMS

MANCHESTER UNITED: Stepney, Brennan, Dunne, Crerand, Foulkes, Stiles, Best, Kidd, Charlton, Sadler, Aston

BENFICA: Henrique, Adolfo, Cruz, Graca, Humberto, Jacinto, Augusto, Coluna, Torres, Eusebio, Simoes

29 May 1968, Wembley (European Cup final)
MANCHESTER UNITED 4 BENFICA 1 (after extra time)

Brian Kidd scores United's third goal on his 19th birthday

Ever since 1956, their great manager Matt Busby had dreamed of Manchester United lifting the European Cup. That night at Wembley Busby – so close to death in the Munich disaster ten years before – realised the dream. United, buoyed by Alex Stepney's magical save from Eusebio, scored a rush of three extra time goals, to become the first English team to win the famous trophy.

United, three times previous semi-finalists , had fought back with verve to reach the final, turning a 3-1 semi-final second leg deficit at Real Madrid into a 3-3 draw. 'We're only 3-2 behind on aggregate,' said Busby at half-time.

'Let's have a go at them in the second half. We might as well lose 6-2 as 3-2!' How United responded, with goals by David Sadler and veteran defender Bill Foulkes.

Benfica had dominated the competition in the early 1960s. Great names were still there – Eusebio, the canny inside forward Mario Coluna; Jose Augusto and Antonio Simoes on the wings, the towering centre-forward Jose Torres. But they had seen better days. This was their last hurrah in a European Cup final. Even so, they proved tough opponents. Tough in more senses than one, as George Best quickly learned when Cruz fouled him early and often.

United, without the injured Denis Law, used Sadler in midfield and sat Nobby Stiles on Eusebio. Midway through the first half, Eusebio escaped his shadow and lashed a right-footed 20-yarder. Stepney was beaten all the way. It took a patriotic goal post to rescue United.

Best was kicked from pillar to post, but John Aston on the left was waltzing past Adolfo at will. It was the final ball that United had to find. Find it they did, after 53 minutes, with the most unlikely of goals. Tony Dunne picked out Sadler on the left. He crossed to the near post where Bobby Charlton rose to loop a header over Jose Henrique. This was akin to Trevor Brooking

heading the winner in a Cup final: so incredible it's passed into legend.

With time running out, Benfica went route one: high balls to the head of Torres. Nine minutes from time, Torres nodded one into the path of Jaime Graca, whose rising shot beat Stepney.

As extra time approached, Jose Henrique saved with his feet from Sadler – then Stepney pulled off the save of the match. Eusebio left Stiles again, broke into the box and smashed a left-foot shot. It might have been his weaker foot, but it was still going like a rocket. Benfica's supporters were about to acclaim the winner, when Stepney somehow arched his body, thrust out a hand and turned the ball away.

Benfica were demoralised. Extra time was all United. They killed the game with three quick goals. Brian Kidd headed on Stepney's clearance to Best, who left the Benfica back line behind him, rounded Jose Henrique and restored United's lead. Kidd himself headed the third after some penalty area pinball following a corner. It was a great way to spend his 19th birthday. Kidd set up the fourth for Charlton, cutting back a centre which the United captain blasted home. United's dream had become reality.

Celtic v Leeds 1970

The Battle of Britain

Leeds' Eddie Gray (white shirt) and Bobby Lennox dispute possession at Hampden Park in 1970

15 April 1970, Hampden Park (European Cup semi-final second leg)
CELTIC 2 LEEDS UNITED 1
(Celtic won 3-1 on aggregate)

This European Cup semi-final was billed as 'The Battle of Britain' – and Celtic deservedly won it.

Leeds could, justifiably, argue they were tired, chasing a treble of League, FA Cup and European Cup. But Don Revie's team met a Celtic side playing their best football since they won the European Cup three years earlier.

Celtic's great manager Jock Stein had done his homework as always. In the first leg at Elland Road, he drafted the brilliant young midfielder George Connelly into a 4-3-3 system, designed to nullify Leeds midfield powerhouse, Billy Bremner and John Giles. Stein's tactics worked perfectly – and Connelly scored the only goal. In the second minute, Paul Madeley failed to cut out Jimmy Johnstone's pass and Connelly drove a deflected shot past Gary Sprake.

Johnstone led Leeds a dance that night – and he did it again in front of a packed Hampden Park. Recognising the phenomenal interest in the match in Scotland, Stein had the second leg moved from Celtic Park to the much bigger national stadium. It was the perfect stage for 'Jinky', who turned England's experienced left-back Terry Cooper inside out.

Stein's trio – Bobby Murdoch, Connelly and Bertie Auld – dominated midfield again. But Leeds called on their last reserves of adrenalin. They had lost the Championship to Everton. They had drawn 2-2 against Chelsea in the FA Cup final the previous Saturday. They met Celtic's poise with desperate determination. They even took a 14th-minute lead when Bremner, himself a Scot, drove a powerful 20-yarder past Evan Williams, off a post to put Leeds level on aggregate.

Celtic poured forward. Johnstone and David Hay tirelessly worked the right flank. Jack Charlton and Norman Hunter could never pin down John 'Yogi Bear' Hughes in the centre.

Two minutes into the second half, Auld centred and Hughes rammed home a header.

Four minutes later, Johnstone set up Celtic's winner. By then David Harvey had taken over from Sprake, who'd left the field following a collision with Hughes. He had no chance as Johnstone sped to the by-line and pulled back a perfect cross for Murdoch to lash in. 3-1 on aggregate: Leeds had been counted out. It was a case of 'so near, yet so far'. They lost the Cup final replay to Chelsea too.

As for Celtic, the hot favourites failed to lift the European Cup. Stein left out Connelly and reverted to 4-2-4 for the final against Feyenoord. Wim van Hanegem dominated midfield and the Dutch side won 2-1, despite Tommy Gemmell firing Celtic ahead. But Celtic fans still remember the 'Battle of Britain' results with pride.

THE GOALS

14 minutes	Billy Bremner shoots Leeds level on aggregate
47 minutes	John Hughes levels to put Celtic ahead on aggregate
51 minutes	Bobby Murdoch hits Celtic's winner

THE TEAMS

CELTIC: Williams, Hay, Gemmell, Murdoch, McNeill, Brogan, Johnstone, Connelly, Hughes, Auld, Lennox

LEEDS: Sprake (Harvey, 48 minutes), Madeley, Cooper, Bremner, Charlton, Hunter, Lorimer (Bates, 70 minutes), Clarke, Jones, Giles, Gray

Brazil v Italy 1970

Brazil's samba con brio

Pele wheels away in celebration after scoring the opening goal in the 1970 World Cup final

THE GOALS

18 minutes	Pele heads Brazil in front
37 minutes	Roberto Boninsegna equalises for Italy
65 minutes	Gerson hits Brazil's second
70 minutes	Jairzinho makes it 3-1
86 minutes	Carlos Alberto glorious strike seals Brazil's victory

THE TEAMS

BRAZIL: Felix; Carlos Alberto, Piazza, Brito, Everaldo; Clodoaldo, Gerson, Rivelino, Jairzinho, Tostao, Pele

ITALY: Albertosi; Burgnich, Cera, Rosato, Facchetti; Domenghini, Bertini (Juliano, 73 minutes), Mazzola, De Sisti; Boninsegna (Rivera, 84 minutes), Riva

21 June 1970, Mexico City (World Cup final)
BRAZIL 4 ITALY 1

Football has rarely seen a clash of such opposites. The Brazilians were the greatest attacking side international football has ever seen. Italy were the masters of defence, unrivalled at frustrating opponents, then swooping in occasional but deadly counter-attacks.

Italy had major talents all right – Sandro Mazzola, Gianni Rivera and Gigi Riva. But coach Feruccio Valcareggi was rarely prepared to gamble on their creative instincts. No wonder that neutrals wanted Brazil to win, to shift football's emphasis from defence to attack again.

The Brazilians had been majestic on their way to the final. Neither the heat nor the altitude deterred them. Gerson, Clodoaldo and Rivelino

were magnificent in midfield. Tostao, Jairzinho – who'd scored in every match – and the incomparable Pele had run defences ragged. The question marks against Brazil were their defence, and the goalkeeper Felix. How would they cope if the opposition somehow fettered Brazil's attackers? Would Italy be that team?

The Italians were tired, desperately tired, after a gruelling semi-final against West Germany. Italy scored early, then sat back behind the ball. Karlheinz Schnellinger managed a late equaliser. Gerd Muller briefly put the Germans ahead in extra time. Somehow the Italians recovered to squeeze a 4-3 win.

The final began as expected. Brazil probed. Italy dropped back. Pele, rising at the far post, broke the deadlock, his precise header guiding a left-side cross past Enrico Albertosi. But Brazil could be careless. Clodoaldo came back to help his defenders, got in a mess with Brito, and

Roberto Boninsegna pounced on Brito's back pass for Italy's equaliser.

The Brazilians seized the initiative again. For 20 minutes of the second half, they pressed and pressed. Suddenly the ball dropped to Gerson on the edge of the box. A swift semi-turn, hardly any backlift – and the ball was nestling in the Italian net. Psychologically it was a killer blow. The drained Italians couldn't fight back a second time. Jairzinho, charging through the box like a runaway bull, finished the third from close range.

Brazil's fourth was another diamond. Pele held and held the ball, with defenders unable to rob him, until he knew Carlos Alberto was overlapping outside him. Pele's flick sent him galloping. The Brazilian skipper's joyous shot finished the job. The most exciting team doesn't always win the World Cup. They certainly did in 1970.

W Germany v Holland
1974

Total Football bombed out

Gerd Muller scores in the 1974 World Cup final

7 July 1974, Munich (World Cup final)
WEST GERMANY 2 HOLLAND 1

Gerd Muller scored many vital goals for Bayern Munich and West Germany. But none as crucial as the shot that won the World Cup final. Holland, the masters of versatility and 'total football' were laid low by the one specialist they never had: an out-and-out penalty box poacher. Muller, 'Der Bomber', was the master in that area. His 43rd-minute goal took West Germany to their first World Cup final victory for 20 years.

There had been times in the previous three weeks when triumph for Helmut Schoen's team seemed far away. They struggled to beat Chile in the opening match, and lost 1-0 to East Germany. It wasn't until they beat Sweden 4-2, a week before the final, that Schoen's men looked a force.

Schoen had stuck with two wingers – Jurgen Grabowski and Bernd Holzenbein – despite domestic criticism. He had defied popular opinion even more, by preferring Wolfgang Overath to the charismatic Gunter Netzer as his midfield general.

But he stung more effort from Uli Hoeness by dropping him against Yugoslavia – and he pulled an ace from his sleeve when he introduced Rainer Bonhof. Netzer's old Moenchengladbach colleague supplied the tackling and running power that Schoen needed. Then there was Muller.

The Dutch by contrast had sailed through the group matches with the world's praise ringing in their ears. Johan Cruyff was majestic. Johan Neeskens was a midfield inspiration. Wim van Hanegem provided a cultured left foot. The full-backs, Wim Suurbier and Ruud Krol, came forward at every opportunity. The Dutch had destroyed Brazil and Argentina in the finals. Yet one important player was missing – the Feyenoord stopper Rinus Israel, injured before the finals began. The Ajax midfield player Arie Haan dropped back to fill the gap alongside Wim Rijsbergen. Would Israel have been a more effective deterrent to Muller in the final?

Holland couldn't have had a better start. Cruyff raced into the box. Hoeness brought him down. English referee Jack Taylor pointed to the spot. Neeskens dispatched the penalty. The Dutch felt that was the only decision Taylor gave them all afternoon. As the teams walked off at half time, Cruyff angrily confronted Taylor, holding up four fingers – the number of times Cruyff reckoned Berti Vogts had kicked him without punishment.

By then, the Germans led 2-1. After 26 minutes, Holzenbein sliced into the Dutch box. He tumbled under Wim Jansen's lunge. Taylor pointed to the spot again and Paul Breitner levelled. Then came Muller's moment. Bonhof

THE GOALS

1 minute	Johan Neeskens scores a penalty
26 minutes	Paul Breitner levels from the spot
43 minutes	Gerd Muller hits Germany's winner

THE TEAMS

WEST GERMANY: Maier, Vogts, Schwarzenbeck, Beckenbauer, Breitner, Bonhof, Hoeness, Overath, Grabowski, Muller, Holzenbein
HOLLAND: Jongbloed, Suurbier, Rijsbergen (De Jong, 68 minutes), Haan, Krol, Jansen, Neeskens, van Hanegem, Rep, Cruyff, Rensenbrink (R.van der Kerkhof, H/T)

burst past Krol and reached the by-line. Muller had advanced too far to meet Bonhof's cross in stride. The ball was slightly behind him. No problem. He checked, half-turned backwards, pivoted again and buried his shot past Jan Jongbloed. Holland never got near him.

Muller had a second-half 'goal' disallowed for offside. But the second half was nearly all Dutch pressure. Johnny Rep missed twice. Sepp Maier pulled off a flying save from Neeskens' volley. Sub Rene van der Kerkhof blazed over a golden chance. So Schoen's team held out, and Beckenbauer lifted the World Cup. 'Der Bomber' had destroyed yet another team's dreams.

Liverpool v B M'Gladbach 1977

The Kop Kings of Europe

25 May 1977, Rome (European Cup final)
LIVERPOOL 3 BORUSSIA MOENCHENGLADBACH 1

During the Second World War, the Liverpool manager Bob Paisley drove into Rome as part of a liberating army. More than 24 years later, he returned at the head of Liverpool and their army of supporters, to liberate the European Cup. It was only the second time an English club had won the trophy, and Liverpool's first triumph. But it wasn't the first time Liverpool had beaten Borussia Moenchengladbach in a European final. Four years earlier, they'd overcome the Germans 3-2 on aggregate in the UEFA Cup final.

Gunter Netzer, Gladbach's midfield inspiration of those days, had left for Real Madrid. But Rainer Bonhof, Herbert Wimmer and Jupp Heynckes were still around. They'd been joined by midfield destroyer Uli Stielike, and the rapier-like little Danish forward Allan Simonsen, later to star for Charlton.

'Super-sub' David Fairclough's goal had been instrumental in Liverpool's crucial quarter-final win over highly fancied St Etienne. But Paisley's team cruised through the semi-final against Zurich – and they didn't need to call on Fairclough in Rome. Centre-half Phil Thompson was injured, so Liverpool brought in the old warhorse Tommy Smith. He would have a major role to play.

The key to Liverpool's victory was the movement of their front men, Kevin Keegan and Steve Heighway. They pulled the Gladbach

Tommy Smith rises to head Liverpool's second goal

THE GOALS

27 minutes	Terry McDermott scores
51 minutes	Allan Simonsen equalises
65 minutes	Tommy Smith makes it 2-1
82 minutes	Phil Neal scores Liverpool's third from the spot

THE TEAMS

LIVERPOOL: Clemence, Neal, Smith, Hughes, Jones, Callaghan, Case, McDermott, Kennedy, Keegan, Heighway
BORUSSIA MOENCHENGLADBACH: Kneib, Vogts, Klinkhammer, Wittkamp, Bonhof, Wohlers (Hannes, 79 minutes), Simonsen, Wimmer (Kulik, 24 minutes), Stielike, Schaefer, Heynckes

defence all over the place. Berti Vogts couldn't get close enough to Keegan to kick him. Heighway led Hans Klinkhammer a dance too. Gladbach's coach Udo Lattek also used the sluggish Hans-Jurgen Wittkamp as sweeper instead of the combative Stielike, a decision that played into Liverpool's hands.

Keegan and Heighway combined for Liverpool's opening goal. Keegan's run tore the Gladbach defence apart. 'Vogts might as well have been selling programmes,' said Paisley wryly. Terry McDermott strode into the gap, controlled Heighway's pass and poked Liverpool in front.

It was unlike Liverpool to concede silly goals. They did though, after 51 minutes. Jimmy Case miss-hit a back pass. On ran Simonsen, past despairing lunges, to beat Ray Clemence. Gladbach, encouraged, hit a brief patch of form. Clemence made a super save from Stielike. Then Liverpool took command again. Heighway swung over a corner. Two defenders followed Keegan – one of the smallest players on the pitch – and Smith loped into a yawning gap to head Liverpool's second. Eight minutes from time, Vogts hauled down Keegan in the box. Phil Neal tucked away the penalty. Liverpool were home and dry.

Argentina v Holland 1978

Argentina win World Cup at home

Mario Kempes takes on Holland's Rudi Krol in the World Cup final

THE GOALS

38 minutes	Mario Kempes gives Argentina the lead
82 minutes	Sub Dick Nanninga equalises to force extra time
104 minutes	Kempes breaks the deadlock
114 minutes	Daniel Bertoni makes sure for Argentina

THE TEAMS

ARGENTINA: Fillol, Passarella, Olguin, Galvan, Tarantini, Ardiles (Larossa, 65 minutes), Gallego, Ortiz (Houseman, 74 minutes), Bertoni, Luque, Kempes

HOLLAND: Jongbloed, Krol, Portvliet, Brandts, Jansen (Suurbier, 72 minutes), Haan, Neeskens, W.van der Kerkhof, Rep (Nanninga, 58 minutes), R.van der Kerkhof, Rensenbrink

25 June 1978, Buenos Aires (World Cup final)
ARGENTINA 3 HOLLAND 1
(after extra time)

This was the year that 'Don't cry for me, Argentina' hit number one in the British charts. But Argentinians were celebrating, not crying, when their team lifted the World Cup for the first time, after a thrilling extra-time finale against Holland. Argentina had home advantage and the backing of passionate crowds. General Galtieri, and the other military men who ran the country, used the World Cup as a showpiece to deflect world attention from the regime's human rights abuses.

If Argentinians were divided politically, then they were united in support of their team. They boasted some wonderful players – the mercurial striker Mario Kempes, winger Daniel Bertoni, midfield maestro Ossie Ardiles, and skipper Daniel Passarella, a dark, brooding defender, who loved to come forward. They had qualified for the final phase despite losing 1-0 to Italy in the group games. A 2-0 win over Poland and a goalless draw against bitter rivals Brazil left a final place still up for grabs. Wednesday, 21 June was the crucial day. In the afternoon, Brazil beat Poland 3-1. That meant Argentina had to see off Peru by four clear goals that evening to reach the final. Argentina won 6-0. 'If they'd had to score ten, they'd have done it,' said the Brazilian coach Claudio Coutinho pointedly. Argentina's coach Cesar Luis Menotti replied: 'I congratulate Brazil on their moral victory. Now I hope Coutinho will congratulate us on our real win.'

Holland had beaten Austria and Italy and drawn with West Germany to reach the final. Their only group defeat was a 3-2 reverse against eliminated Scotland, who'd saved their best for their toughest opponents. Johan Cruyff had retired from international football. But Holland still had Ruud Krol to guide them from the back and Johan Neeskens to lead, going forward.

The Argentinians delayed the kick-off for 10 minutes by objecting to a cast on the injured hand of Rene van der Kerhof. When referee Sergio Gonella passed him fit to play, the Argentinians went off like rockets. They pounded the Dutch from all angles. After 38 minutes, Leopoldo Luque and Ardiles combined on the left and the stretching Kempes toe-poked the centre past the advancing Jan Jongbloed. It was a well-deserved lead.

The Dutch were a different proposition in the second half though. Neeskens was inspirational.

He and and the van der Kerkhof brothers began to dominate midfield. Substitute Dick Nanninga added aerial presence. Eight minutes from time, Rene van der Kerkhof beat the Argentina offside trap and crossed. Nanninga outjumped Passarella and Luis Galvan to nod Holland level. The Dutch took charge. Rob Rensenbrink's shot bounced off a post with time running out. It was not fanciful to wonder about the future of Argentina's generals had that shot won the game.

Instead, the teams went to extra time. Holland had given so much. They'd shot their bolt. Fourteen minutes into the first period, Kempes produced a moment of genius, dribbling past three tackles before sweeping a low shot past Jongbloed. The tired Dutch had to press forward. As they did, Argentina caught them on the counter. With six minutes left, Kempes' pass opened up the Dutch defence and Bertoni's shot sealed Argentina's victory. Maybe 3-1 was hard on the Dutch. But Argentina had gone to town.

Italy v Brazil 1982

Adventurous Brazil pay the price

THE GOALS

5 minutes	Rossi heads Italy into the lead
12 minutes	Socrates equalises
25 minutes	Rossi makes it 2-1
68 minutes	Falcao levels again for Brazil
75 minutes	Rossi nets Italy's winner

THE TEAMS

ITALY: Zoff, Gentile, Collovatti (Bergomi, 34 minutes), Scirea, Cabrini, Tardelli (Marini, 76 minutes), Antognoni, Oriali, Conti, Graziani, Rossi
BRAZIL: Valdir Peres, Leandro, Oscar, Luizinho, Junior, Cerezo, Socrates, Zico, Falcao, Serginho (Paulo Isidoro, 69 minutes), Eder

Paolo Rossi scores for Italy
watched by the Brazilian fans

**5 July 1982, Barcelona (Estadio Sarria)
(World Cup finals)
BRAZIL 2 ITALY 3**

In the end, it was simple. Paolo Rossi's hat-trick won the game for Italy. But Brazil's foolhardiness lost them a prize that was there for the taking. Italy went on to beat West Germany 3-1 in a one-sided Final. How the Brazilians must have kicked themselves, after letting that afternoon slip away.

Once they pulled back to 2-2, they knew they were through to the semi-finals. More cynical teams would have sat on that score. But Brazil wanted to win. In Zico, Socrates and Falcao, they had three of the world's greatest creative players. Their flowing skills gave pleasure to millions.

Yet Brazil were undone by a man who'd only recently returned from a two-year ban after being involved in a bribery scandal - Rossi.

Italy were tough at the back, tough in midfield - with Giancarlo Antognoni the schemer - and hugely reliant on Rossi and Francesco Graziani for goals. They had stumbled through the opening group, drawing all three matches. Come the final phases, they were a different team, vibrant against Argentina when Marco Tardelli and Antonio Cabrini scored in a 2-1 win. But the odds were still against them as they met Brazil for a semi-final place.

The Brazilians had beaten Scotland and the Soviet Union on their way through. Zico, Serginho and Junior scored as they hammered Argentina 3-1 in their opening game of the second round matches. They had superior goal difference. All they needed was to avoid defeat against Italy. Brazil had the best attacking midfielders. But their defence was suspect, especially on crosses - and Serginho and Eder were hardly successors to the great Brazilian forwards of the past.

Even so, Brazil should have qualified. Typically, the Brazilian back line was sleeping when Rossi nodded home Cabrini's centre to give Italy a second-minute lead. Socrates raced on to Zico's through ball to equalise. Brazil in control now? No. Cerezo's defensive blunder presented Rossi with a second.

Falcao levelled midway through the second half, wrong-footing the defence before firing home a left-foot shot. Then Brazil threw it away. With 15 minutes left, Junior failed to clear a corner and Rossi cracked home the loose ball from inside the box. This time Brazil could not recover.

Rossi's hat-trick has gone in history. But Italy owed nearly as much to goalkeeper Dino Zoff. He made save after save from Zico, Socrates and Falcao. So Italy advanced to a semi-final win over Poland then the biggest prize of all. And the Brazilians artistry was sorely missed in those final matches.

Holland v W Germany 1988

Dutch defeat old enemy

**21 June 1988, Hamburg (European Championship semi-final)
HOLLAND 2 WEST GERMANY 1**

'O wat zijn de Duitsers stil?' The Dutch version of 'Can you hear the Germans sing?' ran round Hamburg's Volkspark.

Somehow the Dutch fans had taken over a German stadium. And somehow their team had come from behind to beat a German side that never lost in the closing minutes.

The Dutch were allocated 6,000 tickets in the 61,000 capacity stadium. It was like old England-Scotland games at Wembley. The Scots officially received about 10 per cent of the tickets, but they outnumbered the English come kick-off. The Dutch had a song for it, referring to the German occupation of Holland in 1940: 'In 1940 they came. In 1988, we came.' How the Dutch fans snaffled so many tickets, no-one knows even now. The German midfielder Frank Mill summed up the effect on the 'home' team. 'I think it would have been better if we'd played in Germany,' he said sardonically.

As Simon Kuper wrote in his book *Football Against The Enemy*: 'Hamburg was not only the Resistance we never quite offered (in the war) but also the battle we never quite won.' On the pitch, Ronald Koeman had summed up Holland's problem. 'The Germans aren't as good as us,' he told his team mates. 'But it's when you have to play them that things get hard.'

In the first half, the Dutch, inspired by Ruud

Rijkaard (17) protests his innocence as the referee awards Germany a penalty for a foul on Klinsmann

THE GOALS
54 minutes — Lothar Matthaus scores with a penalty
74 minutes — Marco Van Basten equalises with another spot-kick
87 minutes — Van Basten slots the winner

THE TEAMS
WEST GERMANY: Immel, Kohler, Herget (Pflugler, 44 minutes), Borowka, Rolff, Mill (Litbarski, 84 minutes), Matthaus, Thon, Brehme, Voller, Klinsmann
HOLLAND: van Breukelen, van Aerle, R.Koeman, Rijkaard, van Tiggelen, Vanenburg, Wouters, E.Koeman (Suvrijn, 90 minutes), Muhren (Kieft, 57 minutes), Gullit, van Basten

Gullit and Frank Rijkaard played sublime football, creating chance after chance – and scorning them all. Coach Rinus Michels was tearing out what remained of his hair. In the second half, the Germans came out with new tactics – to kick Dutchmen. Those tactics seemed to work. Romanian referee Ion Igna

couldn't control the conflagration. Nine minutes after the interval, Jurgen Klinsmann fell over Rijkaard's legs in the Holland box. Igna gave a penalty. Lothar Matthaus scored and Holland were incensed.

Twenty minutes later, Igna evened it up. Marco van Basten ran on to Ronald Koeman's pass. Jurgen Kohler challenged him inside the penalty area. The Dutch forward collapsed and Igna pointed to the spot. 'He caught me off balance,' smiled van Basten, who dispatched the penalty. It seemed another harsh decision, yet natural justice had been done.

Three minutes were left when Jan Wouters burst on to another Koeman through ball and picked out van Basten. As Eike Immel came out, van Basten slid the ball across him into the corner of the net. It was Holland's first win over West Germany in 32 years.

The Dutch went on to thrash the Soviet Union in the final. But no victory gave them greater satisfaction than beating the Germans.

Liverpool v Arsenal 1989

Arsenal's last-minute League title

THE GOALS

52 minutes	Alan Smith heads Arsenal's first
90 minutes	Mickey Thomas hits the winner

THE TEAMS

LIVERPOOL: Grobbelaar, Ablett, Staunton, Nicol, Whelan, Hansen, Houghton, Aldridge, Rush (Beardsley, 32 minutes), Barnes, McMahon

ARSENAL: Lukic, Dixon, Winterburn, Thomas, O'Leary, Adams, Rocastle, Richardson, Smith, Bould (Groves, 78 minutes), Merson (Hayes, 75 minutes)

Thomas flicks the ball past a diving Grobbelaar for the winner

26 May 1989, Anfield (League match)
LIVERPOOL 0 ARSENAL 2

'It's up for grabs now... Thomas!' Brian Moore's commentary will be re-played as long as English football lives: the moment that Mickey Thomas's goal won the Championship for Arsenal in the most dramatic title finale ever.

Delight for Arsenal...and a traumatic end to one of the most traumatic seasons in Liverpool's history. They came from mid-table in mid-season to overtake the Gunners in the League. They had already beaten deadly rivals Everton in the FA Cup final. But those feats had been cast into shadow by one tragic afternoon – when more than 90 Liverpool fans died in the tragedy that will forever be known in one word: Hillsborough. The families still fight for justice. Liverpool staff attended every funeral. After Hillsborough, football took on a different meaning. Lord Justice Taylor's report would change the face of English football.

Many of the packed Anfield crowd that night

had relatives or friends who'd died at Hillsborough. Maybe that's why the Liverpool fans were generous in applauding Arsenal at the end. They understood from bitter experience, there were more brutal realities than winning championships. But Arsenal's achievement was immense. Title leaders for most of the season, George Graham's men had faded at the last. A 2-1 home defeat by Derby and a 2-2 draw against Wimbledon left them needing to win by two goals at Anfield to take the title on goals scored (the goal difference would be equal).

Before the game, Arsenal presented a cheque for £30,000 to the Hillsborough Disaster Fund. Once the first whistle blew, though, the goodwill ended. Kevin Richardson had said that, to win, Arsenal had to subdue Liverpool's midfield powerhouse Steve McMahon. They did. The longer it went on, the more Richardson, Thomas and David Rocastle controlled midfield. Lee Dixon marked John Barnes out of the match. Graham's three centre-backs dominated the Liverpool attack.

The injured Ian Rush was taken off and replaced by Beardsley.

The Gunners played with an incredible passion. But the teams were still goalless at half-time. Graham had forecast that. He'd privately predicted that Arsenal would score early in the second half, then grab a late decider. Clairvoyant or what? After 52 minutes, the top division's leading scorer, Alan Smith, made the breakthrough, reacting first to glance home Nigel Winterburn's free-kick while Liverpool defenders stood like statues.

Yet, for all Arsenal's pressure, time began to run out. Another image remains: of McMahon asking the referee how long was left, then holding up one finger. The seconds ticked away. Goalkeeper John Lukic threw out to Dixon. Dixon found target man Smith like he'd been doing all season. 'Smudge' flicked the ball on. On ran Thomas. 'It's up for grabs now.' Thomas buried a shot beyond Bruce Grobbelaar, then turned somersaults towards the Gunners fans. Arsenal were Champions.

England v Germany 1990

England go out on the spot

Gary Lineker scores against Germany in the 1990 semi-final

4 July 1990, Turin (World Cup semi-final)
ENGLAND 1 WEST GERMANY 1
(Germany won 4-3 on penalties)

England fans will always remember this game for two incidents – the penalty shoot-out, and Paul Gascoigne's tears. Gazza's emotions that night have filled TV screens ever since. There he is, clattering into Thomas Berthold. The German coaches and substitutes jump to their feet. Brazilian referee Jose Ramiz Wright reaches for the yellow card. It's Gazza's second of the competition. He realises he won't be able to play if England reach the Final, and the tears begin to well up. It was a mistimed tackle rather than a nasty one. But the groans of English reaction show how important Gazza had become to England's cause.

As in 1986, Bobby Robson got it right at the end of the first stage, after listening to the players. The group had been tough and dour. England squeezed through by drawing against Holland and Ireland and pipping Egypt 1-0. Wins over Cameroon - thanks to Gary Lineker's cool finishing - and Belgium (when David Platt netted a spectacular extra-time winner) had taken England to the cusp of glory. And Gazza was England's surprise package. Robson once affectionately called

him: 'Daft as a brush.' But his creative talent was vital to England's hopes.

The Germans, as ever, had advanced steadily. They never showed their hand until the final stages. They had beaten Yugoslavia 4-1 and the United Arab Emirates 5-1 and drawn 1-1 with Colombia in their group games. Then they knocked out Czechoslovakia to reach the showdown with England.

Robson played three at the back – Mark Wright, Terry Butcher and Des Walker. The England full-backs, Paul Parker and Stuart Pearce, tucked in to support them. It was cat-and-mouse football. Neither side wanted to take a chance. Then, in the 59th minute, Germany got a free-kick on the edge of the box. Andreas Brehme whacked it. The ball struck the unlucky Parker, looped over Peter Shilton's head, and England were one down.

They had to go for it now. Ten minutes from time, Parker's cross caught three German defenders on the hop. Klaus Augenthaler, Thomas Berthold and Kohler were stranded. In raced Lineker, to drive home a close-range shot that kept England alive. Extra time couldn't separate two tired teams, although Waddle hit a post with the goalie beaten. The game had to

THE GOALS

| 59 minutes | Andreas Brehme scores from a deflected free kick |
| 80 minutes | Gary Lineker scores to take the tie into extra time |

THE TEAMS

ENGLAND: Shilton, Parker, Wright, Walker, Butcher (Steven, 69 minutes), Pearce, Gascoigne, Platt, Waddle, Beardsley, Lineker
WEST GERMANY: Illgner, Buchwald, Kohler, Augenthaler, Brehme, Berthold, Matthaus, Hassler (Reuter, 66 minutes), Thon, Voller (Riedle, 36 minutes), Klinsmann

THE PENALTY SHOOT OUT

Gary Lineker (1-0); Andreas Brehme (1-1); Peter Beardsley (2-1); Lothar Matthaus (2-2); David Platt (3-2); Karlheinz Riedle (3-3); Stuart Pearce (saved, 3-3); Olaf Thon (3-4); Chris Waddle (missed, 3-4)

be settled by penalties. The World Cup semi-final had become a lottery.

Lineker despatched England's first kick. Brehme replied for Germany. Peter Beardsley scored. Lothar Matthaus equalised. David Platt shot England's third. Karlheinz Riedle 3-3. Then Bodo Illgner flung himself to save Pearce's blast – and Olaf Thon kept his composure to give Germany the lead.

The pressure was heaped on Chris Waddle. He'd played with such style. Now he had to keep England in the World Cup. He fired. The ball flew over the bar. The Germans were through. They beat a defensive Argentina 1-0 in the final – while England watched and wondered what might have been.

Czech Republic v Germany

1996

Golden Goal bounces Czechs

**30 June 1996, Wembley (European
Championship final)
CZECH REPUBLIC 1 GERMANY 2
(after extra time)**

History was made at Wembley that June
evening. Germany became the first team to win
a major final thanks to a 'Golden Goal'. UEFA had
decreed that, if extra time were needed in the
final, the winners would be the team that
scored first. Twenty years before, the old
Czechoslovakia had beaten the old West
Germany on penalties – after extra time – in
the final in Belgrade. Ivo Viktor, the Czech
goalkeeping hero that night was coach Dusan
Uhrin's assistant at Wembley.

In 1976, Czechs and Slovaks had played
together. There were no Slovaks in the line-up
20 years on. Four years earlier, the Slovaks had
voted to leave the federation set up after the
'Velvet Revolution'.

Re-united Germany could call on players from
the old east, like the Dresden-born Matthias
Sammer. The Germans held a psychological
advantage too: they'd beaten the Czechs 2-0 in
their opening group game, when Christian
Ziege was outstanding.

It was a dour competition, with few goals and
many penalty shoot-outs. But the Czechs had
grown in stature as it went on. Karel Poborsky
became a player to admire - and scored a
sensational quarter-final winner against
Portugal. His Slavia colleague Patrik Berger was
another exciting young talent. So was the left-
side midfielder Pavel Nedved from rivals Sparta.

Bierhoff equalises for Germany

Borussia Dortmund sweeper Sammer, heir to
the tradition of Franz Beckenbauer, was
Germany's guiding light. Thomas Hassler
supplied the midfield spark. Ex-Spur Jurgen
Klinsmann was the cutting edge, though he
would be eclipsed by Oliver Bierhoff at
Wembley.

Both teams reached the final via penalties. On
the Wednesday afternoon, Kadlec's spot kick
took the Czechs through against France. In the
evening the Germans – for the second time in
six years – denied England a place in a major
final on a penalty shoot-out too.

The contest was too tense for neutrals to enjoy.
Neither side wanted to take a chance. It took a
penalty to bring the game to life. After 58
minutes, Sammer checked Poborsky on the
edge of the box. The Germans claimed the foul
was outside. Italian referee Pierluigi Pairetto
pointed to the penalty spot. Berger drove the
kick past Andreas Kopke. Eleven minutes later,
German coach Berti Vogts pulled his master
stroke. He sent on striker Bierhoff for midfielder
Mehmet Scholl and gambled on attack. Within
four minutes, Bierhoff nodded home Ziege's
free kick for Germany's equaliser.

THE GOALS

58 minutes	Patrik Berger shoots the Czechs ahead from the penalty spot
73 minutes	Sub Oliver Bierhoff levels
95 minutes	Bierhoff's shot takes a deflection and wins the game for Germany

THE TEAMS
CZECH REPUBLIC: Kouba, Hornak, Suchoparek,
Kadlec, Rada, Poborsky (Smicer, 88 minutes),
Nemec, Bejbl, Nedved, Kuka, Berger
GERMANY: Kopke, Babbel, Sammer, Strunz,
Helmer, Ziege, Hassler, Eilts (Bode, h/t), Scholl
(Bierhoff, 69 minutes), Klinsmann, Kuntz

Bierhoff was even more decisive in extra time.
Five minutes had gone when he shot from the
edge of the box. The ball struck Czech defender
Hornak on the heel and spun from the hands of
goalkeeper Petr Kouba. Kouba had lost
concentration because he thought linesman
Donato Nicoletti had already flagged German
forward Stefan Kuntz offside. The Czechs
protested long and loud. But Pairetto overruled
Nicoletti. Germany were European champions –
thanks to the first-ever 'Golden Goal'.

Liverpool v Newcastle 1996

Stan Collymore seals seven-goal thriller

Robbie Fowler heads in Liverpool's first goal

3 April 1996, Anfield
(Premiership match)
LIVERPOOL 4
NEWCASTLE UNITED 3

Stan Collymore's last-minute winner effectively killed Newcastle's hopes of their first Championship since 1927. By Christmas, Kevin Keegan's team had built a seven-point lead over Manchester United. But a 2-0 new year defeat at Old Trafford heralded a slide for the Geordies.

Should Newcastle have sacrificed some attacking flair for defensive strength? Was Keegan right to bring in Colombian striker Faustino Asprilla from Parma, when Newcastle had been so impressive in the opening months? Should Lee Clark and Keith Gillespie – unused subs that night – have played more often? The debates continue on Tyneside.

What no-one doubted was Newcastle's role as the most exciting team in the Premiership. Manchester United had caught up in the Championship race. But a Newcastle win would take them level on points with United, with a game in hand.

THE GOALS

2 minutes	Fowler puts Liverpool ahead
10 minutes	Ferdinand levels
14 minutes	Ginola makes it 2-1 to Newcastle
57 minutes	Fowler equalises
60 minutes	Asprilla restores Newcastle's lead
63 minutes	Collymore pegs Newcastle back
90 minutes	Collymore hits the winner

THE TEAMS

LIVERPOOL: James, Jones (Rush, 85 minutes), Wright (Harkness, h/t), Ruddock, Scales, McAteer, McManaman, Redknapp, Barnes, Collymore, Fowler
NEWCASTLE: Srnicek, Watson, Howey (Peacock, 81 minutes), Albert, Beresford, Lee, Batty, Beardsley, Ginola, Asprilla, Ferdinand

Liverpool manager Roy Evans began with three centre-backs – Mark Wright, Neil Ruddock and John Scales – to combat Asprilla and Les Ferdinand. And Liverpool made a flying start. Robbie Fowler headed them into a second-minute lead from Collymore's cross. But it took Newcastle just eight minutes to equalise. Asprilla beat Ruddock and found Ferdinand, whose shot ripped through David James' grasp. Four minutes later, David Ginola held off Jason McAteer and steered Ferdinand's through ball past James. More pragmatic title-contenders would have packed midfield and defence and made sure they hung on. Not Newcastle. They wanted to create, and they gave Liverpool room to create. The home side took advantage after 57 minutes, when Fowler met Steve McManaman's cross with a first time shot to equalise. Now the teams traded goals. The Geordies scored within three minutes. Asprilla raced on to Rob Lee's pass and drove a low right footer past the advancing James. That lead lasted just three minutes too. Collymore darted in between goalkeeper Pavel Srnicek and Steve Howey to tuck away McAteer's cross.

Newcastle could have sat on the draw and hoped to win their game in hand. Instead they kept attacking. James was by far the busier goalkeeper. As Keegan's team pressed for a winner, sub Ian Rush and John Barnes combined to find Collymore inside the box. Collymore shot left-footed. Srnicek was beaten on his near post. Newcastle had no time to fight back. Neutrals would say it had been thrilling entertainment. But Newcastle fans weren't smiling at the finish.

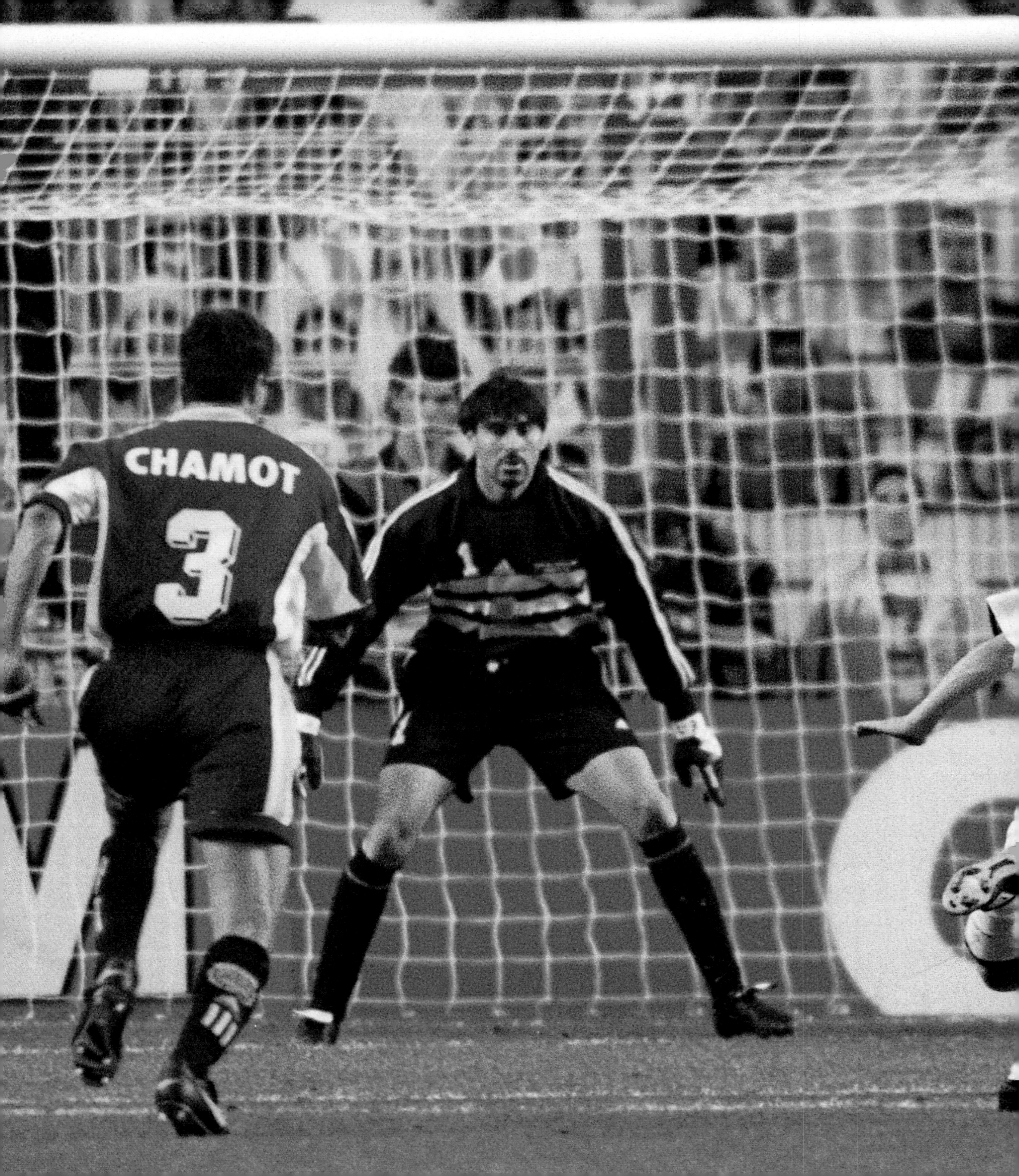
CHAMOT
3

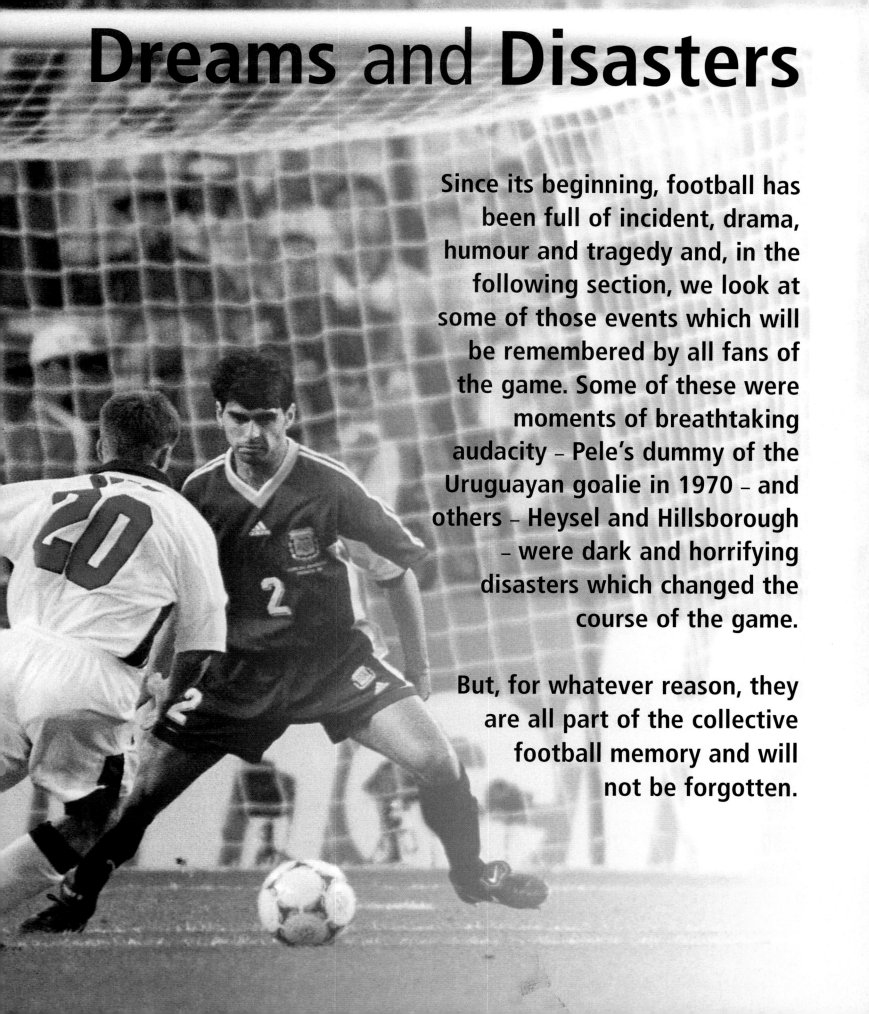

Dreams and Disasters

Since its beginning, football has been full of incident, drama, humour and tragedy and, in the following section, we look at some of those events which will be remembered by all fans of the game. Some of these were moments of breathtaking audacity – Pele's dummy of the Uruguayan goalie in 1970 – and others – Heysel and Hillsborough – were dark and horrifying disasters which changed the course of the game.

But, for whatever reason, they are all part of the collective football memory and will not be forgotten.

Wembley 1923

The White Horse final

The crowd spills onto the pitch, delaying the start of the 1923 final

The FA Cup final had been played at ten grounds, including replays, in its first 51 years, starting at Kennington Oval in 1872 and ending at Stamford Bridge in 1922. In 1923 a new stadium was completed at Wembley for the British Empire Exhibition of 1924. Two years earlier the FA had signed a 21-year agreement with the authorities to hold the Cup final there from 1923.

It was estimated 127,000 could be accommodated in the magnificent new stadium. As the average attendance for Cup finals was around 70,000, and only twice before, in 1901 and 1913, had 100,000 been exceeded, it was not thought necessary to sell all tickets in advance and no special traffic arrangements were made.

But the attraction of a new ground, and a London club, West Ham United, reaching the final (then a rare occurrence), drew well over 200,000 fans, and barriers and turnstiles were over-run. At 3 o'clock, when the match should have started, hundreds were on the pitch. Police hastily called for reinforcements.

A detachment of mounted police arrived at kick-off time. Among them were a man and a horse who became famous, Constable G.A. Scorey and the all-white Billie.

Although there were 12 inspectors, 53 sergeants and 530 policemen trying to clear the pitch, Billie's whiteness shone like a torch in the newsreel film and photos and highlighted his industry. Constable Scorey said:'I felt like giving it up as hopeless.....there was nobody in charge. Anyway Billie knew what to do. He pushed forward quietly but firmly and the crowd made way for him.....they seemed to respect the horse'. The arrival of King George V, and the playing of the national anthem, helped persuade the crowds to the touchlines, and play eventually began at 3.46 p.m.

Bolton Wanderers were West Ham's opponents and with goals from David Jack at three minutes, and J.R. Smith at 55, they won 2-0. Legend has it that the second goal came after the Bolton winger, Ted Vizard, received a wall-pass from a spectator on the touchline, but he denied this. It is true though that wingers taking corners had to plead for a yard of space to swing their legs, and the second goal deceived many fans because the ball came

straight back into play from the spectators behind the net, and was scrambled away. Referee D.H. Asson luckily saw what happened.

The surface, which started green but soft, became a mass of churned-up mud caused by horses' hooves and fans' feet, and apparently clearers-up next day found several banknotes among the tons of litter, broken bottles and twisted metal on the pitch. Questions were asked in the House about the danger to individuals, and Billie and Constable Scorey were cheered for their good work.

The official paying attendance at Wembley was 126,047, but it was estimated that over 200,000 were present. The following year saw the first all-ticket final, and the attendance was limited to 91,695.

Date:	**28 April 1923**
Venue:	**Wembley Stadium**
Event:	**First-ever Wembley Cup final,**
	Bolton Wanderers 2
	West Ham United 0

Wembley Stadium took 300 working days to build and cost £750,000. It was finished only four days before the 1923 Cup final, after an infantry battalion had marked time on the terraces to test their strength. Previously the site was a golf course and a heronry, causing the concrete to be covered by herons' footprints. An accompanying tower like the Eiffel Tower in Paris was begun but abandoned. In 1999 plans were going ahead for the complete rebuilding of Wembley into a national stadium.

Munich 1958

The death of the dream

Bill Foulkes (left) and Harry
Gregg, survivors of the
crash, survey the wreckage

Date: 6 February 1958
Venue: Munich airport
Event: Manchester United's plane
crashes on take-off returning
from a European Cup tie in
Belgrade.

The following season UEFA, as a gesture of
respect, invited Manchester United to take part in
the 1958-59 European Cup together with Wolves,
the new Champions. But the Football League
refused, perhaps not forgetting that it was against
the League directive that Busby and United had
entered European competition in the first place.

The magnificent Manchester United side which
won the Championship in 1955-56 was
nicknamed 'The Busby Babes', after the
manager, Matt Busby. Their average age was
only 22 – in fact it was the youngest side ever
to win the title. The next year, 1956-57, they
won again, and were robbed of the first 20th-
century 'double' only by losing their goalkeeper
to injury after six minutes of the Cup final. In
those pre-substitute days they fought on with
the centre-half in goal, and succumbed to
Aston Villa only by 2-1.

The word 'tragedy' appeared in the reports, but
was put in perspective almost exactly eight
months later when real tragedy struck in
Munich.

At that time United were England's finest club
side. On 1 February 1958, with their sights set
on a hat-trick of Championships, plus the FA
Cup, and the European Cup, United went to
Highbury and in a pulsating, unforgettable
League match before 63,000 fans beat Arsenal
5-4. The same side were in Belgrade four days
later for the second leg of a European Cup
quarter-final: Harry Gregg, Bill Foulkes, Roger
Byrne, Eddie Colman, Mark Jones, Duncan
Edwards, Ken Morgans, Bobby Charlton, Tommy

Taylor, Dennis Viollet and Albert Scanlon.
Missing for one reason or another, but in the
party, were regulars Ray Wood, David Pegg,
Johnny Berry and Liam Whelan.

With a 2-1 lead from the first leg, United were
ahead 3-0 by half-time in Belgrade, but then
had to fight hard as Red Star came back in the
second half to force a 3-3 draw. United's 5-4
aggregate win earned a semi-final place and a
match with AC Milan.

On the way home, the twin-engined
Elizabethan plane stopped to refuel at Munich
airport. Its take-off in snowy conditions was
aborted within seconds because of boost
surging – an over-acceleration of the engines
because of too-rich fuel mixture. Three
minutes later a second take-off was similarly
aborted. After 20 minutes a third attempt was
made but the plane failed to get up and left
the runway, crossing a road to strike a house, a
tree and a hut containing fuel, which exploded.
Of the crew, players, officials, reporters and
others on board, 23 were to die and 20
survived.

Of the great team, Roger Byrne, Geoff Bent,
Mark Jones, David Pegg, Liam Whelan, Eddie

Colman and Tommy Taylor died instantly.
Duncan Edwards and Johnny Berry were
critically injured. Edwards died a couple of
weeks later in a Munich hospital. Berry
recovered but, like Jackie Blanchflower, was
never to play again. Matt Busby, the manager,
was in a critical condition for some weeks in
hospital. He returned home in April, eventually
resumed as manager and later became a
director and president of the club.

With a hastily bought side, United returned to
football with a Cup win over Sheffield
Wednesday two weeks after the tragedy, and
they reached the Cup final again, but lost to
Bolton. Bill Foulkes and Harry Gregg were the
only survivors of the crash to play against
Wednesday, but Charlton, Morgans and Viollet
appeared again before the season's end.

Pele 1970

Moments of genius in Mexico

Pele wrote a book called 'My Life and the Beautiful Game'. The world 'beautiful' is no accident. He regarded football as an art form. He did not want only to win, but to win in stylish and artistic fashion. And since scoring a goal is the climax of soccer artistry, the height of his ambition was to score the perfect goal, the goal which would always be remembered and talked about as the greatest moment in soccer history.

Pele's search for the great goal centred itself upon the World Cup, the biggest stage in sport. In four finals tournaments he scored 12 goals, third in the list behind Gerd Muller and Just Fontaine. His best-known came in the 1958 World Cup final against Sweden, scored when he was only 17 years old. Full-back Djalma Santos sent a long diagonal cross from the left towards the penalty spot where Pele was waiting with his back to goal, closely marked by two defenders. He trapped the ball on his chest and dropped it to his instep, immediately flicking it over his head and over his marker, turning between the two defenders to volley the ball home.

But despite this virtuoso goal, perhaps Pele will best be remembered for three attempts at goal which failed. They all came in the 1970 World Cup finals, after injury had ruined his 1962 and 1966 appearances.

Pele had noticed that European goalkeepers tended to stray from their goal when the ball was in the opponents' half. In Brazil's first game against Czechoslovakia, he tried to exploit this. Receiving the ball well inside his

Pele playing for Santos in the late 1970s. His talent for the unexpected remained with him throughout his career.

Date:	17 June 1970
Venue:	Jalisco Stadium, Guadalajara
Event:	World Cup semi-final, Brazil 3 Uruguay 1

Pele scored 1,281 goals, second in the all-time list. He said: 'I am not proud that I can sometimes make goals out of nothing. It makes me humble because it is a talent that God gave me. All I can do is use it well.'

own half, he saw Viktor well out and to the side of his goal, and without warning launched a terrific shot from around 60 yards. Viktor scrambled back, but was unable to reach the ball which, unfortunately for Pele, just missed the angle of bar and post.

Viktor was one of the world's best keepers, as was Mazurkiewicz of Uruguay, Brazil's semi-final opponents. Once again Pele had spotted a goalkeeping habit – after a save, Mazurkiewicz would often kick the ball from hand to a full-back inside his own half. Seizing his chance, a loitering and uninterested-looking Pele suddenly raced past the full-back, reached the ball first and let fly at goal, forcing a great save from the startled Mazurkiewicz.

The best effort of all, perhaps, but less well documented, possibly because skipper Carlos Alberto did not altogether approve of its extravagance, was Pele's outrageous dummy on the goalkeeper in the same match. A diagonal cross from the left found Pele rushing to meet the ball near the edge of the area, while Mazurkiewicz was dashing from goal to get there first. As both men and the ball arrived together Pele feinted to play the ball to Mazurkiewics's right and sped past on that side. He completely fooled the goalie by letting the ball run on.

Then having passed the goalie at speed, Pele changed direction, caught the ball near the by-line and screwed it back towards goal from a narrow angle. Again, unfortunately for him, it just missed the far post, three exciting near-misses in Pele's quest for the perfect goal.

Banks' Save 1970

The greatest save ever

Banks scoops the ball over
the bar from Pele's header

Pele said: 'At that moment I hated Banks more than any man in football. I just couldn't believe it. But when I cooled down I had to applaud him with all my heart. It was the greatest save I had ever seen.'

Soon afterwards Banks foiled Pele again with another great save from a free-kick, but in the second half Pele laid on the only goal of the match for Jairzinho.

It was one of the best matches of the tournament, and English fans hoped the two teams would meet again in the final, but with Banks absent with a stomach upset England surrendered a two-goal lead to lose to West Germany in the quarter-final. Brazil won the Cup.

Pele's final opinion on Banks was: 'For me Banks was the leading goalkeeper of the 1970 games, and quite possibly the leading defender in any position.

The two best teams in the 1970 World Cup finals were arguably England, the 1966 winners, and Brazil, who went on to win in 1970. Moreover, they sported on one side the player regarded as the best in the world, Pele, and on the other the goalkeeper regarded as the best in the world, Gordon Banks. The two countries were drawn in the same group, and after each had won their opening games they faced each other at Guadalajara. The great attacker found himself facing the great defender, and after only ten minutes the two came together in one of football's most memorable moments.

Jairzinho, Brazil's right-winger, collected the ball near the touchline inside England's half and set off down the wing. He accelerated past his marker, Terry Cooper, on the outside, cut in, and from the edge of the area near the byline sent a perfect cross towards the far post.

Banks was guarding the near post, while Pele and his marker, Alan Mullery, were running in towards the far post. Pele was ideally placed to meet the ball in his run, and seeing Banks

stranded at his left post, leapt high, met the ball on the centre of his forehead, and directed a powerful header down to bounce just before the line and just inside the right-hand post.

Banks described his view: 'As Jairzinho chipped the ball over, I started back across the goal. Halfway across I was sure the ball was too high for anyone to reach, but then I saw Pele. He seemed to climb higher and higher until he got the ball on his forehead, putting everything behind it.'

Pele was already shouting 'Goal' and everybody watching must have thought he'd scored. But Banks' sprint across goal ended with a dive towards the bottom corner. As the ball bounced a couple of feet in front of goal and rose towards the net, so Banks' outstretched right hand managed to reach it and scoop it upwards almost vertically. The ball went away over the bar. It took the television replays to show exactly what happened. At the time itself, at normal speed, Banks' save looked like a conjuring trick.

Date:	7 June 1970
Venue:	Jalisco Stadium, Guadalajara
Event:	World Cup group match, Brazil 1 England 0

In 1966 and 1970 Gordon Banks played in nine consecutive matches in World Cup finals, England winning seven, drawing one and losing to Brazil in perhaps his greatest match. In those nine games he conceded only four goals, and one of those was a penalty from Eusebio.

Charlie **George** 1971

Charlie George lets rip for the winning goal

Charlie lies on Wembley turf

Date:	8 May 1971
Venue:	**Wembley Stadium**
Event:	**FA Cup final, Arsenal 2 Liverpool 1 (after extra time)**

The Wembley scoreboard, the commentators and the Sunday papers all credited Arsenal's equaliser to George Graham. But football history was changed with London Weekend Television's Sunday afternoon recording of the match, which proved that Graham had not touched the ball as it passed Clemence.

In the last decade of the 20th century so much football was being televised in Britain that the fanatical follower at some time or another could see not only almost every goal scored in League and Cup football, but most of the goal celebrations which followed them. Some players went to town with outrageous goal routines, and at some clubs the players rehearsed little group tableaux to express their collective joy at a goal.

However the goal celebration which most fans over 40 will claim was the most memorable of all was the simple, spontaneous act of Charlie George lying prone, arms upraised, on the Wembley turf after the great goal which secured Arsenal's 'double' in 1971. It came during extra time of an energy-sapping FA Cup final against Liverpool.

Charlie George was a charismatic player. He was only 20, a local Islington lad who had been signed at 17 and who had made his debut the season before the 'double'. He was a tall, callow youth, with long, dank hair, who looked as if he should be propping up a dance-hall wall rather than playing at Wembley. But there was a touch of genius about his play, and he was always capable of the imaginative and exciting. He also packed a terrific shot. He cared for nobody, and his enemies called him conceited, peevish and arrogant. But the fans loved him.

Arsenal crept up on the 'double' in 1970-71. Leeds United, the dominant side of the era, gave Arsenal a chance of the Championship by losing at home to lowly West Bromwich Albion to a very controversial 'offside' goal which caused the fans to riot. Arsenal needed to win their last League match at White Hart Lane and did so 1-0, to become Champions by a point. In the Cup semi-final, they had rescued themselves with an injury-time penalty after being two down to Stoke, and won the replay.

The final at Wembley was a hard, defensive slog for 90 minutes, without a goal. In extra time Steve Heighway scored for Liverpool and Eddie Kelly equalised for Arsenal.

Charlie George's golden 'double'-winning moment came in the 111th minute. Liverpool keeper Ray Clemence sent a goalkick towards the Arsenal half but it was immediately headed back towards the Gunners' centre-forward John Radford, a few yards inside both the Liverpool half and the left-hand touchline. Radford nodded the ball forwards and inside to where George was standing, closely marked by Tommy Smith. George volleyed a wall-pass back to Radford, by now advancing up the wing. For the first time since the goalkick, the ball touched the ground as Radford cut inside his marker, Chris Lawler. Tommy Smith went across to tackle him, enabling Radford to slip a short pass inside to the now unmarked George, who had advanced to a few yards outside the box. With Lawler coming across from his left and Larry Lloyd from his right, George carried the ball a couple of paces to the edge of the area and let fly with his right foot just as Lloyd lunged in with a tackle. The ball actually brushed Lloyd's boot as it flew unstoppably into the corner of the net beyond Clemence's dive. George lay back, raised his arms in salute and waited for his team mates' congratulations, one of the enduring images of the FA Cup.

Hat Trick 1973

Stokoe celebrates Sunderland's FA Cup victory

Date: 5 May 1973
Venue: Wembley Stadium
Event: FA Cup final, Sunderland 1
Leeds United 0

Every Leeds player was an international –
none of Sunderland's was. It had been 42
years since a Second Division club won the
Cup – West Brom won in a rainstorm in 1931.
Three years after Sunderland, Southampton
repeated the feat, and Sunderland won
promotion.

In 1973, the sight of a manager dashing across the Wembley pitch, coat flapping, one hand unsuccessfully trying to keep his hat on his balding head, made one of the most joyous images of Cup final history. To understand why, one must consider the two finalists.

Sunderland had four months previously been fighting relegation from the Second Division in 19th place. New manager Bob Stokoe was engineering a recovery. Leeds, the Cup-holders, won between 1965 and 1974 the Championship, two FA Cups, a League Cup and two UEFA Cups.

They were the dominant side of the era. But they were also the most hated side in the country. Mean-spirited, some of their players were unsportsmanlike, tough and occasionally crafty in the tackle, nigglers and, above all, always complaining and trying to influence the referee. So notorious were they that Stokoe said before the final: 'I want Mr Burns, the referee, to make the decisions on Saturday, and not Mr Bremner.' Billy Bremner was the Leeds captain.

Leeds dominated the early play without scoring. In the 32nd minute, Sunderland's commanding centre-half, Dave Watson, advanced for his team's first corner. The Leeds defence watched him closely, but the ball went to Vic Halom, who knocked it back across goal. Ian Porterfield, very left-footed, volleyed home with his right: 1-0 to Sunderland.

Leeds might have had a second-half penalty when Bremner was brought down. Then, with 26 minutes left, came possibly the greatest save ever seen at Wembley.

It began when Leeds' Peter Lorimer centred from the right to the far post where Trevor Cherry was advancing unmarked on goal. From the corner of the six-yard box he headed powerfully towards the opposite corner of goal. Goalkeeper Jim Montgomery, at the near post, dived to his left to push the ball out with both hands. It went towards Peter Lorimer, who had the hardest shot in English football. From the other end of the six-yard box he blasted it at goal. Montgomery flung himself from the ground in the direction of the shot.

The ball hit his arm and was deflected onto the underside of the bar, whence it bounced down at great speed, near enough to the line for Leeds to half-heartedly claim it was over. The ball was scrambled away and Sunderland held on to win.

Danny Blamchflower, who claimed football was all about glory, said it was 'the most gripping, emotional final I have been to, and that includes the two in which I carried off the Cup.'

At the whistle, ITV cameras focussed on Bob Stokoe, who leapt from his touchline seat and ran across the pitch, amidst excited Sunderland fans. Commentator Brian Moore reminisced 26 years later: 'As he started, I said "I wonder where he's going?" My director, Bob Gardam, heard it and decided to follow Stokoe. It was a great example of the director and commentator working together.' Years later, the sight of a beaming Stokoe, minus his hat, hurling himself into an embrace of Jim Montgomery, remains one of Wembley's happiest memories.

Ricky **Villa** 1981

Villa begins his dribble, outfoxing Caton (left) and Ranson

Tricky Ricky bamboozles City

Date:	14 May 1981
Venue:	Wembley Stadium
Event:	100th FA Cup final (replay), Tottenham Hotspur 3 Manchester City 2

In the 20th century, Spurs won more FA Cup finals in the years ending with '1' (five: 1901, 1921, 1961, 1981 and 1991) then all the other clubs put together (there was no Cup final in 1941). Another omen pointing to Spurs' success in 1981 was that it was the Chinese year of the cockerel – the emblem of Spurs.

As the 20th century ended, Premiership-chasing Chelsea could field a side without a single British player and surprise nobody. But 20 years earlier, in 1978, it was sensational news when Spurs manager Keith Burkinshaw spent £700,000 to introduce two World Cup winning Argentinians, Osvaldo Ardiles and Ricardo Villa, to British football.

Both played in the 100th FA Cup final in 1981 against Manchester City. Ardiles, who pronounced 'Tot-ten-ham' as if it were three separate words, was a great favourite with the fans, who put his and Spurs' Wembley disc, 'Ossie's Dream', well up the charts. Villa spoke less English, and was more homesick, becoming a moody player, not always certain of his place in the side.

The first match of the final was drawn 1-1, City's Tommy Hutchison earning fame by scoring at both ends. In the 68th minute, with Spurs one down, Villa was replaced by Gary Brooke. He was distraught, and headed for the dressing room in tears, ignoring his manager. Few thought he would be picked for the replay

However, he was, and the following Thursday, again at Wembley, he gave Spurs a seventh-minute lead. Spurs then went behind, but an equaliser in the second half set the stage for the most famous winning goal in the first 100 FA Cup finals.

It came in the 77th minute, and started with Graham Roberts, a 21-year-old whom Spurs had just bought from Weymouth for £35,000, a record for a non-League player. He had lost two teeth and suffered concussion in the first match. Now he won the ball just outside his own penalty area and passed it to left-winger Tony Galvin, who himself was an unusual Cup finalist – the first to have a degree in Russian. Galvin set off up the wing, was forced inside, and passed square to Villa.

Villa began his breathtaking, mazy run from about ten yards outside the box, in an inside-left position. He was faced by Tommy Caton, and Gerry Gow was tracking back to try to tackle him. Villa went past Caton on the outside, using his right foot. As he entered the area, right-back Ray Ranson challenged, but Villa passed him on the outside, too. He now found Nicky Reid closing in on his left, while Caton had doubled back to keep pace with him on his right.

Using his left foot to play the ball, Villa now dramatically changed direction, turning at right angles to cut between Caton and Ranson, both of whom he'd already beaten, and head towards the spot, with Caton, Ranson and Reid at his heels. Big Joe Corrigan, City's goalie, now rushed out to dive at his feet, and at the same time Caton launched a last desperate lunging tackle with his left foot. But Villa neatly squeezed the ball between the diving keeper and defender with his right foot before tripping over the two bodies at his feet. City's skipper, Paul Power, watched as the only other defender Villa hadn't beaten, Bobby McDonald, chased the ball into the net.

Heysel 1985

Disaster in Belgium

Date:	29 May 1985
Venue:	Heysel Stadium, Brussels
Event:	European Cup final, Juventus 1 Liverpool 0

Shamefully, Everton, Manchester United, Norwich, Southampton and Liverpool unsuccessfully took legal action to get the FA ban on English clubs in European competition lifted. In any case UEFA soon banned English clubs indefinitely, only lifting the ban in 1990-91.

The emergency services examine the destruction at Heysel

The nadir of the hooliganism which troubled football, and English football in particular, for several years was reached in May 1985, at the Heysel Stadium in Brussels. Unspeakable behaviour by a group of people calling themselves Liverpool fans put a stain on the club, the city, the country and the game which can never be removed.

Liverpool were in Brussels to play the Italian club Juventus in the final of the European Cup. Liverpool were the holders, and had won the Cup four times. Large contingents of fans from Liverpool and Turin were in the old, rundown stadium. Security arrangements were poor and there was no closed-circuit television. Many fans were drunk and some took weapons inside including iron bars and bottles. Liverpool fans were put into terrace sectors labelled X and Y, where they were able to pass their tickets over the fence to friends. Sector Z was meant for neutrals, but many Juventus fans obtained tickets there.

An hour before kick-off, bottles began flying over the dozen yards or so between the sets of fans. With police presence at a minimum, some Liverpool fans then charged across. After a second charge, there was a fatal, third charge, when hundreds of Liverpool fans armed with sticks, concrete slabs, fireworks and anything to hand launched an attack. The Juventus fans tried to escape down the terracing, but were crushed against a wall which eventually collapsed. As the English hooligans advanced, many of the crushed were trampled.

Police then waded in with batons to try to clear the terraces on which people were already dead and dying. Eventually some order was restored and police reinforcements and medical assistance arrived. Behind Sector Z, tents were erected in which the injured were tended. Even then the *World Soccer* report of the events contained the chilling fact that some of the English aggressors sneaked back to kick the dead and injured.

The events were witnessed by millions of TV viewers, who were horrified when the match kicked off nearly 90 minutes late. The decision to play was made by UEFA and local officials after discussions with police. It was probably the right decision as it may have prevented further rioting (many in the stadium were unaware of the scale of the tragedy) and it allowed the emergency services to function without interference. Television audiences knew more of the details than the spectators at Heysel – the English commentary was a bizarre and insensitive mix of news and analysis of the tragedy and commentary on the game.

At the end of the day 39 lives were lost, mostly Italian, and over 400 were injured. The FA immediately withdrew all English clubs from European competition for a year. *World Soccer* agreed with the ban: 'It is clear that the only secure way to protect European cities, stadia, fans, and private citizens......is to keep the English hooligans and, yes, murderers, well away.'

The **Good** and the **Ugly**

Diego's two 'divine' goals against England

The 'hand of God' deceives Peter Shilton

In the 1986 World Cup finals, two previous winners, England and Argentina, met in the quarter-finals. They were bitter rivals who had met twice before in World Cup finals, with England winning each time, most recently 1-0 in 1966. On that occasion there was bad feeling between the sides, with the Argentinian captain sent off and England's manager, Alf Ramsey, calling the Argentinians 'animals'. Four years before the 1986 clash, the two countries had engaged in real war over the ownership of the Falkland Islands.

Argentina's captain was now the world's greatest footballer of his era, Diego Maradona.

He excelled against England and scored two of the best-known goals in soccer history – the first infamous for a successful bit of sleight of hand, the second a sublime effort which only he could have scored.

The match was level at half-time, and the deadlock wasn't broken until the 51st minute, when England's Steve Hodge mis-hit a clearance, sending a high ball into England's six-yard area. Goalkeeper Peter Shilton (6ft) came to punch clear, his only challenger Maradona (5ft 9in). As Maradona leapt, he reached upwards with his left hand and pushed the ball past Shilton into the net. The linesman and referee gave a goal, despite England's protests. Shortly afterwards Maradona was to admit his offence and described the goal as being from 'the hand of God'. The referee, Ali Ben Nasser, was immediately banned by FIFA from international duties.

Four minutes later Maradona scored again – and the only way God was involved this time was by giving him his talent in the first place. He collected a pass from Jorge Burruchaga well inside his own half on the right-hand side of the field. His back was to the England goal, and Peter Reid and Peter Beardsley were in close attendance.

A neat shuffle deceived both his challengers at once, and Maradona accelerated past Glenn Hoddle into the England half. He cut inside the challenge of Terry Butcher, past the chasing-back Reid and beat Terry Fenwick's lunge by skppping past him on the outside. Entering the area, he deceived the diving

Shilton who had come out to the six-yard line, on the outside, and as Terry Butcher, who had chased him for most of his 60-yard dribble, slid in with a right-foot tackle, he slotted the ball from the corner of the six-yard box into the net with his left foot. A covering Gary Stevens (Everton) was helpless to intervene. Butcher's tackle knocked Maradona off balance, and might even have helped propel the ball in, but Maradona was not to be denied.

With ten minutes left England reduced the margin of defeat to 2-1, but Argentina, with the help of Maradona's hand and foot, went on to win the World Cup.

A Buenos Aires newspaper celebrated England's defeat: 'We blasted the English pirates with Maradona and a little hand. He who robs a thief has a thousand years' pardon.' It was certainly a match Argentina desperately wanted to win.

Date:	22 June 1986
Venue:	Azteca Stadium, Mexico City
Event:	World Cup quarter-final, Argentina 2 England 1

England met Argentina again in the World Cup finals in 1998. Their second-round clash was marked by the sending-off of England's David Beckham, but despite this the sides were level after extra time at 2-2 in one of the tournament's best matches. Argentina won the penalty shoot-out.

Hillsborough 1989

Ninety-six innocent fans crushed to death

What has come to be known simply as 'Hillsborough' or the 'Hillsborough Disaster' was the worst tragedy in British soccer history. It occurred in April 1989 and 96 soccer fans died.

The occasion was an FA Cup semi-final between Liverpool and Nottingham Forest. Hillsborough had been a venue for semi-finals for most of the century, and there had been no trouble before. Indeed the previous year the same two clubs had contested the semi-final without incident. The situations of the clubs were slightly different in 1989, however. Liverpool were staging a tremendous end to the season, and their fans felt that if they could beat Forest the 'double' was assured. Forest were on an equally impressive run. Between them the two clubs had played 43 games since Boxing Day and lost only three. Fans, some without tickets, flocked to Hillsborough.

Although the match was all-ticket, those without were hoping to buy them outside the ground, as had been possible in previous years. Some hoped to get in without a ticket, as it was rumoured some had at the FA Cup final of 1986, between Liverpool and Everton. This belief contributed to the disaster.

Another contributory cause was that the police authorities, naturally wishing to keep each set of fans apart outside the ground, had arranged for them to occupy the end nearest their arrival points. This meant Liverpool fans, despite being the larger contingent, had the Leppings Lane end, with the smaller capacity. Delays on the M62 meant that as kick-off approached thousands of Liverpool fans were

The scene at Anfield three days after Hillsborough

outside the Leppings Lane entrances trying to get in. Fearing a major disaster in the crush, police opened a gate and fans were pouring in as the match started.

After four minutes, a Peter Beardsley shot struck the Forest bar, and the roar caused the impatient arrivals to push even harder through a central entrance tunnel to the terraces, not knowing this area was already packed, while the side terraces were less so. As fans pressed in, those already there were crushed. Fenced in

Date:	15 April 1989
Venue:	Hillsborough, Sheffield
Event:	FA Cup semi-final, Liverpool v Nottingham Forest (abandoned after six minutes)

Lord Justice Taylor led an inquiry into the disaster which led to a revolution in stadium design and facilities – senior English clubs now have fence-free, all-seater arenas. A failure of command among senior police officers at the ground was identified as a contributory cause of the tragedy, but this remains an ongoing subject of debate and dispute.

at the side, they couldn't reach the pitch because of the perimeter fences – legacies of years of hooliganism in the 1980s – put there purposely to keep supporters off.

After six minutes, when it was clear there was turmoil on the terraces, the match was stopped. But, conditioned to suspect troublemakers, it was a long time before police or onlookers realised the gravity of the situation. Eventually a huge rescue operation was slowly mounted. Somehow dead and injured were brought on to the pitch where advertising hoardings were used as makeshift stretchers to transport them to ambulances and hospitals. After 90 minutes the scale of the tragedy was realised. There were 94 dead immediately, and two more died later. Over 200 people were injured.

Anfield became an enormous shrine of flowers, and tributes to the memory of those killed.

Gazza 1990

Tears on the television

An upset Gazza after the final whistle

Date: 4 July 1990
Venue: Stadio Delle Alpi, Turin
Event: World Cup semi-final, West Germany 1 England 1 (West Germany won 4-3 on penalties)

Retiring manager Bobby Robson said: 'Gascoigne was the best young player of the World Cup. He is special, someone around whom the new manager can build his side'. But England failed to qualify for World Cup 94, and at the last minute Glenn Hoddle omitted a fading Gazza from his World Cup 98 squad.

The outstanding TV image in England of the 1990 World Cup finals was of Paul Gascoigne crying. Newspapers, magazines and book covers later carried the picture of a tearful Gazza wiping his face with his shirt. The whole country felt like weeping with him.

It all came about in a strange way. The 23-year-old Gascoigne was not everybody's choice for the England squad for the finals. For a long time it seemed he would not even be the choice of the England manager, Bobby Robson.

The reason was that Gascoigne was almost two players. He was a genius when things were going well, when he played with great vision and imagination, and with a dainty ball control and sharp acceleration that belied his slightly top-heavy figure. He could pass the ball to perfection and his passes were often unexpected and always probing.

A midfielder, he nevertheless had the true striker's sense of opportunism near goal and was ice-cool when a chance came along. He had a very fierce and accurate right-foot shot, and became the most reliable free-kick expert in the country.

Against all this, he didn't seem to grow up. His only interests outside football appeared to be playing the fool and drinking. And on the pitch he could be easily provoked. If fouled he would retaliate foolishly. If things weren't going right he could sulk, show off, make elementary mistakes. He could put out his tongue like a naughty boy. Off the field he loved practical jokes, like shaking hands while holding an electric buzzer.

He had begun with Newcastle United, where Tyneside hero Jackie Milburn praised his talents. In July 1988 Terry Venables, the manager of Spurs, paid £2 million, then a big fee, to bring him to London. He made his England debut as a substitute at the beginning of the 1988-89 season, and started an international for the first time in a friendly against Czechoslovakia in April 1990, at Wembley. He played brilliantly, making England's first three goals and scoring the fourth himself in a 4-2 win. It booked his ticket to Italy for the World Cup.

Gascoigne was picked for the first group match, and quickly became one of the star players in the England team. England progressed to the semi-final, where the opponents were old football enemies West Germany. By this time Gascoigne was Gazza to the England fans, who were rapidly making him their hero.

Gazza began brilliantly, outshining the German ace Matthaus and looking the most inventive player on the pitch. West Germany took the lead with a somewhat lucky goal in the 59th minute, a freakish deflection from a free-kick. Gary Lineker equalised ten minutes from time and the game went into extra time.

Gazza was playing heroically – and then he went to tackle Thomas Berthold. It was a foul, and Berthold made the most of it, rolling about on the turf. Gazza received a yellow card, his second of the tournament, which meant he would miss the next match – which if England won, would be the final itself. Hence Gazza's uncontrollable tears, and the pictures which went round the world.

Cantona 1995

Date:	25 January 1995
Venue:	Selhurst Park
Event:	Premiership match,
	Crystal Palace 1
	Manchester United 1

Two weeks after the incident, Cantona left with his pregnant wife, Isabelle, and son Raphael for a holiday in Guadeloupe at United's expense. An ITN reporter, Terry Lloyd, and camera crew followed him. Declined an interview, they began filming the family on the beach. During an argument, according to Lloyd, an enraged Cantona launched himself at Lloyd, feet first, knocking him to the sand. Lloyd suffered fractured ribs.

When Crystal Palace played Premiership Champions Manchester United on a damp Wednesday evening in January 1995, the match drew the largest home attendance of the season, 18,224. Sky cameras were also there, to see if United's record £7 million signing, Andy Cole, could score his first goal for the club. He didn't, but fans saw instead one of the most extraordinary incidents ever witnessed in a British football stadium – a kung-fu attack on a spectator by a player.

The culprit was one of the game's greats – the brooding French genius, Eric Cantona. A man with a short fuse, Cantona had scorned authority and restraint all his career. He had been more or less forced out of French football after insulting in turn each member of a disciplinary committee. In three seasons of English football he had collected six red cards and numerous suspensions. But at the same time he helped win Championships in four consecutive seasons – with Marseille, Leeds and Manchester United twice.

At Palace, Cantona was being kept quiet by the

tight marking of Richard Shaw, and was building up resentment at what he regarded as unfair tackling, which was going unpunished by the referee. Early in the second half he appeared to strike out at Shaw but missed, and the incident passed. But the ball came back, Cantona and Shaw became entangled in a challenge and Cantona kicked Shaw. Referee Alan Wilkie sent him off.

Cantona strode, head erect, towards the players' tunnel at the corner of the ground, which meant he had to walk 50 yards along the touchline, before a gesticulating, yelling crowd. One spectator in a black leather jacket came down the terracing and, according to witnesses, shouted obscene racist insults implicating Cantona's mother. Cantona went berserk, leaping into the air and launching a

Kung-fu Eric kicks out

*Eric launches himself
into the crowd*

kung-fu kick over the barrier rail, his right foot ramming into the spectator's chest. Both men fell but rose to exchange punches, the spectator being felled again with a right before the two were separated.

Manchester United immediately fined Cantona and banned him from first-team matches for the rest of the season. The FA, unsatisfied, soon extended the ban until the following 30 September and made it worldwide.

In the extensive press coverage of the incident (12 pages in the *Sun*) the spectator was named as Matthew Simmons, a man who had been connected with extreme right-wing politics and who had been ejected from Selhurst Park the previous season after a pitch invasion.

Cantona was charged with common assault at Croydon magistrates court in March, pleaded guilty, and was sentenced, to general astonishment, to two weeks imprisonment. He was given leave to appeal, and in the Crown court eight days later Judge Ian Davis reduced his sentence to 120 hours of community service, teaching youngsters how to play football. Over 600 hopefuls benefited from his conscientious coaching.

At the Croydon Park Hotel, on the evening he learned he had escaped a spell in prison, the enigmatic Frenchman gave a press conference, saying: 'When the seagulls follow the trawler it is because they think, perhaps, sardines will be thrown into the sea'. An amused *Daily Telegraph* summed it up: 'Cantona free, philosophy nil'.

Owen 1998

Owen's screamer in vain

Date: 30 June 1998
Venue: St Etienne, France
Event: World Cup second round tie, Argentina 2 England 2 (Argentina won 4-3 on penalties)

England had not practised penalties, and Batty had not taken one before, so England's continuing 1990s frustration was largely self-inflicted.

Owen's shot heads for goal

Losing important matches on penalties became an English habit in the 1990s: the 1990 World Cup semi-final to West Germany, the 1996 European Championship semi-final to a now combined Germany and the 1998 second-round World Cup finals tie to bitter footballing rival Argentina. In each case a different outcome to the penalty shoot-out would have left England with an excellent chance of winning the tournament – in the first two examples an odds-on chance.

The 1998 failure was a particularly hard blow because England had played superbly for 73 minutes with only ten men after David Beckham's foolish sending-off, and because they had scored possibly the best goal of the tournament courtesy of their new young superstar, 18-year-old Michael Owen.

The first half of the match was one of the most exciting of all the tournament's 64 matches, with the quality of the football matching the drama. The pattern was set when after only two minutes Owen ran at the Argentine defence, and Roberto Ayala's tackle merely diverted the ball to Graeme Le Saux, whose far-post cross was just missed by a lunging Alan

Shearer. After six minutes Argentina went in front. Goalkeeper David Seaman dived at the feet of Diego Simeone, who was chasing a through ball, and brought him down. Gabriel Batistuta powered in the penalty.

Four minutes later Owen again raced through the defence. This time Ayala fouled him in the box, and Shearer banged in the spot kick to equalise.

After 16 minutes Owen scored his great goal. David Beckham found him with a pass on the halfway line, and Owen again set off to arrow in at great speed on the Argentine goal. Jose Chamot was just not quick enough to get in a tackle and Ayala was again the last line of defence. Owen went past him like a blur on the outside – only another foul could have stopped him. Bearing in on goal from the inside-right position Owen found Paul Scholes in support but almost brushed him aside with the impetus of his run. The finish matched the run as Owen shot across goalkeeper Carlos Roa into the far corner of the net for a wonderful goal.

England might have increased their lead two

or three times, particularly when Scholes missed when clean through, before Argentina levelled with a clever goal from a free-kick, awarded when Sol Campbell pulled back Claudio Lopez by his shirt. Batistuta dummied and Lopez played a gentle ball to Javier Zanetti, who had crept round the wall and emphatically beat Seaman with a shot to the far top corner.

After two minutes of the second half, Beckham was fouled by Simeone, and as he lay on the floor gently kicked his tackler and was sent off. England switched to 4-4-1 and defended superbly for the rest of the match, including extra time. With nine minutes left Campbell even nodded the ball home from a corner, but Shearer had unnecessarily elbowed the keeper and it was disallowed.

In the penalty shoot out, Hernan Crespo and Paul Ince missed each country's second effort, but at 4-3 to Argentina David Batty missed the last penalty and England were out.

'To send the English back home is wonderful', said the Argentina coach, Daniel Passarella. 'But the English, what passion!'

Glory Skills

Moments of football genius

Poborsky scores his stunner
against Portugal in Euro 96

Poborsky scores his stunner against Portugal in Euro 96

'Football is about glory.....doing things in style......doing them with a flourish,' said Danny Blanchflower. When fans discuss their memories, it is not results but special players and moments that most warm the hearts.

Sometimes it is a player's attitude, for example that of the arrogant, rebellious Len Shackleton, who once dribbled round an entire defence, including the goalie, and passed back from an empty goal with a contemptuous invitation to his Sunderland colleague Trevor Ford, with whom he did not get on, to put the ball in the net. Or Scotland's Jim Baxter, who at Wembley in 1967 against the recent World Cup winners, England, took the mickey by playing 'keepie-uppie' on the edge of his own penalty area. Scots laughed while the world champions fumed.

Dribbling is perhaps what most excites, and there have been great practitioners through the century from Alan Morton to George Best and Diego Maradona. But the man called 'The Wizard of Dribble' was Stanley Matthews, who for years beat full-backs who knew exactly what he was going to do. From outside-right he made a slow approach, a dip of the left shoulder as if to go inside, and using the outside of the right foot to play the ball, he would accelerate away on the outside. For years clubs' biggest gates were for the visit of Stoke or Blackpool – and Matthews.

Special tricks excite. Johan Cruyff beat defenders with a move so unique it bears his name, the 'Cruyff turn'. Pretending to run round one side of a player, Cruyff could suddenly stop dead, play the ball behind his 'standing' foot and shoot off at right angles to the previous run. It always drew gasps. Older fans still rejoice in a piece of 'sleight of foot' performed by Ferenc Puskas, when Hungary beat England 6-3 at Wembley in 1953. To the right of goal, Puskas showed the ball to defender Billy Wright. As Wright began his tackle, Puskas rolled the ball back with the sole of his right boot, pushing it to the right as Wright's momentum took him past to the left, and lashed it into the net. It was a trick that many players – most notably George Best – would adopt in the proceeding years.

Passing draws quieter satisfaction. David Beckham's chipped passes, centres and shots, clipping the ball with pin-point accuracy while on the run, delight spectators as the century ends. The backheel was raised to a new height in 1999 when Arsenal's Nwankwo Kanu magically backheeled a quick cross which was appearing to pass him into the corner of Middlesbrough's net.

Goals always excite. The best in the 1996 European Championship was scored by the Czech Karel Poborsky against Portugal with a scoop shot, made after a dribble while on the run. An unforgettable moment.

In the 1960s the Brazilian Garrincha amazed with his 'banana' kicks. Several players have now mastered the swerving free-kick, none more so than another Brazilian, Roberto Carlos, who against France in 1997 curled a 40-yarder which started out as if it would pass halfway between goal and corner flag. It swerved several yards to curl into goal to fool a thunderstruck keeper and thunderstruck crowd. One could imagine Blanchflower smiling.

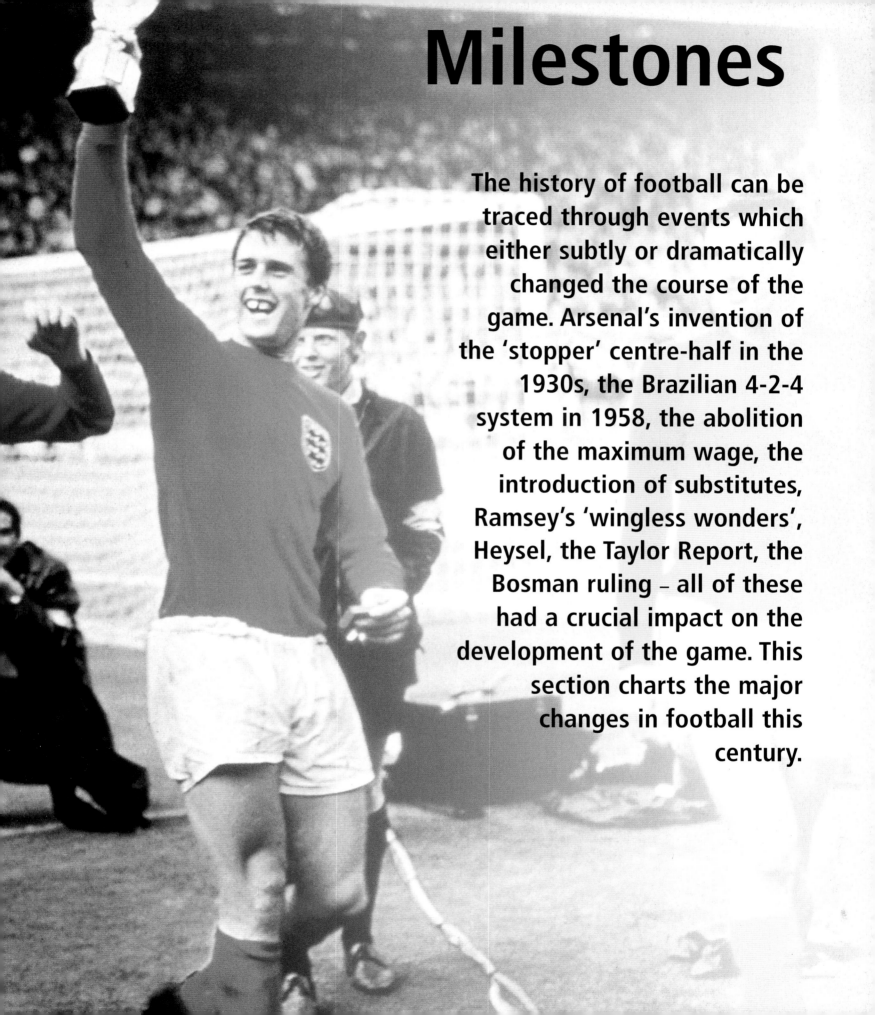

Milestones

The history of football can be traced through events which either subtly or dramatically changed the course of the game. Arsenal's invention of the 'stopper' centre-half in the 1930s, the Brazilian 4-2-4 system in 1958, the abolition of the maximum wage, the introduction of substitutes, Ramsey's 'wingless wonders', Heysel, the Taylor Report, the Bosman ruling – all of these had a crucial impact on the development of the game. This section charts the major changes in football this century.

The team of the 1890s:
Aston Villa with the FA Cup and
League trophies in 1897

Football was well-established in Britain as the 20th century started, but a present-day fan with a time machine who could go back 100 years to watch, say, the first FA Cup final of the century would immediately spot vital differences to today's game.

First of all, the markings on the pitch (which had been written into the laws only five years earlier) were different. There was no six-yard box; instead two overlapping semi-circles of a radius of six yards with their centres the two goalposts. The resulting area looked like a letter 'M' with no straight lines. Goalkicks could be taken from anywhere within this area. The penalty area was not today's familiar box, but a line 12 yards from the goal line which stretched from one touchline to the other. A penalty kick could be taken from anywhere on this line.

The idea of the penalty kick itself was only ten years old. At one time referees could punish foul play which prevented a certain goal by actually awarding a goal, like the penalty-try in rugby, but this idea lasted only one season.

Our hypothetical fan might have been amazed to see the 1900 goalkeeper going unpunished for handling outside the area. In 1900 the goalkeeper could handle anywhere in his own half. Until the 1890s he could handle anywhere on the pitch, and it wasn't until 1912 that the goalkeeper's handling was restricted to the penalty area.

The pitch markings changed radically in 1902, mainly to make the penalty area nearer to the goal instead of being the full width of the pitch. Nearly all of today's markings were then in place, including the penalty spot for the first time, the exception being the arc of the circle outside the penalty area and the little quarter-circles at the corner flags. The arc was not added until 1937, and it is not part of the penalty area, its purpose being to ensure that all players, except the kicker, are ten yards from the ball when a penalty is taken. The corner-flag quarter-circles were added in 1938.

Shirts, shorts and stockings

The 1900 Cup final players were wearing big heavy boots with metal toe caps of the kind which lasted until after the Second World War. They wore shirts with collars and long sleeves (though some were rolled up) and long shorts and socks which almost met, allowing no more than a few inches of knee to be seen.

The players of the day were paid about 7s 6d per week - the pay of Steve Bloomer, England's top goalscorer, during the 1890s. In 1901, a maximum wage for footballers was established at £4 per week, but few attained this level. The great Welsh winger, Billy Meredith, itemised his activities in the week of his first cap for Wales in 1895. This was against Ireland in Belfast on Saturday (journeys by boat). On Monday, he played against England in London, on Wednesday for his club City in Manchester, on Saturday for Wales against Scotland in Wrexham. Between times he did shifts down the pit. The three internationals were drawn, and Meredith's fee was £1 each. He estimated that his average wage from football over 30 years (he played till after the First World War) was £4.15s (£4.75) per week. The maximum would rise in 1910 to £5 per week, and in 1920 to £9, but in 1922 it was reduced again to £8 in the season and £6 in summer. Amazingly, this remained the maximum wage until after the Second World War.

In 1900, the Football Association had been in existence for 37 years, the FA Cup for 29 years, the Scottish FA for 27, the Football League for only 12 years, the Scottish League for nine. The Football League was so called (rather than English League) because it was hoped it would later include Scottish clubs.

North-South divide

The soccer power axis at the beginning of the century could be seen by a glance at the First Division, which contained not a single southern club. Villa were Champions, with

Billy Meredith, the Welsh winger, whose 30-year career earned him an average wage of £4.75 per week

other midlands clubs in Wolves, Derby, Forest and Stoke in the top nine. West Brom were 13th and Notts County were 15th. The north-east were strong, with Sunderland and Newcastle third and fifth, and so were Lancashire, although their top club, Manchester City, were only seventh. Liverpool, Everton, Bury, Blackburn, Preston, Burnley and Glossop were behind with Yorkshire's Sheffield United in second place. The highest southern club was Woolwich Arsenal, eighth in the Second Division. Unfamiliar Second Division names were Small Heath (now Birmingham City) and Newton Heath (Manchester United).

In Scotland, the first four had a still-familiar look: Rangers, Celtic (the Cup-winners), Hibernian and Hearts, although the amateurs, non-League Queen's Park, were still a great strength in Scotland and lost the Cup final only by 4-3. Scottish clubs in 1900 to since disappear from the League were: Third Lanark, St Bernards, Port Glasgow, Leith, Abercorn and Linthouse. Queen's Park joined the League in 1900-01, having already won the Scottish Cup ten times in its first 20 seasons.

So far as the game at large in Britain was concerned, the number of clubs affiliated to the FA had grown to around 10,000. FA Cup entrants had risen from 15 in the first year, of which four scratched, to 270 by the turn of the century. The game had changed from its public school and middle-class origins to a game of the working classes. Many of the 10,000 clubs belonging to the FA were local sides, works sides, Sunday school or old boys' sides.

A great British export

In the world outside the British Isles, the game spread best in those countries where it was taken by British servicemen or workers overseas. By 1900 Denmark, Holland, Switzerland, Belgium and Italy in Europe had formed Football Associations and Argentina and Chile had done likewise in South America.

By 1910, of the major nations, other countries formed FAs as follows: 1900, Germany, Uruguay; 1901, Hungary, Czechoslovakia; 1902, Norway; 1904, Austria, Sweden; 1906, Paraguay; 1907, Finland; 1908, Romania, Luxembourg. Portugal, Spain, Brazil, Canada and the USA had Associations before the First World War. Most other European and South American countries soon formed Associations. Japan, China and South Korea formed Associations in the 1920s, and with a few exceptions no other countries had a Football Association until after the Second World War.

FIFA itself was founded in 1904 in Paris. Representatives from France (although that country had no official FA at the time), Belgium, Holland, Denmark, Switzerland, Sweden and Spain were the founders. The British Associations, as is the way of British institutions, remained aloof at first, but England joined in 1905 and the rest in 1910, although they all withdrew again in 1920 because of the membership of Germany after the First World War. By 1912 other countries, including Austria, Czechoslovakia, Hungary, Luxembourg and Norway, were members. The first of the American countries – Canada, USA, Argentina and Chile – had also joined.

Although the home countries had been playing international matches since the first England-Scotland match in 1872, it was not until 1908 that any team from abroad was played, England going on a summer tour and beating Austria 6-1 and 11-1, Hungary 11-0 and Bohemia (later part of Czechoslovakia) 4-0. Hungary and Austria were well beaten again the following year to end overseas internationals until after the war. Meanwhile Argentina and Uruguay had met in the first international not involving British teams in 1901.

The Fatty Foulke final

There was a historic event in the first complete season of the century in Britain, as Tottenham Hotspur, then in the Southern League, won the FA Cup, thus becoming the only non-League club to win the Cup since the formation of the League. They beat Sheffield United in a replay. United's goalkeeper, Willie Foulke, is worth

Sheffield United's Willie 'Fatty' Foulke, the 20 stone, 6ft 2in goalkeeper

mentioning as a symbol of the times. He stood 6ft 2 in, and weighed 20 stone, yet was extremely successful in a long career. The gate for the first match at Crystal Palace, was 114,815, the first-ever six-figure soccer gate, setting a record that has since been beaten in the final only twice – in 1913 and 1923.

Just before the 1902 Cup final there occurred soccer's first mass tragedy, during the Scotland-England international at Ibrox Park. Two years before, huge open terraces had been built of timber supported by steel pylons. Soon after the match had started in pouring rain, newcomers charged up the staircase to an already packed west terrace and the crowd began to sway and the terrace to tremble. Finally, with a great cracking sound, some of the timber gave way, creating a hole some 21m x 4m, 70ft x 13ft, through which hundreds of fans fell, piling up on each other several feet below. Twenty-five died and about 500 were injured. Amazingly, the match went ahead after 20 minutes or so, and ended 1-1. The result was later declared unofficial.

Professionalism sweeps the game

The last great fling of the public school and university players before professionals took over completely came in 1903. Corinthians, an amateur side for whom C.B. Fry played, beat many top pro clubs in the 1890s and in 1903 took on the FA Cup winners, Bury. Despite going two down they ran out 10-3 winners.

Professional clubs were now making big profits – Newcastle in 1904-05 took over £25,000 at the gate, with profits approaching £10,000. Their neighbours Middlesbrough paid Sunderland a record £1,000 for the transfer of Alf Common. This caused an outcry against players being sold like cattle, and in 1908 the authorities put a ceiling on transfer fees of £350. But clubs soon overcame this, by selling players in twos or threes, to include the wanted player plus a makeweight or two to bump up the overall fee, and the limit was withdrawn after three months.

In 1905 the Football League expanded from 36 teams to 40. Among the newcomers was Chelsea, for whom H.A. Mears built a magnificent new stadium at Stamford Bridge, which he claimed seated 5,000 and could accommodate another 95,000. Chelsea were formed on 14 March 1905, bought their first player on 26 April and were elected to the Second Division on 29 May before they'd played a single match. Captained by the aforesaid Willie Foulke (now 22 stone) they finished third in their first season and were promoted the next.

In Scotland, Rangers and Celtic had established their supremacy over other clubs from the beginning of the Scottish League and in 1905 Celtic became the first Scottish club to perform the 'double'. They were in the middle of six consecutive title wins, and as they repeated the 'double' the following year were enjoying a spell of complete domination. They might have completed a hat-trick of 'doubles' in 1908-09 but after two Cup final draws with Rangers, the crowd at Hampden Park rioted and the Cup was withheld. The rules allowed for extra time to be played after a third draw, but the newspapers wrongly stated there would be extra time after the second. When there wasn't, the crowd set fire to buildings and hundreds were injured.

The Outcasts FC

With English clubs making large profits and forming themselves into limited liability companies, while players' wages were derisory by comparison, the Players Union, which had existed for a couple of years up to 1900, was revived in 1907, and applied for affiliation to the Federation of Trades Unions. This frightened the League and FA and, five days before the 1909-10 season they decided that union members should be suspended without wages and banned from taking part in any game. Clubs hastily began signing on amateurs to get the new season started. The Manchester United players, who the previous season had won the FA Cup for the first time, stood solid led by Billy Meredith, and United were in danger of being unable to play. Together with an Everton player, United pros formed the Outcasts FC. On the day before the season, the authorities gave in - just as well for Manchester United, who in February opened their splendid new ground at Old Trafford.

CROWD TRAGEDIES THROUGH THE CENTURY

1902	Glasgow	25 killed, 517 injured, Ibrox Park stand collapses
1946	Bolton	33 killed, 400 injured, Burnden Park wall collapses
1964	Lima, Peru	318 killed, 500 injured in riot when referee disallows goal
1968	Buenos Aires, Argentina	74 killed, 150 injured, crushed against locked exits
1971	Glasgow	65 killed, Ibrox Park, staircase crush after late equaliser
1974	Cairo, Egypt	49 killed, 50 injured, barriers and wall collapse
1979	Nigeria	24 killed, 27 injured, stampede after floodlight failure
1981	Piraeus, Greece	24 killed, crushed, stampede at exits
1982	Moscow, USSR	66 killed, crushed after late goal in UEFA Cup match
1985	Bradford	56 killed, 250 injured, Valley Parade fire in stand
1985	Brussels, Belgium	39 killed, 400 injured, wall collapses during riot, European Cup final
1988	Tripoli, Libya	30 killed, 40 injured, stand collapses after man with knife causes panic
1988	Kathmandu, Nepal	70 killed, electric storm provokes stampede to locked exits
1989	Sheffield	96 killed, 200 injured, crushed at FA Cup semi-final
1991	Transvaal, South Africa	40 killed, 50 injured, fighting and stampede after a refereeing decision
1992	Bastia, Corsica	15 killed, stand collapses at French Cup semi-final
1996	Guatemala City	81 killed, 147 injured, crushed after World Cup qualifier

For the first time royalty, in the person of King George V, attended the Cup final in 1914. The following season was played out in England despite the outbreak of war. The last eight clubs in the FA Cup reflected that the balance of football power remained firmly in the north, as only one, Chelsea, was based south of Sheffield. In addition, the top five clubs in the First Division (Everton, Oldham, Blackburn, Burnley and Manchester City) were from Lancashire, while three more of the 20 clubs came from Lancashire, four from Yorkshire (the two Sheffield and Bradford clubs), three from the north-east, three from the midlands and two from London - the bottom two, Chelsea and Tottenham.

Arsenal's dubious promotion

Chelsea had finished in the relegation position only because the club above them, Manchester United, had fixed their match with Liverpool to end 2-0 for betting purposes (they got 7-1 for a correct score). Although there were widespread confessions, and four players from each side were banned for life, the League table remained unaltered. An interesting situation arose after the war, when the two divisions were expanded by two clubs each. Chelsea argued successfully they should not be relegated because of Manchester United's crime, so three teams were required to replace Spurs. Naturally these included the top two teams from the Second Division. The third team to be promoted, for some obscure reason, was decided by ballot. There were seven applicants, including an incensed Spurs, who felt they should not be relegated.

As a result of a conspiracy between the chairman of Arsenal, Sir Henry Norris, a notoriously devious character, and the chairman of Liverpool, John McKenna, the League president, Arsenal got the verdict, despite having finished only fifth in the table, behind Wolves, who also applied. Ironically, Arsenal have not since been relegated and at the end of the century enjoyed the longest unbroken presence in the top flight.

After one year of post-war football the Football League was extended further to take in another 42 clubs, 22 in the Third Division (South) and 20 in the Third Division (North). After two seasons two extra clubs were added to the northern division, to make 22 clubs in each of the four divisions. Promotion and relegation was by two clubs up and two down in each division (one each being promoted from the two Third Divisions). In 1921-22, the Scottish League, which had been reduced to one 22-club division after the war, reverted to two divisions, which soon comprised 20 clubs each.

The look of English football changed considerably in 1923 when the new Wembley ground staged the FA Cup final. It has continued to do so since, except for a 1970 replay at Old Trafford.

The Rules take shape

A curious law change in 1924 made it legal for a goal to be scored direct from a corner-kick, although the law needed changing again a year later after Everton winger Sam Chedgzoy dribbled the ball in from the corner flag. The goal was wrongly disallowed, and the rule altered to state the kicker could not play the ball twice. But in 1925 came a more important law amendment that changed the face of the game altogether.

Charlie Buchan, the Arsenal captain and instigator of Arsenal's domination of English football in the 1930s.

It concerned the offside law. In effect, until then to be onside a player needed three opponents (one, of course, usually the goalkeeper) between him and the opposing goal-line at the time the ball was played to him. Some full-backs had developed into an art the practice of moving up at critical times to throw opposing forwards offside. Sometimes matches would be disjointed by as many as 40 offside decisions. The Newcastle pair of Irish international Bill McCracken and his English international partner, Frank Hudspeth, became notorious in this respect. The International Board in charge of the laws agreed in 1925 to a Scottish FA proposal that the critical number of opponents should be reduced from three to two.

On the opening day of the new season, Villa scored ten against Burnley. At season's end, the total number of goals scored in the Football League had risen from 4,700 the season before to 6,373, an increase of 28 per cent. The following season, George Camsell scored a still-standing record of nine hat-tricks in the Second Division for Middlesbrough and hoisted a new League individual scoring record of 59. Alas for Camsell, Dixie Dean scored 60 for Everton in 1927-28, so his record lasted only one season. Dean's has never been beaten as defences learned to cope with the new rule.

The man who worked out the counter was Charlie Buchan, who later published a famous football weekly which lasted many years. Buchan played for Arsenal, who were managed by the first outstanding manager in League football, Herbert Chapman. Chapman had been manager of Huddersfield Town when they became the first club to win the Championship three times in succession, 1923-24 to 1925-26, although before the third of these seasons he had left to manage Arsenal.

In the 1930s, Arsenal were to become the second club to perform the hat-trick but, ironically, Chapman was to die during the third season. The hat-trick wasn't to be performed again for 49 years, until Liverpool achieved it in the 1980s.

Buchan's plan was to convert the centre-half, then much more of an attacking player, to a central defender, playing between the two full-backs. It was called the 'third-back' game and Chapman found exactly the man to fill the role in Herbie Roberts, who arrived at Highbury from Owestry for £200. Not particularly skilful, his sole job was to block the middle, and head away all the high balls before the likes of Dean could nod them in. He did it well, and became known as 'Policeman' Roberts.

Gunners dominate inter-war years

Arsenal's day was not long in coming. In October 1928 they broke the £10,000 transfer barrier by paying £10,890 to Bolton for inside-forward David Jack. The club's first honour came in 1930 when they won the FA Cup, the Championship followed the next season, and Arsenal went on to dominate the 1930s. In the ten seasons before the Second World War, they won the Championship five times, the FA Cup twice and were finalists once. In only two seasons were they not Champions or Cup

The Graf Zeppelin looms over the 1930 FA Cup final between Arsenal and Huddersfield Town at Wembley

Old Firm duopoly in Scotland

The picture in Scotland was amazing. From 1903-04 until the Second World War, Rangers had won 19 Championships and Celtic 15, with Motherwell the only club to break the duopoly with a win in 1931-32. The Cup was different, with Rangers going 25 years between victories, and with 12 clubs outside the 'old firm' having claimed the trophy between 1900 and 1939.

One of soccer's biggest individual tragedies occurred in an 'old firm' match in 1931 when Celtic's brilliant 22-year-old international goalkeeper, John Thompson, died after fracturing his skull diving at the feet of Rangers' Sam English. Thousands packed the streets for his funeral, but poor English never recovered. Although he set a Rangers goalscoring record that season, barracking forced him to leave for Liverpool where after two seasons he drifted out of football.

Celtic's Jimmy McGrory ended his career with Clydebank in 1938, having scored 410 goals in 408 League matches for the two clubs, the only player in British football to have averaged over a goal a game.

British attendance records were set in Scotland in the 1930s: 149,415 (plus some 10,000 gate-crashers) saw Scotland beat England 1-0 at Hampden Park on 17 April 1937; 144,303 saw Celtic beat Aberdeen 2-1 in the Scottish Cup final at Hampden Park a week later on 24 April 1937; and a record League attendance of 118,567 saw Rangers beat Celtic 2-1 at Ibrox Park on 2 January 1939.

finalists. Arsenal's tactical pioneering with the central defender had now been adopted by most clubs, and extended to the extent that one or both inside-forwards dropped back to become attacking midfielders, in those days called 'schemers', as they schemed the attacks. Arsenal had the schemer par excellence in Alex James. With both inside forwards dropping back, the forward line played in a combination resembling a 'W', and the whole formation, linked with the defensive 'M', became the standard, known as the 'WM' formation. In these days of numbers, it would be called 3-2-2-3.

Arsenal's 1930 Cup win was famous because the huge Graf Zeppelin airship hovered over Wembley, dipping in salute at kick-off. In football terms, the match could be seen as a symbolic shifting in soccer power south. It was the first of many honours for Arsenal, whereas the defeated Huddersfield Town, the team of the 1920s with three Championships, two seconds, and three Cup final appearances, once winners, have never since won a major honour.

A remarkable feat of the 1930s was that of Joe Payne, such a failure he had even been dropped from the reserves at Luton Town. But with all their centre-forwards injured, Luton called up Payne against Bristol Rovers on 13 April 1936 and he proceeded to score ten in a 12-0 victory. For the rest of his career, the best of which was at Chelsea during the war, he was known as 'Ten-goal' Payne.

The first World Cup

Meanwhile, on the international scene, all four British unions withdrew from FIFA in 1928. The reason was a disagreement over amateurism in connection with the Olympic Games. Previously the Olympic Committee had followed strict British views on amateurism but, at a meeting in 1927, they agreed to FIFA demands that 'broken time' payments (i.e. payments to players for lost earnings) would not affect a player's amateur status. The British could not agree with this view and subsequently withdrew from FIFA.

This decision meant that the home countries could not take part in the new World Cup. Two Frenchmen, Jules Rimet and Henri Delaunay, had proposed a World Cup in 1904 at the inception of FIFA, and after years of discussion and organisation the first took place in Uruguay in 1930.

At that time matches between the British and other countries were usually played near the beginnings or ends of seasons, or on summer tours. England's first such match had been in Vienna in 1908, and by 1930 they had played fewer than 40, often one-sided, games on tours of emergent soccer nations like South Africa and Australia. They met their first defeat in Madrid in May 1929, when Spain won the first meeting between the countries 4-3.

Scotland didn't play Continental opposition until 1929, with matches against Norway, Germany and Holland, and remained unbeaten by the time of the first World Cup. Wales and

WORLD CUP FINALS		
1930	(Montevideo)	Uruguay 4
		Argentina 2
1934	(Rome)	Italy 2
		Czechoslovakia 1 (aet)
1938	(Paris)	Italy 4
		Hungary 2
1950	(Rio de Janeiro)	Uruguay 2
		Brazil 1
1954	(Berne)	West Germany 3
		Hungary 2
1958	(Stockholm)	Brazil 5
		Sweden 2
1962	(Santiago)	Brazil 3
		Czechoslovakia 1
1966	(London)	England 4
		West Germany 2 (aet)
1970	(Mexico City)	Brazil 4
		Italy 1
1974	(Munich)	West Germany 2
		Holland 1
1978	(Buenos Aires)	Argentina 3
		Holland 1 (aet)
1982	(Madrid)	Italy 3
		West Germany 1
1986	(Mexico City)	Argentina 3
		West Germany 2
1990	(Rome)	West Germany 1
		Argentina 0
1994	(Los Angeles)	Brazil 0
		Italy 0
		(Brazil won 3-2 on
		penalties aet)
1998	(Paris)	France 3
		Brazil 0

Northern Ireland hadn't played outside the home countries but the Republic of Ireland had beaten Belgium three times and lost home and away with Italy.

So the first World Cup, won by the home country Uruguay from 12 other entrants, only four from Europe, made little impression in Britain. England's match with Austria at Stamford Bridge in September 1932 was seen as much more significant, and considered the unofficial championship of Europe. From 2-0 at half-time, England scraped home 4-3, and it was generally acknowledged that the Austrian 'Wunderteam' had outplayed them.

The 1934 World Cup was also won by the hosts, this time Italy, from an entry of 32, which required a qualifying competition. The Republic of Ireland, then called the Irish Free State, failed to qualify on goal average, having drawn 4-4 with Belgium and lost 5-2 in Holland. In November England played the winners at Highbury and won an extremely dirty match 3-2, captain Eddie Hapgood's broken nose being only the worst of several injuries. The match became known as the 'Battle of Highbury' and one newspaper by-lined its report as 'From our War Correspondent'. This, plus a 6-3 victory over Germany in Berlin in May 1938, after the English players had been required to give the Nazi salute during the anthems, was sufficient to persuade the English that they were the world masters for at least another 12 years.

Italy had better cause to claim the title by retaining the World Cup in France. Thirty-seven countries initially entered, but ten withdrew without playing. The Republic of Ireland lost their two-legged qualifier with Norway.

A break for war

In the last season before the Second World War, England beat the Rest of Europe 3-0 at Highbury in a match to celebrate the 75th anniversary of the Football Association. The 1939-40 season was abandoned after a few matches because of the outbreak of war, but it was the first in which shirt numbering was compulsory in the Football League.

Football resumed in Britain in 1945-46 with the FA Cup, played up to the semi-final stage on a two-leg basis. Soccer-starved fans flocked to the matches, and on 9 March 1946 in a sixth-round tie at Burnden Park, Bolton, where Stoke with Stanley Matthews were the visitors, a crash barrier gave way with 60,000 present and 33 people lost their lives.

The home countries rejoined FIFA in 1946, allowing them entry into the World Cup, to be held in Brazil in 1950. To mark their return, FIFA staged a match at Hampden Park between Great Britain and the Rest of Europe. Great Britain won 6-1 before 135,000 spectators, and their share of the receipts made FIFA financially sound for the first time. There were 73 members in 1950, but with the austerity of the aftermath of war and the long journey to Brazil for the European sides, there were only 31 entries for the World Cup. FIFA made the Home Championship a qualifying group, the first two to qualify, but the Scottish FA decided they would only take part if they won, and, finishing

second, declined their place. England failed to win their group in the finals, and humiliatingly lost 1-0 to the United States.

Hungary show way forward

Scotland lost at home to a Continental side for the first time in 1950, Austria winning 1-0 at Hampden Park, and England, after a last-minute penalty, saved their home record in a 4-4 draw with the Rest of Europe in October 1953, but lost it comprehensively to Hungary five weeks later 6-3. Hungary won a return in Budapest 7-1, England's worst-ever defeat. Hungary baffled England with a new development in tactics – the deep-lying centre-forward. Nandor Hidegkuti, Hungary's number 9, played in midfield, with licence to roam in all directions, a ploy which completely non-plussed England's marking system.

However, Wolverhampton Wanderers gave English supporters something to cheer in the 1954-55 season with floodlit victories over the Moscow teams Spartak and Dynamo and a 3-2 victory over Honved, the Hungarian army side which included six of the players who had outclassed England. This persuaded English papers to describe Wolves as Europe's champion club side, and led Gabriel Hanot, editor of the French sports paper *L'Equipe*, to propose a competition to decide the matter - the European Cup, which came into being the following season.

The four home nations all reached the World Cup finals in 1958, and Wales and Northern Ireland reached the quarter-finals. Brazil won,

and their formation, with four attackers, four defenders and two in midfield, led to the modern habit of describing formations with numbers, in this case 4-2-4. Brazil's system became over the years more of a 4-3-3, as their left-wingers, Zagalo and Rivelino, dropped back into midfield.

Catenaccio sweeps soccer

Just as Hidegkuti roamed in the Hungarian attack, a similar mobile role developed in defence, and the term 'sweeper' was born. It started in Switzerland between the World Wars, when a defender had the role of dropping behind the last line of defence with the purpose of shuttling from wing to wing to deal with attacks as appropriate. It was called *verrou*, or 'the bolt', and it reached its peak after the Second World War in Italian football, where it was called *catenaccio*. It became very defensive, and 1-0 was the typical score in Italian League games for many years.

When England won the World Cup in 1966, manager Alf Ramsey began the finals with orthodox wingers – John Connelly, Terry Paine and Ian Callaghan all played – but from the quarter-finals onward he dispensed with them, leading to his winning team being called 'Wingless Wonders'. In effect, he used a system in which the full-backs were expected to overlap and become acting wingers. Ramsey's backs – George Cohen and Ray Wilson – were not, in fact, particularly skilful as wingers, but nowadays, with the system widely adopted, such men are known as wing-backs. England's current left wing-back, Graeme Le Saux, began

The development of formations

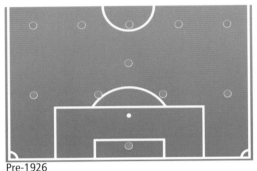

Pre-1926

Arsenal 1926 (the 'WM' formation)

'stopper' centre-half

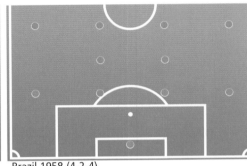

Brazil 1958 (4-2-4)

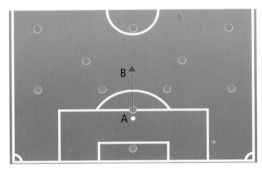

Catenaccio (A). The sweeper can also initiate the attack (B)

4-4-2 (the typical modern formation)

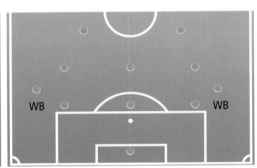

3-5-2 (wing-backs defend and attack)

as a winger and reverted to full-back, and fills the role very well.

In 1974, West Germany won the World Cup using Franz Beckenbauer in a new role, as a 'sweeper' playing mainly in front of the back four, in a system which could be described as 4-1-2-3. Beckenbauer was at liberty to drop back behind the defenders, as a conventional sweeper, to roam to the wings or to advance in attack. The role required a complete footballer, at home anywhere on the pitch, and Beckenbauer fitted the role perfectly.

The best team of the 1970s, however, Holland, required all their players to be comfortable in any position on the field, playing a fluid form of football which was called 'total football'. This did not preclude specialists such as strikers and defenders - but it gave individual players more flexibility and freedom to follow their instincts.

At the end of the century, elements of all these formations and tactics are used, plus others, such as enveloping the opposition in a five-man midfield, with only one striker in operation.

The European Cup is born

Meanwhile, the enterprise of L'Equipe had resulted in the first European Champion Clubs' Cup in 1955-56. The first English team to qualify were Chelsea, but the Football League strongly advised them against taking part, so Hibernian were the sole representatives from Britain. Real Madrid won the first five European Cups, as it was popularly called. The first English club to take part were Manchester United, in 1956-57, their manager, Matt Busby, defying the Football League. The following year, in United's second European season, the Munich air crash destroyed their great side while they were returning from a European Cup quarter-final.

Celtic became the first British team to win the European Cup in 1967, and Manchester United the first English club the following year. Since then, Liverpool (four times in the 1970s and 1980s), Nottingham Forest (in 1979 and 1980), Aston Villa in 1982 and Manchester United

EUROPEAN CLUB COMPETITIONS

Winners, country by country, of the three major European club competitions in the 20th century are as follows:

European Champion Clubs' Cup (since 1956)	
Italy 9	Germany 5
England 9	Belgium 3
Spain 8	USSR 3
Holland 6	Scotland 2
Germany 5	Portugal 1
Portugal 3	Czechoslovakia 1,
Scotland 1	Holland 1, France 1
Romania 1	
Yugoslavia 1	**UEFA Cup** (since
(Marseille won for	1972)
France in 1993, but	Italy 9
were stripped of the	Germany 6
title following a	England 5
bribery investigation)	Holland 3
	Sweden 2
	Spain 2
European Cup Winners	Belgium 1
Cup (1961 to 1999)	
England 8	(Germany's totals
Spain 7	include West and East
Italy 7	Germany. English clubs
	were barred 1985-90)

again in 1999 have won for England. In the first season of 1999-2000, the Champions Cup was enlarged to take in extra clubs from the stronger countries, with Germany, Italy and Spain each getting four entrants.

In 1960-61 a European Cup Winners Cup was started and ran for 39 seasons, the 1998-99 competition being the last. It was discontinued in conjunction with the enlargement of the Champions Cup. Winners for England were Chelsea (2), Spurs, West Ham United, Manchester City, Everton, Manchester United and Arsenal, and for Scotland, Rangers and Aberdeen.

During the 1950s a third European competition was for cities which held trade fairs, called the Inter-Cities Fairs Cup. The first winners in 1958 were Barcelona, who beat London. The competition became the UEFA Cup in 1971-72. Since then English winners have been: Spurs (2), Liverpool (2) and Ipswich Town.

Disaster strikes twice in 18 days

Tottenham Hotspur, winners of the Cup Winners Cup in 1962-63, were the first English team to win in Europe. Because of the tragedy at the Heysel Stadium in 1985, when Liverpool were playing Juventus in the European Cup final, English clubs were banned from all European competition until 1990-91.

The Heysel tragedy happened only 18 days after another major tragedy in English football. On 11 May 1985, fire raged in the old wooden stand at Valley Parade, Bradford City's ground, during a match with Lincoln. Bradford fans were celebrating their team's promotion to the Second Division. Rubbish under the stand caught fire, possibly because of a discarded cigarette butt, and 56 died and 200 were hurt. Television audiences saw the horror unfold.

Evolution of League football

The structure of the Football League changed in the 1950s. First, in 1950-51 four new clubs were incorporated into the Third Divisions, making 92 League clubs, a number which, including the Premiership, remained to the end of the century. In 1958-59, the two regional Third Divisions were re-arranged into a Third and Fourth Division. Between these two divisions, four clubs were promoted and relegated each season. In 1973-74, promotion and relegation between the top three divisions was changed from two clubs to three, and in the 1976-77 season, teams level on points were differentiated by goal difference rather than goal average. The idea was to encourage attacking football, and from 1981-82 three points were awarded for a win (instead of two) to further discourage teams from playing for a draw.

For two seasons from 1986-87, the First Division was reduced by a club a season, and the final promotion/relegation places decided by play-offs between the divisions, including the First. This meant that by the 1988-89 season the First Division was reduced to 20 clubs, the other three divisions consisting of 24 clubs. The play-offs continued, but now concerned only the three lower divisions.

The top League clubs then broke away from the rest, and in 1992-93 the Premiership was formed, reverting to 22 clubs. The Football League then labelled the three remaining divisions First, Second and Third, causing confusion for all historians and statisticians. Promotion between the Premiership and

League remained the same, with play-offs in all the League divisions. The League switched from goal difference to goals scored to differentiate teams equal on points.

The Scottish League had adopted goal difference before the Football League, in 1970-71, and also preceded the Football League with a ten-team Premier Division, formed in 1975-76. The Scots retained a First and Second Division of 14 clubs each, so the total number of clubs remained the same. In 1994-95, a Third Division was added, the Scottish League at this time consisting of ten clubs in each of the four divisions.

The Football League began a new Cup competition in 1960-61, the Football League Cup. Some of the top clubs shunned it at first, as it was seen to be an irrelevant burden on their fixture lists. It was not until 1969-70 that all 92 clubs took part for the first time, and entry was made compulsory in 1971-72. It became established when winning it ensured entry into the UEFA Cup, but it remains much the least valued of the three main English domestic competitions.

Subs brought in

One of the biggest law changes in the second half of the century occurred in 1965-66 when substitutes were allowed in British domestic football for the first time. At first there was considerable opposition to the plan, as critics feared the law would be 'abused', and only one substitute was allowed per team, and that for injury only. It was not until 1973-74 in Scotland and 1986-87 in England that a second substitute was allowed. Nowadays different competitions allow different numbers, and for Premiership matches the substitutes' bench has as many as five players ready to come on. Nor is injury any more a requirement for making a substitution.

More small changes to the role of goalkeepers have been incorporated in the laws, all intended to speed up the game. In 1967-68 goalkeepers were limited to taking four steps before releasing the ball from hand, in 1992-93 they were not allowed to handle a ball deliberately passed to them from the foot of a colleague, and four years later they were not allowed to hold the ball for longer than six seconds. The 'pass-back' rule certainly improved the game.

Another rule change in the 1990s that helped improve the game was a change to the off-side law. Instead of requiring at least two opponents between him and the opponents' goal-line at the time the ball is played for a player to be onside, he now requires merely to be not nearer the goal-line than at least two opponents. In other words, if the attacker and the relevant opponent or opponents are level, the attacker is now onside. A law change brought in at the same time was that a 'professional' foul was subject to an automatic sending-off. That is, a defender who commits a foul when he is the last line of defence, thus depriving the attacker of a clear run on goal, is to be sent off.

A player sent off in English football is shown a red card. The Football League introduced a system of the referee showing players a yellow card for a caution and a red card for a sending off in 1976-77, eight years after FIFA had introduced the system in the 1968 World Cup. A second yellow card offence in a match automatically meant a red. The system was dropped in England in 1981 but reintroduced in 1987. The use of cards, and the suspensions for accumulating too many, has certainly helped clean up the game.

The World game expands

The number of international matches played by England against opposition from outside the home countries grew enormously in the second half of the century. Of approximately 200 internationals played by England before 1950, 86 were against 'foreign' opposition – all friendlies, including unrepresentative tours of Australia and South Africa. Between 1950 and 2000, England will have played nearly 400 matches against 'foreign' opposition alone. This growth was partly the reason the Home International Championship was discontinued after the 1983-84 season, 100 years after it began.

As well as the World Cup, the home countries entered a European Championship, the first tournament of which was played from 1958 to a final in 1960. Known until 1966 as the European Nations Cup, it was a French initiative, being the idea of Henri Delaunay. Nowadays the finals are held every four years, halfway between the World Cup finals. The ten tournaments to 1996 inclusive were won by

The first time football was televised – a practice match at Highbury in September 1937

runners-up), 4 FA Cups (3 times beaten finalists), 4 League Cups (twice beaten finalists), 4 European Cups (once beaten finalists), 2 UEFA Cups (once beaten finalists) and were beaten finalists in the Cup Winners Cup. In this period they performed the Championship/FA Cup 'double'.

Spurs, Arsenal (twice) and Manchester United (3 times) have also performed the 'double' in the 20th century and in 1998-99 Manchester United added the European Cup for a unique 'treble', thus ending the century the dominant club in England.

In Scotland, the 'old firm', Rangers and Celtic, ruled nearly as much in the second half of the century as the first, winning between them 39 Championships to 11 by other clubs (up to 1949 the ratio was 39 to 4). They each won nine Championships running. They have been slightly less dominant in the Cup competitions, but throughout the century have consistently won over two thirds of the honours on offer.

The television era

The biggest changes in football in the last decades of the century lie in its social and financial status, and these have been largely triggered by television. The first match to be shown on TV was an Arsenal practice match in 1937, followed by parts of the 1937 FA Cup final. With the exception of 1952 when the FA refused the BBC permission, the Cup final has been shown live on TV every year since 1938. A League match was first televised live on a Friday night in 1960, but Friday night football

eight nations, only (West) Germany winning more than once, as follows: Germany 3, USSR, Spain, Italy, Czechoslovakia, France, Holland and Denmark. The only consolation for England was to win a match arranged in 1987-88 to celebrate the centenary of the Football League, when the Football League beat a Rest of the World XI 3-0 at Wembley.

Axis of Power shifts south

As the 20th century ends, a comparison between the 20 Premiership teams of 1999-2000 with the 18 First Division teams of 1899-1900 shows that six teams are common to both: Aston Villa, Sunderland, Newcastle United, Derby County, Liverpool and Everton. Representation by region shows (Premiership first, 1900 in brackets): Lancashire 3 (8), London and the South 7 (0), the Midlands 4 (7), the North-East 3 (2), Yorkshire 3 (1). The advance of London (in particular with Arsenal, Chelsea, Spurs and West Ham) in soccer power can be seen to be at the expense of Lancashire and the Midlands (in particular the Lancashire clubs of Preston and Burnley have declined while Glossop has disappeared).

The most sustained period of one-club supremacy in recent times has been enjoyed by Liverpool who, in 27 years between 1964 and 1990 won 12 Championships (7 times

PREMIERSHIP FINANCES 1997-98

Club	Turnover £ million	Wage bill £ million	Wages % of turnover	Highest wage (per week)	Pre-tax Profit (loss) £ million
Manchester United	87.8	26.9	31%	£25,000	14.1
Newcastle United	49.2	22.4	45%	£25,000	3.7
Chelsea	47.5	27.0	57%	£32,000	2.1
Liverpool	45.5	24.1	53%	£30,000	0.7
Arsenal	40.4	21.9	54%	£25,000	5.9
Tottenham Hotspur	31.2	17.0	54%	£20,000	(0.9)
Blackburn Rovers	19.4	19.0	98%	£22,000	(3.7)

Based on figures published in The Guardian

did not catch on. The BBC's 'Match of the Day' highlights programme first appeared in 1964 and became very popular.

Television started to become a big influence on football in 1988, when the BBC and ITV battled for the rights. ITV paid £44 million for live League football for a period of four years and the BBC £30 million for internationals and FA Cup ties. The arrival of satellite TV in the 1990s soon made this small beer, and the Premier League's four-year-deal with BSkyB some ten years later was worth £670 million, a 15-fold increase. During this time the rights to show the last three World Cups of the 20th century cost £215 million, whereas the first three of the next century will cost £1.37 billion, a six-fold increase.

Wide exposure on television has made football attractive to sponsors. A four-year deal with Carling brings in £36 million for the Premiership, AXA pay £25 million for a four-

year FA Cup deal, Worthington £23 million for a five-year League Cup deal. Nationwide are paying £15 million to sponsor the England team for 3½ years and £9 million for a two-year extension to their Football League sponsorship. Examples of contracts existing with individual clubs for sponsorship over various periods are £12 million for Celtic and Rangers from NTL, £10 million for Arsenal from Sega, £4.8 million for a two-year extension to their contract with Manchester United from Sharp, £4 million from Newcastle Brown Ale for United. In 1976 the total sponsorship money available to football in the whole of Britain was £2 million.

The wealth in football and its TV connection persuaded BSkyB to offer £623 million for Manchester United, a bid accepted by the club but, in April 1999, blocked by the Monopolies and Mergers Commission as anti-competitive, against the public interest and damaging to the quality of British football.

The new wealth of football, at least at Premiership level, and the improvement to the stadia enforced upon the clubs by the Hillsborough tragedy in particular, has provoked a change in the kind of people who follow football. The traditional fan who never missed watching his team on a Saturday afternoon after knocking off work at lunchtime nowadays often cannot afford to attend so regularly, with ticket prices costing £25 and upwards.

Modern fandom requires much more of an outlay than it did, say, 25 years ago, especially if the fan wants to buy one of the facsimile club shirts and other artefacts that have boosted club finances in recent years. Some of the many thousand supporters who travelled from Britain to Barcelona to be present when Manchester United won the last European Cup of the century in 1999 paid over £1,000 in air fare and black market ticket for the privilege.

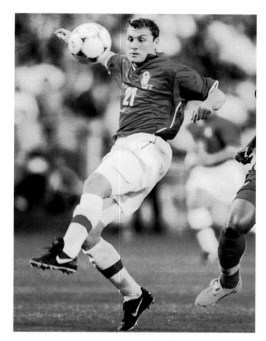

Christian Vieri, who moved from Lazio to Inter in the summer of 1999 for a staggering £30 million

SOME TRANSFER RECORDS OF THE CENTURY

Year	Player	Clubs	£
1905	Alf Common	Sunderland to Middlesbrough	1,000
1912	Danny Shea	West Ham United to Blackburn	2,000
1922	Syd Puddefoot	West Ham United to Falkirk	5,000
1928	David Jack	Bolton to Arsenal	10,890
1932	Bernabe Ferreyra	Tiger BA to River Plate	23,000
1952	Hans Jeppson	Amateur to Napoli	52,000
1961	Luis Suarez	Barcelona to Internazionale	142,000
1968	Piero Anastasi	Varese to Juventus	500,000
1973	Johan Cruyff	Ajax Amsterdam to Barcelona	922,000
1975	Guiseppe Savoldi	Bologna to Napoli	1,200,000
1982	Diego Maradona	Boca Juniors to Barcelona	3,000,000
1984	Diego Maradona	Barcelona to Napoli	6,900,000
1987	Ruud Gullit	PSV Eindhoven to AC Milan	6,000,000
1990	Roberto Baggio	Fiorentina to Juventus	8,000,000
1992	Jean-Pierre Papin	Marseille to AC Milan	10,000,000
1992	Gianluigi Lentini	Torino to AC Milan	13,000,000
1997	Alan Shearer	Blackburn to Newcastle	15,000,000
1997	Ronaldo	Barcelona to Internazionale	17,800,000
1998	Denilson	Sao Paulo to Real Betis	21,500,000
1999	Christian Vieri	Lazio to Internazionale	30,000,000

Players reap financial rewards

All the money in the game has made the biggest difference of all to the players. Since 1961, when the maximum wage in the Football League was lifted, and Johnny Haynes' wage packet improved from £20 to £100 overnight, players have won two big legal battles. Before 1963, a 'retain-and-transfer' system operated, whereby a club could keep a player on their books indefinitely by retaining him each season. Otherwise they could sell him to another club. When George Eastham of Newcastle United wanted a transfer, Newcastle refused, Eastham refused to play for them and was thus effectively frozen out of the game. Eastham, backed by the Professional Footballers Association, took his case to the High Court, where Judge Wilberforce ruled that the 'retain-and-transfer' system was an unlawful restraint on trade. From then on footballers could negotiate a contract with their clubs for a fixed number of years and at the end, if they did not like the renewal option, they were free to sign for another club. If clubs could not agree a suitable transfer fee, then a special 'transfer tribunal' would decide the appropriate fee.

In 1996 the European Court of Justice issued a judgement in the case of Belgian Jean-Marc Bosman, who in 1990 had claimed restraint of trade when his Belgian club Liege, with whom his contract had expired, put a transfer fee of £250,000 on his head, to which the French club he wanted to join, Dunkerque, objected. The free movement of players from country to country within the European Community became incorporated in the case, and the Court decided that footballers, like other workers when out of contract, should be free to work where they liked without their previous employer/club demanding a fee. This allowed footballers higher wages from new clubs who were not required to pay transfer fees for them. Clubs began to sell players before their contracts expired - the only way they could cash in on their asset.

The other result of the 'Bosman ruling', was that clubs became increasingly keen to extend the length of top players' contracts. By the end of the century, five- and six-year deals were fast becoming the norm, and the best players could command salaries more in line with entertainers of the pop music industry. Wages in the Premiership of over £25,000 per week were not uncommon and, of course, players could more then double their basic salaries with sponsorship and advertising deals.

It is the players whose lives have changed most in the development of football from 1900 to 2000, and their fortunes have changed mostly in the last quarter of the century.

If a fan from 1900 could be brought back to watch a top game now, he would see the pitch markings changed, the kit changed (sponsors' names on the front and players' names on the back), a huge upsurge in speed and skill on the pitch, and comfort and facilities off it and so unbelievable a change in the finances, merchandising, fanaticism of fans and media attention as to make it seem a different game. But the game itself - well, it's practically the same.

Index

Page references in italics are to photographs of players or teams, but are not shown if there is already a reference in the index to the text on the same page as which the photograph appears.

It will be appreciated that the index cannot include references to every mention of a player, team or match, but those of most significance are included.